A Land Full of God

A Land Full of God
Christian Perspectives on the Holy Land

Edited by
Mae Elise Cannon

Forewords by
Aziz Abu Sarah and Daniel Roth

CASCADE Books · Eugene, Oregon

A LAND FULL OF GOD
Christian Perspectives on the Holy Land

Copyright © 2017 Wipf and Stock Publishers. All rights reserved. Except for brief quotations in critical publications or reviews, no part of this book may be reproduced in any manner without prior written permission from the publisher. Write: Permissions, Wipf and Stock Publishers, 199 W. 8th Ave., Suite 3, Eugene, OR 97401.

Cascade Books
An Imprint of Wipf and Stock Publishers
199 W. 8th Ave., Suite 3
Eugene, OR 97401

www.wipfandstock.com

PAPERBACK ISBN: 978-1-4982-9880-3
HARDCOVER ISBN: 978-1-4982-9882-7
EBOOK ISBN: 978-1-4982-9881-0

Cataloguing-in-Publication data:

Names: Cannon, Mae Elise, ed. | Roth, Daniel, Foreword | Sarah, Aziz Abu, Foreword

Title: A land full of God: Christian perspectives on the holy land / Cannon, Mae Elise, ed.

Description: Eugene, OR: Cascade Books, 2017 | Includes bibliographical references and indexes.

Identifiers: ISBN 978-1-4982-9880-3 (paperback) | ISBN 978-1-4982-9882-7 (hardcover) | ISBN 978-1-4982-9881-0 (ebook)

Subjects: LCSH: 1. Arab-Israeli conflict—Peace. | 2. Jews Restoration. | 3. Middle East Palestine. | I. Title.

Classification: DS119.76 L345 2017 (print) | CALL NUMBER (ebook)

Manufactured in the U.S.A.   MAY 12, 2017

The opinions expressed in this book are those of the individual authors and do not necessarily reflect the views of Churches for Middle East Peace (CMEP) and its membership denominations.

To the men and women of Israel and Palestine who are holding
firmly to the olive branch of peace . . .

Blessed are the peacemakers,
for they will be called children of God.
—MATTHEW 5:9, NIV

In memory of my father, Michael Patrick Cannon . . .
who loved boldly, gave generously, fought courageously, and always
encouraged . . .
"Make a memory."

The land was not holy at the time of Terah or even at the time of the Patriarchs. It was sanctified by the people when they entered the land under the leadership of Joshua . . . . We do not worship the soil. The land of Israel without the God of Israel will be here today and gone tomorrow.

—RABBI ABRAHAM JOSHUA HESCHEL
(FROM *ISRAEL: AN ECHO OF ETERNITY*)[1]

In Jerusalem, and I mean within the ancient walls,
I walk from one epoch to another without a memory
to guide me. The prophets over there are sharing
the history of the holy . . . ascending to heaven
and returning less discouraged and melancholy, because love
and peace are holy and are coming to town.

—MAHMOUD DARWISH (FROM "IN JERUSALEM")[2]

---

1. Heschel, *Israel: An Echo of Eternity*. 120.
2. Darwish, "In Jerusalem."

Contents

Permissions | xi

Contributors | xiii

Multiple Narratives Toward Peace: Foreword by Muslim and Jewish Leaders | xxiii
    Aziz Abu Sarah and Rabbi Dr. Daniel Roth

Acknowledgments | xxix

Introduction | 1
    Rev. Dr. Mae Elise Cannon

Part I: Contextualizing the Israeli-Palestinian Conflict

1. Beginning to Understand the Israeli-Palestinian Conflict | 17
    Dale Hanson Bourke
2. "We Need One More Common Friend" | 25
    David Neff
3. How Should Christians Relate to the State of Israel? | 34
    Rich Nathan
4. Speech at the Presidential Palace with Palestinian Authorities in Bethlehem | 41
    His Holiness Pope Francis

Part II: God's Chosen People and the Family of Abraham

5 I am Jewish: Reflections on Jewish Identity in the Holy Land | 47
   Dr. Judith Mendelsohn Rood

6 The Holy Land and the Larger Family of Abraham | 56
   Dr. Tony Maalouf

7 Will God Really Bless Those who Bless Israel Today? | 67
   Dr. Michael L. Brown

8 The Land of Israel and the Problem of Supersessionism | 75
   Rev. Dr. John E. Phelan Jr.

Part III: Intersections of History

9 Land & People | 89
   Dr. Andrea Lee Smith

10 Martin Luther King, Jr.'s Hope for a Better Israel | 99
   Dr. Clayborne Carson with Rev. Dr. Troy Jackson

11 A Very Short History of Christian Zionism | 108
   Dr. Donald M. Lewis

12 Christian Just Peacemaking and Israel-Palestine: A Quick and Dirty Historical Account of What We are Calling Israel-Palestine | 123
   Dr. David P. Gushee

Part IV: Political Paradigms and Perspectives

13 Across the Israel Divide | 135
   Susan Michael

14 Palestine and Apartheid | 146
   Archbishop Desmond Tutu

15 Remarks at the Gaza Donors Conference | 152
   The Honorable John Kerry

16 Protestifying: A Pentecostal Reflection on Interfaith Learning and Political Action | 157
   Dr. Paul Nathan Alexander

Part V: An End to Violence and Vision for Peace

17 Millennial Voices for Peace Statement of Principles | 173

18 Barriers to Peace | 175
   Dr. Bob Roberts

19 Middle East Crisis and Peace Building | 182
    Dr. David A. Anderson

20 Hope in the Midst of a Mess | 188
    Dr. Darrell L. Bock

21 Navigating Minefields: Explosive Wisdom for Modern Pilgrims | 193
    Jerry White

Part VI: We Belong to Each Other: Relationship Across Divides

22 Standing Beside the Vulnerable | 205
    Shane Claiborne

23 The Power of Unlikely Relationships | 211
    Carolyn Custis James

24 A Truer and Deeper Peace | 218
    Lynne Hybels

25 Overrated: The Holy Land and Discipleship | 227
    Rev. Eugene Cho

Part VII: Future Hope: Action & Engagement toward a Just Peace

26 Praying for Peace in Jerusalem | 237
    Jim Wallis

27 Jews, Christians, and Muslims: Finding a Way to Peace | 246
    Dr. Joel Hunter

28 How to Create a New Conversation about Israel-Palestine in Your Church | 256
    Rev. Bill Hybels

29 Christians as Agents of Reconciliation | 263
    Dr. Tony Campolo

Epilogue | 271
    Rev. Dr. Mae Elise Cannon

Pursuing Peace and Strengthening Presence: The Atlanta Summit of Churches in the USA and the Holy Land | 272

Subject Index | 283

Names and Organizations | 291

Permissions

Scripture quotations marked (ESV) are from the ESV® Bible (The Holy Bible, English Standard Version®), copyright © 2001 by Crossway, a publishing ministry of Good News Publishers. Used by permission. All rights reserved.

Scripture quotations marked HCSB®, are taken from the Holman Christian Standard Bible®, Copyright © 1999, 2000, 2002, 2003, 2009 by Holman Bible Publishers. Used by permission. HCSB® is a federally registered trademark of Holman Bible Publishers.

Scriptures marked (KJV) are taken from the KING JAMES VERSION (KJV): KING JAMES VERSION, public domain.

Scripture quotations from THE MESSAGE. Copyright © by Eugene H. Peterson 1993, 1994, 1995, 1996, 2000, 2001, 2002. Used by permission of NavPress. All rights reserved. Represented by Tyndale House Publishers, Inc.

Scripture quotations marked (NASB) are taken from the New American Standard Bible® (NASB), Copyright © 1960, 1962, 1963, 1968, 1971, 1972, 1973, 1975, 1977, 1995 by The Lockman Foundation. Used by permission. www.Lockman.org.

Scripture quotations marked (NIV) are taken from the Holy Bible, New International Version®, NIV®. Copyright © 1973, 1978, 1984, 2011 by Biblica, Inc.™ Used by permission of Zondervan. All rights reserved worldwide. www.zondervan.com. The "NIV" and "New International Version" are trademarks registered in the United States Patent and Trademark Office by Biblica, Inc.™

Scripture quotations marked (NKJV) are taken from the New King James Version®. Copyright © 1982 by Thomas Nelson. Used by permission. All rights reserved.

PERMISSIONS

Qur'an Shakir Version

Chapter 4 © LIBRERIA EDITRICE VATICANA

Chapter 12 © Dr. David Gushee. This essay appeared in substantially similar form in the author's book *In the Fray* (Wipf and Stock, 2014).

Chapter 13 © Susan Michael, International Christian Embassy Jerusalem-USA, INC.

Chapter 14 © 2007 by Archbishop Emeritus Desmond Tutu. Used with Permission. All Rights Reserved.

Epilogue: © Atlanta Church Summit Executive Committee. Used with Permission.

Contributors

Dr. Paul Nathan Alexander is the former Ronald J. Sider Professor of Theology, Ethics, and Public Policy at Palmer Seminary of Eastern University, Director of the Sider Center, President of Evangelicals for Social Action, and Co-Founder of Pentecostals and Charismatics for Peace and Justice. He is an alumnus of the Christian Leadership Initiative of the American Jewish Committee and Shalom Hartman Institute in Jerusalem and he has worked with and learned from Palestinian Christians, Palestinian and Israeli Muslims, Israeli and American Jews, and Israeli and American Messianic Jews in Israel, Palestine, and the United States. He earned his PhD from Baylor University.

Dr. David A. Anderson is an author and the founder and Senior Pastor of Bridgeway Community Church, a nondenominational and multicultural church. He is one of the world's leading authorities on building bridges across the deep divides of race, faith, culture, and wealth. His work has brought hope and healing to communities, families, and people in Africa, Asia, Europe, the Middle East, and North America. Wherever there is a divide, Anderson seeks to build a bridge through relevant and intelligent conversation. Inviting robust dialogue across tough topics, Anderson is a radio and television talk show host in the nation's capital. His insight, vision, and passion have made him a widely sought speaker, writer, and consultant for major national and international events and policy initiatives.

CONTRIBUTORS

Dr. Darrell Bock is the Executive Director of Cultural Engagement and Senior Research Professor of New Testament Studies at Dallas Theological Seminary, engaged in the historical study of Jesus, biblical theology, and messianic Jewish ministries. He is an editor-at-large for Christianity Today and serves on the board of Chosen People Ministries and Wheaton College. He co-edited the 1992 book *Dispensationalism, Israel and the Church: The Search for Definition* and *Israel, the Land, and the Future* (2012).

Dale Hanson Bourke has traveled extensively and served on the boards of World Vision (US and International), International Justice Mission, Opportunity International, Sojourners, ECFA, and MAP International. She is author of The Skeptic's Guide series, including *The Israeli-Palestinian Conflict* as well as ten other books, including *Embracing Your Second Calling*.

Dr. Michael L. Brown is the founder and president of FIRE School of Ministry in Concord, North Carolina, Director of the Coalition of Conscience, and host of the daily, nationally syndicated talk radio show, *The Line of Fire*, as well as the host of the apologetics TV show, *Answering Your Toughest Questions*, which airs on the NRB TV network. He has preached throughout America and around the world, bringing a message of repentance, revival, reformation, and cultural revolution. He holds a PhD in Near Eastern Languages and Literatures from New York University and has served as a visiting or adjunct professor at Southern Evangelical Seminary, Gordon Conwell Theological Seminary (Charlotte), Trinity Evangelical Divinity School, Fuller Theological Seminary, Denver Theological Seminary, the King's Seminary, and Regent University School of Divinity. He has contributed numerous articles to scholarly publications, including the *Oxford Dictionary of Jewish Religion* and the *Theological Dictionary of the Old Testament*. Dr. Brown is the author of more than twenty-five books, including *The Real Kosher Jesus: Revealing the Mysteries of the Hidden Messiah*. Dr. Brown is a national and international speaker on themes of spiritual renewal and cultural reformation, and he has spoken on radio, TV, and college campuses. He is widely considered to be the world's foremost Messianic Jewish apologist.

Dr. Tony Campolo is professor emeritus of sociology at Eastern University, a former faculty member at the University of Pennsylvania, and the founder and president of the Evangelical Association for the Promotion of Education. He has written more than thirty-five books and is one of the founders of the Red Letter Christian movement and blogs regularly at his website, RedLetterChristians.org. An ordained minister, Campolo has served American Baptist churches in New Jersey and Pennsylvania and is a frequent commentator on religion and politics. Tony formerly served as a spiritual counselor to President Bill Clinton.

CONTRIBUTORS

Dr. Clayborne Carson has devoted his professional life to the study of Martin Luther King Jr. and the movements King inspired. Since receiving his doctorate from UCLA in 1975, Dr. Carson has taught at Stanford University, where he is now professor of history and founding director of the Martin Luther King, Jr., Research and Education Institute. Carson's scholarly publications have focused on African American protest movements and political thought of the period after World War II. His other publications include *In Struggle: SNCC and the Black Awakening of the 1960s* (1981); *Malcolm X: The FBI File* (1991); *African American Lives: The Struggle for Freedom* (2005, coauthor); and a memoir, *Martin's Dream: My Journey and the Legacy of Martin Luther King, Jr.* (2013). In 1985, the late Coretta Scott King invited Dr. Carson to direct a long-term project to edit and publish the papers of Dr. Martin Luther King, Jr. In 2005, Carson founded the Martin Luther King, Jr. Research and Education Institute to endow and expand the work of the King Papers Project. Under Carson's direction, the King Papers Project has produced seven volumes of *The Papers of Martin Luther King, Jr.*—a projected fourteen-volume comprehensive edition of King's most significant speeches, sermons, correspondence, publications, and unpublished writings.

Rev. Eugene Cho is the founder and Lead Pastor of Quest Church—an urban, multicultural, and multigenerational church in Seattle, Washington. He is also the founder and visionary of One Day's Wages (ODW), "a grassroots movement of people, stories, and actions to alleviate extreme global poverty." The vision of ODW is to create a collaborative movement by integrating human relationships, social media/technology, and the power of story. ODW promotes awareness, invites simple giving (one day's wages), and supports sustainable relief through partnerships, especially with smaller organizations in developing regions. Since its launch in October 2009, ODW has raised over $4 million dollars for projects to empower those living in extreme global poverty. Eugene's first book, *Overrated: Are We More in Love with the Idea of Changing the World than Actually Changing the World?* was released in 2014.

Shane Claiborne is a best-selling author, renowned activist, sought-after speaker, and self-proclaimed "recovering sinner." Shane writes and speaks around the world about peacemaking, social justice, and Jesus, and is the author of numerous books including *The Irresistible Revolution*, *Jesus for President*, and his newest book, *Executing Grace* (2016). He is the visionary founder of The Simple Way in Philadelphia, and director of Red Letter Christians. His work has been featured in Fox News, Esquire, *SPIN*, the *Wall Street Journal*, NPR, and CNN.

CONTRIBUTORS

Dr. David Gushee is Distinguished University Professor of Christian Ethics and Director for the Center of Theology and Public Life at Mercer University. He is a scholar, activist, and churchman. As an author and editor of twenty books and hundreds of articles in his field, he is widely regarded as one of the leading moral voices in American Christianity. His research interests focus on the ethical teachings of Jesus Christ and the Christian theological-ethical tradition, together with its contemporary implications for Christian discipleship and public witness. He has traveled to Israel/Palestine on two separate initiatives, and is a fellow of the Christian Leaders Initiative of the American Jewish Committee.

Dr. Joel Hunter is senior pastor of Northland, A Church Distributed, a pioneering congregation of 20,000 focused on building communities of Christians around the world. A nationally and internationally recognized bridge-builder among religious and mainstream leaders, his challenge to Christians is to be the church everywhere, every day. He speaks and writes on contemporary issues and finding common ground so that issues of compassion can be addressed in ways that benefit all. Hunter is the author of several books, including *A New Kind of Conservative*, which outlines a nonpartisan approach to political involvement, and *Church Distributed*, an explanation of how the church can thrive in an era of connection.

Bill Hybels is the founding and senior pastor of Willow Creek Community Church in South Barrington, Illinois, and chairman of the board of Willow Creek Association. He convened The Global Leadership Summit in 1995, following a God-given prompting to help raise and develop the spiritual gift of leadership for the local church. Both visionary and passionate about seeing every local church reach its full God-given potential, he speaks around the world on strategic issues related to leadership, evangelism, and church growth. An exceptional communicator, he is a best-selling author of more than twenty books, including *Axiom, Holy Discontent, Just Walk Across the Room, The Volunteer Revolution, Courageous Leadership,* and *The Power of a Whisper: Hearing God and Having the Guts to Respond.*

Lynne Hybels has been an active volunteer at Willow Creek Community Church since she and her husband, Bill, started it in 1975. For the last twenty years she has engaged in ministry partnerships in under-resourced communities in Latin America and Africa, and has advocated for comprehensive immigration reform on behalf of the hundreds of undocumented immigrants who call Willow Creek their church home. Since 2009, Lynne has been actively trying to learn what it means to follow Jesus into places of conflict. In the Democratic Republic of Congo, where the deadliest conflict since World War II still rages, she has partnered with local churches that are caring for women who have been brutally raped, and are initiating grassroots peacemaking efforts in their villages. In Israel-Palestine she hosts groups of American Christians who want to learn from Jews, Muslims, and Christians—both Israeli and Palestinian—who are working for dignity, security, and freedom for all the people in the Holy Land. Lynne also raises awareness and funds to empower followers of Jesus in the Middle East who are serving Syrian refugees and displaced Iraqis.

Carolyn Custis James is an award-winning author whose speaking and writing ministry is dedicated to addressing the deeper needs that confront both women and men as they endeavor to extend God's kingdom together in a messy, complicated world. She blogs at MissioAlliance.com and *Huffington Post/Religion*. She is an adjunct faculty member at Biblical Theological Seminary in Pennsylvania, a consulting editor for Zondervan's Exegetical Commentary Series on the New Testament, and a contributing editor for *Leadership Journal*. In 2013, *Christianity Today* named her one of the fifty evangelical women to watch. She speaks regularly at church conferences, colleges, and other Christian organizations both in the US and abroad and is a visiting lecturer at various theological seminaries.

Rev. Dr. Troy Jackson is the director of the AMOS Project in Cincinnati, an organization that works with congregations, clergy, and faith leaders to work for racial and economic justice, and co-founder and director of Ohio Prophetic Voices. Previously, Troy served as pastor of University Christian Church in Cincinnati for nearly nineteen years. He has an MDiv from Princeton Theological Seminary and a PhD in United States History from the University of Kentucky. He is the author of *Becoming King: Martin Luther King, Jr. and the Making of a National Leader* and editor of *Volume VI: Advocate of the Social Gospel* in The Papers of Martin Luther King, Jr. Project.

John Kerry is the former US Secretary of State. Secretary Kerry joined the State Department after twenty-eight years in the United States Senate, the last four as Chairman of the Senate Foreign Relations Committee. Secretary Kerry has worked extensively on issues regarding the Middle East.

Dr. Donald M. Lewis is an alumnus of Regent College who went on to do doctoral work at Oxford University before coming back to Regent as a faculty member. He is a specialist in the history of evangelicalism in the Victorian era and has written and published extensively in this area. He has written numerous articles and book reviews for both popular and academic periodicals, including *Fides Et Historia* and *The American Historical Review*. He has recently completed a book on the nineteenth-century background to the rise of Christian Zionism: *The Origins of Christian Zionism: Evangelical Support for a Jewish Homeland*. Don Lewis has served as Regent's Academic Dean, and is currently the Secretary of the college's Anglican Studies Program. He is also a Fellow of the Royal Historical Society.

Dr. Tony Maalouf is Professor of World Christianity and NAME Studies, and Director of the Islamic Studies Program at Southwestern Baptist Theological Seminary in Fort Worth, Texas. Maalouf has served as professor of biblical studies at Jordan Evangelical Theological Seminary in Amman, Jordan. He is a regular visiting professor at the Arab Baptist Theological Seminary in Beirut, Lebanon as well as JETS in Amman. He is the author of *Arabs in the Shadow of Israel* (2003), and has several published articles on the subject of biblical Arabs and early Arab Christianity.

Rich Nathan has been serving since 1987 as the first senior pastor of the Vineyard Columbus, a large multiethnic congregation in Columbus, Ohio. The church is especially known for its outreach to immigrants, to the poor, and to the vulnerable in the community. Prior to pastoring, Rich taught business law at Ohio State University for seven years. He is a graduate of Case Western Reserve University in Cleveland, Ohio, and received his Juris Doctorate with honors from the Ohio State University College of Law in 1980. Rich serves as the Large Church Task Force leader for the Vineyard. He is a popular national and international conference speaker. Rich wrote *Who is My Enemy? Welcoming People the Church Rejects* (2002), coauthored the book *Empowered Evangelicals* (2009) with Ken Wilson, and coauthored the book *Both-And: Living the Christ-Centered Life in an Either-Or World* (2013) with Insoo Kim. Born and raised in New York City, Rich and his wife, Marlene, have been married for forty years. The Nathans have two adult children and six grandchildren.

David Neff retired in 2013 after twenty-eight years at *Christianity Today*, where he was editor-in-chief and an editorial vice-president. While at *Christianity Today*, he also supervised *Books & Culture* and *Christian History & Biography*. Mr. Neff currently serves on the board of the Ecumenical Institute at St. Mary's Seminary and University in Baltimore. He formerly served on the boards of Bread for the World, the Association of Theological Schools, the National Association of Evangelicals, and the Robert E. Webber Institute for Worship Studies. He is the co-convener of a national Evangelical-Jewish conversation and participated for over a decade in Evangelical-Mormon dialogue. He is also the past president and chair of Evangelicals for Middle East Understanding.

CONTRIBUTORS   xix

Susan Michael has pioneered the development of the International Christian Embassy Jerusalem in the United States and around the world for more than thirty-five years. She currently serves as the ministry's USA Director and is a member of the ICEJ's international Board of Directors. Susan's involvement with the ICEJ began as a graduate student at Jerusalem University College in 1980, the same year that the Christian Embassy was first established. Upon completing her masters degree in Judeo-Christian Studies she returned from Israel with a heart to further the embassy's mission among fellow Americans. A graduate in Theology from Oral Roberts University, Susan is often called upon to address complex and sensitive issues such as anti-Semitism, Islam, Jewish-Christian relations, and current events in the Middle East to a diverse range of audiences. Her experience working with Arabs, Jews, and Christians from many national and denominational backgrounds has equipped Susan to handle delicate topics central to an understanding of Israel with extraordinary clarity and grace. In recent years she has pioneered a number of educational tools to enable other Christians to do the same, including the IsraelAnswers.com website, a series of highly accessible educational seminars and educational tours to Israel. Susan and her husband lived for many years in Washington, DC, where she developed a close working relationship with the US Jewish community. George, a Coptic Christian, served the US government as Middle East Analyst. They currently reside in South Florida.

Dr. John E Phelan Jr. is Senior Professor of Theological Studies at North Park Theological Seminary, where he teaches Introduction to New Testament, Eschatology, and a Wendell Berry seminar. As a pastor in the Evangelical Covenant Church, Dr. Phelan knows the value of theological education, particularly in the serious study of the biblical text. He served as the seminary's president and dean until 2010, when he became a full-time faculty member. Dr. Phelan has served as a pastor to congregations in Florida and Kansas, and in the ECC denomination as executive director of Covenant Publications. He is passionate about engaging Evangelical-Jewish dialogue, a conversation that continues to reward his life and ministry.

His Holiness Pope Francis was elected Pope of the Catholic Church on March 13, 2013. His tenure in office has included a loud and clear call for peace and justice in many areas, including in the Middle East.

Dr. Bob Roberts Jr. is the founding pastor of NorthWood Church in the Dallas/Ft. Worth area. Bob works extensively globally, having traveled to over sixty-five nations. In the US he has helped plant over 200 churches. Bob is a graduate of Baylor University (BA), Southwestern Baptist Theological

Seminary (MDiv), and Fuller Seminary (DMin) with an emphasis in church planting.

Dr. Judith Mendelsohn Rood is Professor of History and Middle East Studies at Biola University, La Mirada, CA. Previously she was Associate Professor at William Tyndale College where she was Director of the Middle East Studies and Global Studies programs. She has published extensively in the field of Ottoman and Modern Middle Eastern History. Her scholarly publications have appeared in the *International Journal of Turkish Studies*, *The Encyclopedia of Modern Asia*, *The Arab Studies Journal*, *The Jerusalem Quarterly*, *The Review of Faith and International Affairs*, and other journals. At Biola University she teaches the history of the Middle East and Islam and historiography. She specializes in the history of Jerusalem and its environs. She has been a member of numerous professional societies including the Association for Middle East and African Studies, the American Historical Association, the Middle East Studies Association, the Turkish Studies Association, and the Conference of Faith and History. She conducts research in Arabic, French, Turkish, Ottoman Turkish, and Hebrew. Dr. Rood received her doctorate in Modern Middle Eastern History from the University of Chicago in 1993. She conducted research in the Islamic Court in Jerusalem as a Lady Davis Fellow of the Hebrew University. The resulting book, *Sacred Law in the Holy City* (2004), is a widely cited resource on the Ottoman rule of Jerusalem.

Dr. Andrea Lee Smith is an academic and activist. Smith's work focuses on issues of Native Americans. A co-founder of INCITE!, Women of Color Against Violence, the Boarding School Healing Project, and the Chicago chapter of Women Nations, Smith centers the experiences of women of color in both her activism and her scholarship. Smith is currently an associate professor in the Department of Media and Cultural Studies and Ethnic Studies at the University of California, Riverside.

Archbishop Desmond Tutu was the first black South African Archbishop of Cape Town, South Africa, and a key player in the fight against apartheid. In 1984, he received the Nobel Peace Prize in recognition of his efforts in fighting this injustice. After becoming archbishop in 1986, Desmond Tutu became a principal mediator and conciliator in South Africa's transition to democracy. In 1995, President Nelson Mandela appointed him to be the Archbishop Chairman of the Truth and Reconciliation Commission. In addition, Desmond Tutu has been active in advocating for peace and reconciliation in Israel-Palestine. He was an advisory member for the 2012 Global March to Jerusalem, led a UN investigation into Israeli bombings in Gaza in 2008, and became a patron of Sabeel International beginning in 2003 to offer support to Palestinian Christians.

Jim Wallis is a *New York Times* bestselling author, public theologian, speaker, and international commentator on ethics and public life. He formerly served on the White House Advisory Council on Faith-based and Neighborhood Partnerships and was former vice chair of and currently serves on the Global Agenda Council on Values of the World Economic Forum. Jim is president and founder of Sojourners, where he is also editor-in-chief of *Sojourners* magazine, which has a combined print and electronic media readership of more than a quarter million people. Jim frequently speaks in the United States and abroad. He has written eleven books, and his columns appear in major newspapers, including *The New York Times, Washington Post, Los Angeles Times*, and *The Boston Globe*.

Jerry White has over twenty-five years' experience leading change-making campaigns to prevent mass destruction and increase civilian security worldwide. A social entrepreneur and senior *Ashoka Fellow*, White has helped train next-generation leadership in scores of countries to transform highly contentious issues into opportunities to unify communities, generate jobs, and build stability and hope. White currently serves as Deputy Assistant Secretary of State in the new Bureau of Conflict and Stabilization Operations, where he is responsible for the Burma and Libya portfolios, as well as three new offices: Policy, Partnerships, and Training. He cochairs the State Department's sub-working group on religion and conflict mitigation, responsible for outreach to diverse civil society leaders and religious actors working to break cycles of violence.

Foreword

Multiple Narratives Toward Peace

Aziz Abu Sarah and Rabbi Dr. Daniel Roth

We all have a narrative—a way we see the world around us. As people who examine conflicts and seek ways to build peace—*shalom*—our work has taught us the importance of hearing and learning narratives from multiple perspectives. If we fail to open our minds beyond a single perspective, we eventually cage ourselves into the limitations of one narrative, one story.

When this happens, our narrative becomes the *only* truth; we become limited in our ability to live in this world alongside of people with different perspectives. When only one narrative is "true" then everyone else becomes an enemy, rather than just someone with a perspective different from our own.

The word for *shalom* in Hebrew or *salaam* in Arabic, is translated "peace" in English. *Shalom/Salaam* is about the unity of opposites. *Shalom/Salaam* brings together seemingly contradictory ideas about truth and justice. This idea extends far beyond the overly simplistic English definition as "peace." Pursuing *shalom/salaam* means pursuing conflicting interpretations of an idea, not just insisting that one's own idea is correct. As advocates of holistic peace, we need people to be curious and engaged with the justice of others.

When we learn the narratives of others, it doesn't negate one's own life and experience. It just helps us to understand the world differently, to understand the people we are talking to, and to have more compassion and understanding for others in this world. Many people fear if we explore other narratives, it will weaken one's own story. From our experience that is not true. Other people's stories might reshape your understanding of your narrative, but learning other narratives does not make one's own narrative wrong or "weak." Rather, listening builds better bridges. It is important to learn diverse narratives if you are planning on working with people in fields like conflict resolution.

As Christians, you may also fear that if you open your hearts and minds to the stories of others that you might have to compromise your theological convictions. We believe that religious actors can maintain their own theological integrity while still creating space for the narratives of others who have different beliefs and experiences.

Whether it's the Bible or the Koran, stories of people like Mohammed or Jesus or Abraham or Moses—none of them went through life in comfortable surroundings. Their learning experience was not in their own "comfort zone." These spiritual leaders went to places that were scary. In reality, we can grow in our own life is if we put ourselves in uncomfortable situations so we can listen and grow and understand. Then we can think together to find where there might be common ground. There are places where we might disagree—but we can disagree without hating or killing each other or seeing the other person as an enemy.

Many people play all different sides of the conflict in the Holy Land—holding various narratives and perspectives that relate to the religions, politics, and traditions of the region. There are many different narratives—to the point that there is not even one name for the conflict. Some call it the Israeli-Palestinian conflict, some call it the Jewish-Arab conflict, others by a different name.

Similarly many people have different ideas about what peace and justice look like. It's important to distinguish between the pursuit of justice or peace. Many people say peace, but they are really involved in one-track justice work. That is, their own particular understanding of justice. Their issue is often one worth fighting for, but they make it the only issue without seeking to build bridges and intersectionality in regards to the multiple perspectives, narratives, and needs that are all part of the conflict. Rather than seeking peace, people are trying to advance their own specific understanding of justice. We have a lot of people pursuing justice, but not enough people holding up conflicting interpretations of justice and pursuing peace.

We do not know of a mass movement with people like Rev. Dr. Mae Elise Cannon who are able to try and border-cross between different groups and break down barriers while seeking to help others to also cross that border. Instead, we see people strengthening each side of the border, building up taller and stronger walls of division.

By definition, American Christians are already engaged in the conflict in the Holy Land because they have so much at stake in the land. The question is, how can Americans most helpfully engage? American Christian engagement has played an important role in perpetuating the conflict precisely because there are different American Christian groups supporting polar opposite sides of the conflict. This is not the most helpful!

American Christians can invest in the work of interreligious dialogue and intra-religious dialogue by investing their volunteering, resources, and political advocacy towards Track 3 diplomacy—creating a healthy and thriving civil society. Religion can be a place of bridge building, and American Christians have a role to play. This happens through interreligious dialogue and by meeting with Jews and Muslims separately. The conflicts are so deep that often the people who most need to be engaged are not the ones willing to meet with people from the "other" side. But working through some of these issues in parallel—in areas where US Christians can help to bridge the divide—can help move the conversation forward.

The American Christian community can go back and forth in helping people from different perspectives in non-threatening ways by beginning to expand the space for the narratives of others. This is a critical role for the American church and for other religious actors who desire to contribute toward efforts of peace.

For many secular Americans, the conflict is about scarcity of resources such as land and water. Thus any solution focuses on how to creatively divide things up. Using maps and generals, one could literally decide who gets what over the course of a few short weeks. However the tangible division of resources, Christians in the United States need to not forget the symbolic value of so many of the issues at stake, which cannot easily be divided by a map. Many aspects of the conflict are not about scarcity of tangible resources; but rather a scarcity of space in our identity to allow in the identity and narratives of the "other."

We have seen this take place in a variety of ways, not the least of which is through MEJDI Tours. MEJDI is a socially conscious tour company that seeks to promote efforts toward peace by creating increased space for multiple narratives about the Israeli-Palestinian conflict and other conflicts around the world. MEJDI is holy work. It allows for the different voices directly impacted by what's happening in the Holy Land to be heard in a way that suspends judgment. Instead, the stories and the narratives focus on the importance of learning to heal.

When MEJDI started, specifically with the idea of offering multiple perspectives through Jewish, Muslim, and Christian guides—both Israelis and Palestinians—the idea scared many of our friends. They said, "No guides will ever want to work together and nobody wants to listen to both narratives side by side." The assumption that people don't want to hear conflicting narratives is absolutely wrong. MEJDI thinks of ways to facilitate that experience—having an Israeli and Palestinian work together—listening and learning from one another's narratives and changing the way the story may be understood. They disagree sometimes, but they do it in a way that is friendly and with respect; the guides work side by side and actually like each other! Sometimes they disagree and sometimes they agree. They eat together, work together, and respect each other. This changes the narrative of "us vs. them." People see a whole new reality, their willingness to work side by side, to listen to each other's stories and perspectives, shifts the whole paradigm of how Israelis and Palestinians are viewed in the world. People disagree, but even in their disagreement they agree it is possible for them to care about each other.

Those who travel with MEJDI share the stories of the people they meet on their MEJDI trip. Many of the people they meet will never be able to meet with each other, because of travel restrictions and barriers, but in this story-sharing, the stories cross borders. This border-crossing experience can empower both those who travel and those who live in the land and have relationships with people in different communities.

MEJDI also speaks directly to the way we learn rabbinic text. A core value in Jewish rabbinic theology is the concept of *machloket leshem shamayim*, which means "disagreement for the sake of Heaven," where contradictory opinions are deemed to both be correct. Every line has a disagreement and a disagreement for how to understand that disagreement. With MEJDI, we lead people back to a place of ambiguity. One person says it says "this" and another says it says something else. How can we uphold and understand two contradictory statements? MEJDI asks people to look at all these ideas and see them together.

If you are only reading the commentary of one news agency and never having any respect for another news agency—there is a lack of appreciation of different interpretations. People's narratives are becoming more extreme because they only see one viewpoint. MEJDI allows people to get out of that filter to experience the actual places themselves and get as many interpretations as possible on that issue.

What travelers do with MEJDI afterwards matters. They go back to their home communities and attempt to build bridges—understanding different interpretations and stories while bringing that complexity back home to help people better understand their own stories.

May this book, *A Land Full of God,* be a starting point to expanding your understanding of the Israeli-Palestinian conflict. Read with an open mind and learn from the narratives of Christians who view the conflict in a variety of ways. In whatever ways you can, listen and hear the stories of the people who live in the land—Israelis and Palestinians, Jews, Muslims, Christians, and other communities. Travel if you are able and see the beauty of multiple narratives at work in the Holy Land.

Pursue peace, but do not do so with only one interpretation of peace in mind. Pursue peace that honors and respects all of the opposing narratives of God's children in *A Land Full of God*.

Rabbi Dr. Daniel Roth is the director of the Pardes Center for Judaism and Conflict Resolution. He holds a PhD from Bar Ilan University's Program for Conflict Resolution, Management, and Negotiation, writing on Jewish models of conflict resolution, peacemaking, and reconciliation. Daniel has been teaching advanced rabbinics, Bible, conflict resolution, and other subjects at Pardes for over fifteen years. He is also a lecturer on religion and conflict resolution at Bar Ilan's Program for Conflict Resolution, and has been speaking to MEJDI groups for over five years. Daniel was also a senior research fellow at George Mason University's Center for World Religions, Diplomacy, and Conflict Resolution and an Israeli certified court mediator. He holds an MA in Talmud from Hebrew University, a BEd in Jewish Philosophy and Talmud from Herzog Teachers' College, and studied for eight years in Yeshivat Har-Etzion, during which time he received rabbinic ordination. Daniel is married with four children and lives in Jerusalem.

Aziz Abu Sarah is an entrepreneur, speaker, peace builder, and author. He is a National Geographic Explorer and a TED Fellow. In 2009, Aziz co-founded MEJDI Tours, a cultural exploration vehicle for an ever-changing travel market. He is a seasoned tourism professional with over a decade of experience in the industry. In 2014, he gave a TED Talk about his vision for redefining tourism. Aziz has spoken at countless of international organizations and universities, including The United Nations, Nexus, TED, BMW, European Parliament, Georgetown, Yale, and Harvard. He has published articles in *The New York Times, National Geographic, TED, Haaretz, The Jerusalem Post*, and others, and regularly contributes analysis for CNN, Fox, and Aljazeera among others. Aziz is the recipient of the Goldberg Prize for Peace in the Middle East from the Institute of International Education, the European Parliament's Silver Rose Award, the Eisenhower Medallion, and the Eliav-Sartawi Award for his Middle Eastern Journalism. He was named one of the 500 most influential Muslims in the World by the Royal Strategic Centre in Jordan for 2010, 2011, 2012, 2013, 2014, and 2015. He won the Intercultural Innovation award from the UN Alliance of Civilizations and the BMW Group. He was also recognized by UNSG Ban Ki Moon for his work in peace building.

Acknowledgements

THE COMPILATION OF *A Land Full of God: Christian Perspectives on the Holy Land* has taken several years and the dedication of an incredible group of people. I am grateful for the courage and kindness of each of the contributors and their teams of support. It is a profound privilege to work alongside such influential and committed global leaders—each compelled by Christian conviction and committed to the pursuit of peace in a land we all love. I am indebted to Aziz Abu Sarah, Daniel Roth, Scott Cooper, and the team at MEJDI Tours for their ongoing commitment to providing multi-narrative pilgrimages to the Holy Land with aspirations toward social change.

My own experiences in the Holy Land have been deeply shaped by the families who have adopted me into their communities. For many years, the Mascobi family provided a home away from home and opened my eyes to the treasures of the Old City of Jerusalem and the beauty of the Palestinian people. My friends and extended family in the region are too extensive to be named, but my heart has grown as a result of your vulnerability, generosity, and love. A few colleagues on the journey have been stalwart supporters of my work including Charlie Abou Saada, Shireen Awwad Hilal, Jack Sara, Salim Munayer, Yohanna Katanacho, Sami Awad, Munther Isaac, Daoud Nasser, and many other Christians from the community in Israel, Jerusalem, the West Bank, and Gaza. I am grateful for their steadfast hope while living under the realities of occupation.

In Israel and in the United States, I am grateful for the influence of significant leaders within the Jewish community, including individuals at the Jewish Council of Public Affairs, the Jewish Federation of Chicago, the Simon Wiesenthal Center, J Street, Religious Action Center of Reform Judaism, and the Anti-Defamation League. I hope these leaders will continue to challenge me and hone my thinking. I have learned much from the courageous efforts toward peace by Daniel Sherman, Sahar Vardi, Daniel Seidemann, Yakir Englander, Daniel Roth, Peter Ochs, Lara Friedman, and many others. Out of respect for my closest Jewish friends, I hold your struggles close to my heart and cheer on your advocacy efforts and pursuits toward peace.

This book would not have been possible without the hours of work tirelessly given by Nicole Morgan, Craig Swandby, and Natalie Wisely. Without their contributions—in both content and form—this book would never have come to completion. Nicole handled the painstaking task of organizing, compiling, editing, and formatting. Craig's thoughtful diligence in reviewing and editing the manuscripts only sharpened our understanding of the authors' perspectives and provided greater insight into the content at hand. Natalie's clear thinking and focus contributed to the organization, flow, and overall direction of the manuscript. I am grateful also for the editing and administrative efforts of Sara Burback and Anna Baker. This incredible team of writers, editors, and activists reflects the growing movement of Millennials dedicated to new ways of pursuing peace. Any errors are my own. I couldn't have completed this project without the loving support of my husband, Paul, who teaches me more about God's love than anyone I know.

I am thankful for the time and investment by the Cascade team at Wipf and Stock Publications, including Matthew Wimer, Rodney Clapp, Brian Palmer, and Ted Lewis.

My prayer is that God might be glorified by our efforts.

Introduction

Rev. Dr. Mae Elise Cannon

WATCHING THE FOOTAGE AND images of the 2014 Gaza War between militants and Hamas in Gaza and the Israeli Defense Forces (IDF) was one of the most tragic things I have ever seen. At the time, I was serving as the Senior Director of Advocacy and Outreach for World Vision and was well acquainted with the realities affecting Palestinian children living in the West Bank and Gaza. I also had many Jewish friends who talked about the penetrating fear of attack and violence against their friends and families living in Israel. My advocacy work focused primarily on calling for a cease-fire and raising awareness about the disproportionate effect of the war on children.[1]

The significant disparity between perspectives in the United States about Israel and the Palestinians came to a head for me during one of the weeks of fighting in early August 2014. At the beginning of the week, I joined several representatives from nonprofit organizations at an advocacy meeting at the Israeli Embassy in Washington, DC. Our main message was calling upon the Israeli government for a cease-fire. We had a similar message, through public statements, directed toward the perpetrators firing rockets from Gaza: "Stop the violence." During the meeting with the Israeli official, I learned he had two children actively serving in the IDF—at least one of whom was directly involved in the Gaza War. Understandably, he feared for their safety. During the meeting, I spoke about the effects of the Israeli bombing campaigns upon children living in Gaza. After the group had shared our concerns, the official stated his appreciation of our

---

1. For more of my involvement in calling for a cease-fire, see "Children in Gaza."

perspective. Then he looked at me and said, "I know you mean well . . . but, even without intending it, you are inadvertently serving as a handmaiden for Hamas." I couldn't believe my ears. How could he think my concern for children meant that I supported a terrorist organization that regularly had inflicted so much pain upon the people of Israel?

A few days later, after having worked long hours and joining several team members committed to raising awareness about the Gaza conflict, I was having a conversation with an expat working closely with the Palestinian NGO community in Jerusalem. As a colleague, I figured this man would empathize with the struggles we were having in the United States context to get people to care about what was happening in Gaza. We had successfully published several press releases and even had a piece featured on CNN highlighting the effects of the Gaza War on children. Yet, during a Skype call with this advocate for the Palestinians, he was furious that I, and my American counterparts, weren't doing enough to promote an end to the violence. He said to me something very similar to what I had heard at the Israeli Embassy. The main idea of his message was: "I know you mean well . . . but you are inadvertently supporting the bombing of innocent Palestinian children." I didn't understand how he could say such a thing . . . I could list a litany of activities, efforts, and hours spent doing our best to advocate for a cease-fire. Certainly in the grand scheme of things, our efforts were insignificant. Yet for this advocate, our limited efforts constituted an offense against the Palestinian people. How could that be?

I learned a lot during that summer. It was a stark reminder to me about how binary and divided discussions about Israel are in the United States. In the US, discussions about Israel and the Palestinians are incredibly broken and bifurcated. The issue is viewed from a false binary perspective—you are either on one side or the other. This polarization demands a false choice. Why can't American Christians hold firmly to theological convictions and support of the Jewish people while also caring deeply about the lives and impacts of the conflict on Palestinians?

One of the goals of *A Land Full of God* is to provide a more holistic space for discussion about the Holy Land and the Israeli-Palestinian conflict. I first learned of the idea of what might it mean to be pro-Israeli, pro-Palestinian, and pro-peace from Greg Khalil and Todd Deatherage of The Telos Group. Their goal is to equip and engage Americans to build a transformative pro-Israeli, pro-Palestinian, and pro-peace movement. When I speak alongside Israelis and Palestinians about holistic engagement in the conflict, we often use this language with the addition of "pro-justice" and ultimately "pro-Jesus."

Martin Luther King, Jr., said, "Peace is not the absence of tension, but the presence of justice." Sometimes we can get into trouble when we talk about peace, because peace means that we're just going to "get along" or that we're going to pretend things are okay and not address core issues. In the Middle East, some Palestinians think *peace* is a dirty word, because it can be used as an excuse to not address injustices. On the other hand, if you talk to Israelis, "justice" can be used as an abusive term, because "justice" can be used to justify any action—even violence. So how do we, as followers of Christ, reconcile these two tensions? The Scriptures call upon the people of God to both "seek peace and pursue it" (Ps 34:14, NIV) and "do right; seek justice" (Isa 1:17, NIV).

Another goal of *A Land Full of God* is to create space for constructive questions, robust conversation, and even divergent views about the conflict and Christian interest in the region. As Palestinian American Aziz Abu Sarah and Israeli American Rabbi Doctor Daniel Roth described in the foreword, constructive space to listen and learn from differing viewpoints, narratives, and perspectives is critical if a path to peace will ever be forged.

Because the land is sacred to Jews, Muslims, and Christians, there are many topics about the region that can be divisive. Even how we identify the land can be an issue of contest. Should we call it the Holy Land? And can we do so in a way that doesn't recreate the historical zealousness of the Crusader mentality—which assumed that the land only belonged to followers of Jesus? If we do not call the region the "Holy Land" what is the most appropriate term? Certainly "Israel" is an appropriate title as the Jewish people reestablished their historic homeland in the contemporary nation-state in 1948. At the same time, it is important to distinguish the modern nation-state of Israel from the Israel written about in the Hebrew Scriptures. Are they one in the same? And today, what do we call the rest of the land outside of the modern nation-state of Israel? How do we designate the territory to the west of the Jordan River that hasn't been annexed by Israel and has yet to become a state of its own? Should we call it Palestine? Or should we call it Judea and Samaria, referencing the historic Jewish presence in the land? Is occupied Palestinian territories (oPt) a legitimate political definition, as it is used even by allies of Israel like the United States? This book seeks to address these kinds of questions. Throughout this work, I often use the technical term *occupied Palestinian territories* when referring to the West Bank and Gaza.

Terminology can quickly reflect someone's perspective and bias about the conflict. For example, consider the separation barrier that currently exists between Israel and communities in the West Bank. If someone calls the barrier the "Security Fence," it denotes that they believe the barrier is a necessary structure for the security of those living in Israel. If someone calls the barrier the "Apartheid Wall," one immediately understands that person is coming from a perspective more sensitive to the experience of the Palestinians living in the West Bank. For those only cursorily educated about the conflict, one can get lost in terminology and different analysis of the "facts on the ground." On July 9, 2004, the International Court of Justice (ICJ), in The Hague, gave its advisory opinion regarding the legality of the separation barrier being built by Israel. According to B'Tselem, an Israeli human rights organization, the ICJ ruled that the separation barrier violates the rights of the Palestinians.[2] Israel did not agree that the court had jurisdiction. The barrier is just one of many realities dividing the Jewish community and Palestinians in Israel and Jerusalem from Palestinians living in the West Bank.

One of the most common things I hear about the Israeli-Palestinian conflict is the desire to have a "balanced" perspective. Balance means to give equal weight to two different sides of an equation. While it is important to give equivalent consideration to multiple perspectives, *balanced* is not the most helpful designation. First of all, there are many more perspectives than two monolithic "sides" to the conflict. Further, there are also significant power differentials at play in the Israeli-Palestinian conflict: there is the occupying power, and the occupied. Israel's military occupation of the Palestinian territories presents an imbalanced power dynamic that makes negotiation difficult, and some say impossible, for Palestinians. At the same time, Israel is a small country, roughly the size of New Jersey, and is confronted by hostile Arab states that for several decades have not acknowledged its right to exist. These are some examples of differentials in power and access to resources and do not necessarily reflect ideas of "balance."

So, what does it mean to have a more holistic perspective of the conflict? Part of that equation is creating space for disparate narratives. This book seeks to be attentive to facts and realities on the ground and to not distort data to serve any ulterior motive. How do we hold differing multiple perspectives to be true? We must wrestle with the tensions of what it means to hold the reality of the Israeli narrative and the fact anti-Semitism exists alongside of the truth that there is serious suffering for the Palestinian people in the West Bank and in Gaza. The goal is not to disparage the state of Israel or to demonize the Palestinians, but rather to more holistically understand the history and the multiple perspectives of individuals in different sectors of society who have different vantage points. *A Land Full of God* seeks to sit in those places of tension. We must wrestle, engage, discuss,

---

2. B'Tselem.

lament, grieve, celebrate, and pursue justice and reconciliation across the divides of different opinions and perspectives.

A Land Full of God gives Christians an opportunity to promote peace and justice in the Israeli-Palestinian conflict. It shows them how to understand the enmity with brief, digestible, and comprehensive essays about the historical, political, religious, and geographical tensions that have led to the dynamics we see today. Many of the essays offer differing and contradictory perspectives, with the hopes of expanding the dialogue and creating space for a more constructive conversation regarding the Israeli-Palestinian conflict and more broad Christian engagement in the Middle East. All the while, *A Land Full of God* walks readers through a biblical perspective of God's heart for Israel and the historic suffering of the Jewish people, while also remaining sensitive to the experience and suffering of Palestinians. The prevailing wave of Christian voices are seeking a pro-Israeli, pro-Palestinian, pro-peace, pro-justice, pro-poor, and ultimately pro-Jesus approach to bring resolution to the conflict.

Currently, in 2017, violence and opposing ideologies are intensifying in the Middle East and in domestic conversations within the United States about Israel and the Palestinians. As Americans witness the growing concern, they step into a web of confusion. Where did the hostility begin, and why is it so entrenched in the culture? Is there anything they can do to create peace and positive change? How does their faith relate to the dynamics that feel worlds away? How can they orient themselves to the continual headlines about Israel and Palestine, Judaism and Islam, peace and terror-filled violence?

In light of the summer 2014 war in Gaza, the ongoing civil war in Syria, the recent Arab Spring, the increasing radicalization of Islam, and the genocide of minority groups at the hands of ISIS, Christians throughout the Middle East face an uncertain future. *A Land Full of God* lifts up Christian voices in America as an act of solidarity with our brothers and sisters in Israel, Palestine, and the Middle East. Personal narratives of Christian world leaders will show readers how we can come alongside the disappearing church in the West Bank, Gaza, and the surrounding Arab world. More than following the headlines, Christ followers have an important role to play as we turn our eyes to the Middle East and to the Holy Land.

The authors of *A Land Full of God*, with the exception of the forward authors, are all believers in Jesus, although from different Christian traditions. Some are Catholics, most are Protestant, several self-identify as evangelicals. Some profess to be Christian Zionists and others are more ardent advocates of the Palestinians. The authors are theologians, historians, world politicians, Middle East experts, religious leaders, and pastors of local congregations. While I may disagree with some of the views stated in the following chapters, I believe respect is a foundational component of reconciliation. I believe each of these authors has a perspective that needs to be heard and sought to be understood. These chapters challenge me to think differently, inspire me to action, and hold out a light that there is hope for the future.

A Land Full of God is divided into six sections to bring a multifaceted understanding to the pressures facing the Middle East, keeping in the mind the context, history, theological reflections, personal experiences with both Israelis and Palestinians, ways for readers to enter the conversation, and practical steps they can take to help bring hope and alleviation to the most contested place in the world.

Part I provides a backdrop for contextualizing the conflict. Christians care deeply about the Holy Land. From the time many of us were in Sunday school, we learned about the land in the Bible stories of the Near East referenced throughout the Hebrew Scriptures—from Tyre to Sidon in ancient Philistia (Joel 3:4); to the wilderness of the Egyptian desert (Exod 16:32); to the coastline of the Mediterranean Sea (Num 34:6); to the shores of the Jordan River (Josh 1:2); to the waves of the Sea of Galilee (Mark 4:39); to the most holy and sacred of cities—Jerusalem (Ps 122:6).

Many of these sites and sacred cities are not only precious to Christians, but also to Jews and Muslims around the world. Jerusalem is the city of Christ's crucifixion and is also the city where the sacred temple of the Jews once stood; the Western wall in the Old City of Jerusalem is the holiest of places in the Jewish tradition. After Mecca and Medina, Jerusalem is the third most sacred city to followers of Mohammad and adherents of Islam. Jews, Muslims, and Christians have been living in Jerusalem, the historic land of Palestine, and modern-day Israel for thousands of years. Has there always been war? Have there been divisions between these communities since the time of Abraham? What is the history of conflict in the region and how has Christian faith, theological presuppositions, and politics contribute to what now amount to some of the greatest divides in our twenty-first–century world? How do we talk about these things in ways that are constructive and helpful rather than causing further division, strife, and hatred? How do we converse without further perpetuating historic Christian presuppositions that are inherently anti-Semitic? And how do we avoid further fanning the flames of Christian Islamophobia as we talk about Muslim extremism and terrorism in the Arab world?

In chapter 1, Dale Hanson Bourke provides a beginning for how to start to engage in the complexities and issues surrounding the Israeli-Palestinian conflict. Bourke reflects on her Christian upbringing and wonders how to relate what she learned in church to the headlines in the newspaper. Tasked with writing a book on the Israeli-Palestinian conflict, she set out to memorize all the terms, understand their origins, and become conversant in the nuances, only to find the people of the land won't fit into boxes. Her chapter provides an introduction of the things she discovered on her journey.

David Neff, former editor-in-chief and an editorial vice-president of *Christianity Today*, stands in the midst of a tragically broken relationship, with friends deeply invested on opposing sides of the Israel-Palestine conflict. Chapter 2 describes his journey: Rather than joining one side over and against the other, he responds to the call of Archbishop Elias Chacour, an Israeli citizen of Palestinian descent, "[Israelis and Palestinians] need one more common friend. We do not need one more enemy, for God's sake."

For Rich Nathan, Senior Pastor of the Vineyard Church of Columbus, Ohio, the issue of Israel is not just academic. Raised in a Jewish family, Nathan consider himself to be a Jew who believes that Jesus is the Jewish Messiah, the one promised by the God of Abraham, Isaac, and Jacob. Nathan explores the implications of this claim on his life and approach to the Israeli-Palestinian conflict. He writes about how Christians should relate to Israel in chapter 3.

Perhaps one of the most provocative and beloved Holy Sees in contemporary times, His Holiness Pope Francis gave a moving speech at the Presidential Palace with Palestinian Authorities in Bethlehem on Sunday, May 25, 2014. The manuscript of his words during his first pilgrimage to the Holy Land concludes Part I and the contextualization of the Israeli-Palestinian conflict in chapter 4.

The second part of *A Land Full of God* is about God's chosen people and the family of Abraham. This section begins to wrestle with questions surrounding the Jewish people, their chosenness before God, and the significance of their having had a remnant dwelling in the Holy Land for millennium. From various different perspectives, authors discuss the significance of Jewish return to the land as a fruit of the Jewish Zionist movement and the subsequent establishment of the modern state of Israel. *A Land Full of God* is also about the "other" people of the land, the Palestinian Arab Muslims and Christians who have also been residents in the region for thousands of years.

The restoration of the Jews to their historic homeland, for a people decimated by the *Shoah* (Holocaust) was experienced as a miracle. Thousands of refugees who had lost parents, grandparents, siblings, and extended family at the hands of the Nazi regime were rejected by the global community. Limited international immigration meant that Jewish refugees had no place to turn. The establishment of the State of Israel represented hope for a new future rising up out of the ashes of near annihilation. At the same time, the 1948 Israeli-Arab War resulted in the forced removal and displacement of more than 750,000 Palestinian Arabs, a refugee population that has grown to more than five million people today.

In chapter 5, Dr. Judith Rood talks about her Jewish heritage and identity as a Messianic follower of Jesus. Rood, serving as professor of History and Middle Eastern Studies at Biola University, shares a compelling account of her personal narrative as a Jewish activist and scholar of Islam. She issues a call to both Palestinians and Israelis to build bridges and to overcome the hatred and evil that has been directed toward both of their communities over the past several decades of history.

Many of our presuppositions about the Israeli-Palestinian conflict are based on false information or limited knowledge. Some people believe the conflict between the Arabs and Jews has been raging for thousands of years since the division between Ishmael and Isaac. In chapter 6, Lebanese Christian Tony Maalouf, World Christianity and Director of the Islamic Studies Program at Southwestern Baptist Theological Seminary, shows an alternative perspective, citing how the Scriptures prove that Ishmael and biblical Arabs are not the sworn enemy of biblical Israel, but actually were "blessed" descendants of Abraham.

Author, radio broadcaster, and Messianic Jewish leader Dr. Michael Brown asks the poignant question about the significance of the Jewish people as God's chosen ones in chapter 7, "Will God Really Bless Those who Bless Israel Today?" Brown explores the importance of American Christians understanding Jewish ties and connection to the Holy Land from the twentieth-century restoration to their historic homeland through other current events.

In chapter 8, Biblical scholar Rev. Dr. John Phelan Jr. tells of what he believes the Scriptures teach about the place of Israel in God's divine plan. Based on his recent book, *Essential Eschatology,* Phelan describes how the study of eschatology often gets bogged down in minutiae that rarely affects daily life. Phelan seeks to identify how Christians should wait for God's future to be fully revealed and what role the Jewish people and the modern nation-state of Israel plays in the divine scheme of the universe.

Part III shifts away from theological considerations and includes reflections about the intersections of the Israeli-Palestinian conflict with other relevant historical periods. Native American scholar Dr. Andrea Smith writes in chapter 9 about "Land and People." Smith grew up relating the state of Israel to the Cherokee nation. She reasoned that just as the Cherokee people should have the right to their land in Georgia, so too do the Jewish people have the unconditional right to their historic homeland

land in Israel. Over time, her views have changed. She still does not question the relationship between the Jewish people and Israel; but rather, the relationship between people and land. She challenges the assumption that the attainment of a nation-state should be the goal for any liberation struggle.

In chapter 10, Dr. Clayborne Carson with Rev. Dr. Troy Jackson, write about Martin Luther King, Jr.'s "Hope for a Better Israel." Carson serves as the Director of the Martin Luther King, Jr. Research and Education Institute at Stanford University. Recounting a 2011 journey to the Holy Land, Carson tells of leading a mostly African American delegation to the region to perform the play "Passages of Martin Luther King." This collaboration between African American musicians and Palestinian actors would result in the first Arabic-language play about King. Carson's work helps integrate the legacy of King's allegiances with the Jewish people, struggle for liberation, human rights, and justice with the on the ground experiences of Palestinians living under occupation.

In chapter 11, Donald Lewis, Professor of Church History at Regent College and author of "The Origins of Christian Zionism," describes the history of Christian Zionism. Lewis writes that over the past five centuries it has been associated with very different theological frameworks and prophetic views; it is a movement in the sense that it is "on the move" and continues to morph.

The final chapter focusing on intersections of history looks with broad brushstrokes at the modern political history of the conflict. In chapter 12, Dr. David Gushee, distinguished University Professor of Christian Ethics and Director for the Center of Theology and Public Life at Mercer University, reviews core geopolitical disagreements and highlights the distinctive characteristics American evangelicals bring to the global discussion and potential resolution of the Israel-Palestine problem.

Part IV continues the discussion of different political paradigms and perspectives. In chapter 13, Susan Michael, Director of the International Christian Embassy in the United States reminds readers of the weight and magnitude of how Christian beliefs about Israel and the Jewish people are critically important. She calls Christians to take a stand. Michael believes "Israel presents a moral and ethical challenge to the world and will become the ultimate fault line." She writes about how the Jewish people play a vital role in God's divine plan for the redemption of the world.

Archbishop Desmond Tutu, in chapter 14, reflects on the profound inspirational biblical accounts of the Hebrew people brought to South Africa's anti-Apartheid movement. The liberation of the Jewish people was a reminder that God hears the cries of the oppressed, even in Palestine. Tutu highlights his observations about realities affecting the Palestinian community in the West Bank and Gaza in his chapter on "Palestine and Apartheid."

Responding to the 2014 War in Gaza, the United States' Secretary of State John Kerry traveled to Cairo, Egypt to speak at the international Donor conference on Gaza's reconstruction. In chapter 15, Secretary Kerry's message goes beyond the needs of immediate reconstruction: "I say clearly and with deep conviction here today: The United States remains fully, totally committed to returning to the negotiations not for the sake of it, but because the goal of this conference and the future of this region demand it. There is nothing sustainable about the status quo. In the end, the underlying causes of discontent and suspicion and anger that exist in Israel, the West Bank, and Gaza can only be eliminated by resolving the conflict itself."

Chapter 16 ends the section on political paradigms in Dr. Paul Nathan Alexander's "Protestifying: A Pentecostal Reflection on Interfaith Learning and Political Action." As former professor of Christian ethics and public policy at Palmer Theological Seminary of Eastern University, Alexander recounts his dive into behind the scenes interfaith discourse on the Israeli-Palestinian conflict. After years of study, dialogue, and wrestling, Alexander finds that the only way forward is to let hope die.

Though violence sweeps across the Middle East, we are witnessing a growing tide of pro-peace, pro-justice American Christians who want to see restoration and reconciliation, particularly in the Holy Land. Part V focuses on what it might take to bring an end to violence and a vision for peace.

Chapter 17 lifts up the voices of millennials engaged in policy work and advocacy in Washington, DC, and around the country. Their efforts seek to mobilize a growing movement of "Millennial Voices for Peace" (MVP) who are committed to a new way of entering into relationships with Israelis, Palestinians, and people with divergent perspectives about the conflict in the Middle East. MVP invites you to consider signing their Statement of Principles recounted in this chapter.

Dr. Bob Roberts, founding pastor of NorthWood Church in Dallas/Fort Worth, continues the discussion in chapter 18 about how Christians might overcome "Barriers to Peace." Roberts reflects on tribalism and prejudice and his unexpected journey into the Israeli-Palestinian conflict confronts the human temptation to categorize a group of people as less than or more than others. A seed of discrimination against a single person or group opens the door to discrimination amongst all groups and people.

In chapter 19, Dr. David A. Anderson, author, founder, and Senior Pastor of Bridgeway Community Church, reflects on an old African Proverb: "From afar, I thought you were a monster. When you got closer, I thought you were just an animal. When you got closer I noticed that you were a human, but when we were face to face, I realized you were my brother." With this in mind, Anderson proposes five ways to effect peace.

Dr. Darrell L. Bock of Dallas Theological Seminary and *Christianity Today* explores the complexities resulting from competing religious claims to the Holy Land in chapter 20. Muslims, Christians, and Jews in the land are in a cycle of suffering with plenty of blame to go around; is there a way forward? Bock's chapter focuses on "Hope in the Midst of a Mess."

As one of the primary leaders of the International Campaign to Ban Landmines (ICBL), Jerry White received the Nobel Prize in 1997. In chapter 21, "Navigating Minefields: Explosive Wisdom for Modern Pilgrims," White tells parts of his riveting personal story of the loss of his leg because of a landmine in Israel and the lessons he learned as a result of his personal loss and advocacy to have a world free of landmines.

I first learned the phrase "We Belong to Each Other" from Lynne Hybels as she taught me the famous quote of Mother Teresa: "If we have no peace, it is because we have forgotten that we belong to each other." Part VI focuses on relationships across divides as one of the primary ways we remember that we belong to each other.

Focusing on relationships, Shane Claiborne writes in chapter 22 about how his heart was broken after serving alongside of the Ecumenical Accompaniment Program in Hebron, Palestine. Claiborne writes about his personal encounters with both Palestinians and Israelis and about peacemaking, social justice, and Jesus.

Carolyn Custis James, President of the Whitby Forum, writes about "The Power of Unexpected Relationships" in chapter 23. James recounts her experience in Oxford, England during the launch of Operation Desert Storm. Oxford proved to be a global village with neighbors from all over the world sharing meals, talking politics and religion, and encountering a cornucopia of cultural diversity. These neighbors exposed perspectives Carolyn hadn't considered and introduced her to realities she could no longer ignore.

Throughout Lynne Hybels' travels and ministry she continues to ask herself: "What does it mean to follow Jesus into a place of violent conflict?" In chapter 24, Hybels' reflects "A Truer and Deeper Peace." Through encounters with the Holy Land and its people—Muslims, Christians, and Jews —Hybels encourages us to listen with a discerning ear, to study well, to question what we hear, and to learn from a wide variety of people.

Rev. Eugene Cho writes in chapter 25 about the Holy Land and discipleship. He emphasizes the idea that we are often more in love with the idea of changing the world than actually changing the world. Many Christians have been in love with Israel or Palestine, with the Holy Land, with our Christian heritage therein, but few allow the land and its people to impact us, change us, make us think and grow. As a result, we have ignored the truth of our Holy Land; it is full of pain, suffering, hate, prejudice, and deep wounds. If we seek to confront this reality, to be peace builders, to heal wounds, and to see justice in the land; if we seek to follow Jesus into the land of his birth, we must accept the reality that we ourselves need to be changed in the process.

The final section, Part VII, focuses on "Future Hope" and action and engagement toward a just peace. Over and over again, I have heard it said that the Israeli-Palestinian conflict is intractable. It will never be solved. Yet, in my heart of hearts, I do not believe that to be true. Pragmatically, numerous global crises have raged for decades with the belief that they might never end. Consider the violent division between Catholics and Protestants in Northern Ireland and apartheid in South Africa. In South Africa, 1989 marked the end of a decades long regime that had been marked by racial disparity where the rights, movement, and freedoms of individuals were significantly limited based on race. Similarly, no one ever believed there would be peace in Belfast. Yet on Good Friday in 1998 an agreement was signed that eventually led to a more lasting peace. Even in the most hopeless of situations, we must hold out for the future hope of peace.

In chapter 26, Jim Wallis, *New York Times* bestselling author and President/Founder of *Sojourners*, suggests that Christians in the United States have become an obstacle to peace in Israel and Palestine. Wallis suggests the North American Church must take a new approach; one that is pro-Israeli, pro-Palestinian, and pro-peace by "Praying for Peace in Jerusalem."

Joel Hunter is a national evangelical voice, spiritual advisor to President Barak Obama, and pastor in Orlando, Florida. He has had the opportunity to interface and work closely in partnership with followers of Islam, Judaism, and other religions outside of Christianity. In chapter 27, Hunter highlights the importance of relationships across religious divides particularly as Christians, Jews, and Muslims are deeply invested in the future of Jerusalem, Israel, Palestine, and the land Christ followers call holy.

Bill Hybels, founder and Senior Pastor of Willow Creek Community Church, draws from his experience to recommend best practices in creating a new conversation on Israel-Palestine in the local church in chapter 28. Above all, Hybels believes the American attitudes toward Israel and Palestine have an unavoidable impact on what happens in the Holy Land; it is critical for American Christian leaders to promote a conversation that is authentically pro-Israeli, pro-Palestinian, and pro-peace.

The final chapter by Tony Campolo addresses practical considerations of how Christians can be "Agents of Reconciliation." A prolific speaker, author, and cofounder of Red Letter Christians, Campolo looks at the intersection of racism, divisive policies, and a responsible preaching and teaching of Scripture. He asks us to remember Galatians 3:28, where we are told that in Christ such prejudices and discrimination are contrary to the spirit of Christ, who seeks to make us one people.

What role can Christians play as we seek to constructively engage in the land and with the people of the Holy Land? Christ followers can pray for the people of Israel; pray for the peace of Jerusalem; pray for the Palestinians; pray for the manifestation of justice; and pray for peace.

One of the unique roles American Christians can play in promoting peace in the Holy Land is to be agents of hope as we engage in peacebuilding, reconciliation, and advocating for justice for all people in the Holy Land. The Scriptures promise there will be trials and challenges in the world, but the good news of the Gospel is that peace is possible. John 16:33 says, "I have told you these things, so that in me you may have peace. In this world you will have trouble. But take heart! I have overcome the world." Might we be hope to one another as Christians and all people around the world diligently encourage efforts toward peace, while holding onto the belief that an end to the conflict is possible in *A Land Full of God*.

Bibliography

B'Tselem. "Opinion of the International Court of Justice." Jan 1, 2011. Accessed June 25, 2016. http://www.btselem.org/separation_barrier/international_court_decision.

"Children in Gaza sponsored by Christian charity killed." *The Lead with Jake Tapper*, CNN. Atlanta: August 1, 2014. http://thelead.blogs.cnn.com/2014/08/01/children-in-gaza-sponsored-by-christian-charity-killed/.

Part I

Contextualizing the
Israeli-Palestinian Conflict

©Mae Elise Cannon
Haram al-Sharif, the Temple Mount—Old City of Jerusalem.

1

Beginning to Understand the Israeli-Palestinian Conflict

Dale Hanson Bourke

MY VERY FIRST BOOK was a Bible, and even before I could read its words, the colored pictures and the shaded maps of a place called the Holy Land captivated me. In those earliest days of spiritual education and Sunday school stories, I somehow confused the Holy Land with heaven. I heard stories about Jesus in places like the hills of Judea or the Sea of Galilee, and then we prayed to Jesus in heaven. Sitting squarely in the middle of the flat Midwest, I assumed a place with hills and a sea had to be in heaven.

Although I eventually sorted it out, it wasn't the last time I was confused about the Holy Land. Like many Christians, I spent most of my adult years wondering how to relate what I learned in church to the headlines in the newspaper. Was the Israel I read about in the Bible the same one I saw on the evening news? Were the Christians in the Middle East the descendants of those early church members Paul wrote about in the New Testament?

As a friend of mine observed, "After all those years in church I feel like I should know more about the issues in the Middle East, but I don't know where to start." I knew exactly what she meant.

But there was more. There was a strong sense of avoidance and even denial. When I was around my Jewish friends, I was always careful to avoid the subject. I didn't know what terms to use and what might be offensive. I sometimes heard my liberal Jewish friends criticize the actions of Israeli politicians, but I always felt I should steer clear of those conversations.

In my Bible study, some of my Christian friends began to talk about Palestinian rights, while others defended Israel, often basing their arguments on the Bible. In the interest of harmony, we banned all such discussions from our Bible study and went back to safer topics.

For many years, I was happy with that approach. I equated peace with avoidance. After all, every time the subject came up, arguments seemed to follow. If there was ever a topic that seemed to attract conflict, it was the mere mention of Israelis and Palestinians. My view of peacemaking was to gently change the subject.

Eventually my ignorance began to frustrate me. I wanted to know more—just the facts—about the region and the issues. When I began my own search for answers I ran into a new challenge. Even a simple question could bring a barrage of strong opinions. Some of my most mild-mannered friends moved from placid to angry at the mention of Israelis or Palestinians. It seemed like many people had strong opinions—on both sides—and wanted to tell me what to believe.

Many of those people recommended books for me to read and most of those books were aimed at convincing me that one side was right and the other was wrong. But I wasn't ready to take sides. I wanted to understand the basics first.

And so began my journey to find others, like me, who wanted to know more. I collected the questions people wanted to ask, the terms that confused them, and the events they had heard so much about but didn't really understand. I discovered that many people were like me, trying to connect the dots from biblical knowledge to historical understanding to current events.

My search for answers took me to some of those places I had first seen on the map in the back of my childhood Bible. Most lacked the ethereal glow I had imagined. But instead I found amazing people—Israelis and Palestinians—who generously shared their experiences and opinions with me.

Some conversations were disturbing. I found some Israelis who believed the worst about Palestinians and some Palestinians who wanted only to tell me bad stories about Israelis. I was surprised to discover most had never had a conversation with the other, except at a checkpoint.

But I also found remarkable people who wanted only peace. One of my first encounters was with an Israeli woman named Robi Damelin, who had lost her son David in the conflict. Now part of an organization that brings Palestinians and Israelis who have lost family members together,

Robi's advice to well-meaning people around the world is this: "Don't be pro-Israeli. Don't be pro-Palestinian. Be pro-peace, or leave us alone."[1]

As I did research, I tried to heed Robi's advice. I talked to Palestinians and Israelis, read books representing various points of view, and interviewed experts on all sides. As an American and a Christian, I have to acknowledge that my identities may create more bias than all my attempts at objectivity can overcome.

When I was asked to write a book on the Israeli-Palestinian conflict, I of course said no. Who was I to write a book on a subject I had avoided for most of my life and then tiptoed into just far enough to know that the waters were cold, shark-infested, and full of currents that could easily pull me under? Because I had already written a series of books on complex subjects called The Skeptic's Guides, my publisher and others believed I might be able to treat this subject the same way. But I knew that wasn't possible. This subject was more than complex. It was fraught with emotion and agendas and stories within stories.

Learning to Listen

I never really said yes. The best I could say was, "I'll try." And thus began the most difficult year of my life. I became intellectually insecure and frustratingly unproductive. Days of research often produced just one written page. More than once, I considered quitting the project and taking up something more manageable. But in retrospect, the lessons of that year were not so much about choosing my subject more carefully, but about what I learned and how I learned it. Taking on a topic that was so complicated and potentially polarizing taught me lessons I had never learned from writing about subjects closer to my comfort zone. And because the subject was not just about facts but also about beliefs, I spent a good amount of time interviewing people who held a variety of opinions.

If there was a theme for that time, it would have to be the year of asking questions. I asked dozens of questions, not in the way I had ever asked questions before. I asked to understand points of view I found confusing and disturbing. I listened to people share stories of pain and anger, sorrow and frustration. I heard theories and diatribes, proposed solutions and defiant declarations. It was important to understand each so thoroughly that I could explain them. So instead of pushing back, I asked to hear more.

1. Parent's Circle.

People from completely different points of view took the time to talk to me, to explain themselves, to answer my often ignorant questions. They were mostly kind, extravagantly patient, and willing to share resources. I rarely offered an opinion or reacted to what I heard. It wasn't my place and my lack of expertise was profound. I needed to take in what was offered without filters.

Some of the people I interviewed wanted me to engage. It is, after all, a topic that elicits strong reactions from almost anyone. But most just seemed surprised and then grateful that I was truly listening to a view they held dear. The longer I spent listening, the more I realized that my ignorance was a gift. I wasn't being disingenuous when I said, "I don't really know enough to offer an opinion." I asked to truly understand, not to argue.

In the end, I came to a place of empathy for a variety of opinions. Almost every person I interviewed graciously offered to help. Many spent hours reviewing my drafts and helping me articulate their point of view clearly. I made new friends so diverse I dare not mention one to the other. And even when I found some of their beliefs disturbing, I came to understand why they held them. Instead of stereotyping points of view or types of people involved in this conflict, I came to a new appreciation for the painful realities and conflicting narratives.

I learned to ask questions, not to be polite, or to elicit a quote for a story, or to act like I cared. I asked questions to truly understand. Not only did I learn a great deal about the subject, I learned even more about people. We are very much alike, even when we hold very different opinions. We mostly care about the people we love and about being safe. We care about justice even though we define it in many ways. And we want to be respected. We want someone to listen to our thoughts and try to truly understand who we are.

Rejecting Labels

Here's the problem: You can memorize all the terms, understand their origins, become conversant in the nuances, and even know when not to use them. The Zionists and Palestinians. The settlers and the freedom fighters. Those who support Fatah or Hamas or Likud or Labor.

But then you meet the people and they confuse you. Like the proud Zionist who uses his brilliant legal mind to represent Palestinians. Or the Palestinian who studies Buddhism and pacifism and teaches peaceful resistance to his people. Or the settler who has come to love his Palestinian neighbor. Or the Christian Palestinian citizen of Israel who believes Jesus wants him to help all people. It never really adds up. The labels never really help define any of these people.

But Americans like labels. I like labels. It helps me sort people into good and bad. Saint and sinner. It makes sense of messiness and explains the reason why people act the way they do. Labels take away some of my discomfort and impotence.

After writing *The Skeptics Guide to the Israeli-Palestinian Conflict* (InterVarsity Press, 2013), I was asked to speak on the subject from time to time. I tried to remain neutral, offering history and definitions in careful tones.

Whenever I spoke, I worked hard to sound almost clinical and detached, but then I would think of the people. Good people. Loving people. People like you and me who simply want to live quiet lives with their families. I was tempted to talk about the people who told me stories of losses and agony I could barely stand to hear. I wanted to talk about weeping with Israelis and Palestinians and laughing with them too. But that would only confuse my audience. More often than not I was asked questions like, "Which side are you on?" "Who do you think is right?" "Isn't this all the fault of _____?"

I would carefully explain that most Israelis have never met a Palestinian. It's easier that way. You can believe Palestinians are different kinds of people if you don't know any. Most Palestinians have only met Israeli soldiers. They see Israelis as occupiers and, too often, brutes. I explain this to help Americans understand why loving Israelis and loving Palestinians can hate each other and call each other vile names.

I know that the labels are useful for slogans and sound bites and wars. But the names and the stories would undo all of that. Perhaps that's why the political leaders work so hard to keep people apart. It would be harder to launch a missile toward the home of someone you might know. It would be harder to drop an explosive on an apartment where a friend might live.

During the conflict in the summer of 2014, I watched the images from Israel and Gaza, and I looked at the faces. Now I actually know people in these places. It is no longer an abstract concept or a place I read about in my Bible. I thought knowledge would help me become objective. But the people have undone me.

Changed by Individuals

A skeptic at the beginning of my journey, I was first surprised and then greatly moved by the people I met there who are working—often sacrificially—for peace.

My heart was changed as I watched Robi Damelin, an Israeli Jew, embrace Bassam Aramin, a Palestinian Muslim, as they each told of losing a child to the conflict. As members of the Parents Circle/Family Forum, they join dozens of other Israelis and Palestinians who meet together and speak out about their own losses, determined to find a way to keep others from experiencing the same pain they have endured. Their friendships don't come easily. But perhaps more than any other people in the region, they understand the cost of conflict.

My mind was changed as a Muslim man in Nazareth directed me to what he called the "Christian hospital," assuring me, "They are good people. They help everyone, not just Christians." I walked the halls of Nazareth hospital and heard patients and their families thank God and Allah for this historically Christian hospital.[2] I learned that people come from miles around, not just for physical healing, but also for psychiatric therapy that is rarely available to the Arab population of Israel, as well as help with parenting and family problems. A volunteer program called SERVE Nazareth brings Christians from around the world to help comfort patients and pray for them as they receive dialysis or chemotherapy.[3]

In Haifa, the House of Grace ministers in the name of Jesus to the most needy citizens, including ex-prisoners, whether they are Muslim, Jewish, or Christian.[4] The entire town takes pride in the work done by this thirty-year-old ministry, and the fact that everyone is treated like family, whatever their background.

In the town of Bethlehem, I listened to Sami Awad talk about how his ministry, Holy Land Trust, teaches Palestinians that every encounter with an Israeli soldier is an opportunity to show love.[5] I heard stories of Israeli soldiers, who had entered the West Bank afraid and full of hatred for Palestinians, but now had true friendships with those they once considered the enemy.

---

2. Nazareth Trust, "Nazareth Hospital."
3. Nazareth Trust, "Serve."
4. House of Grace.
5. Holy Land Trust.

I saw how Bethlehem Bible College equips pastors and lay leaders to minister creatively, regardless of the circumstances.[6] I was amazed to learn that despite their own hardships, mission teams are going out from the college to help Syrian refugees.

I was moved to tears as I heard Daoud Nassar, a Palestinian Christian, explain how he and his family live out the sentiment painted on a rock at the entrance to their family farm in the West Bank, nearly surrounded by an Israeli settlement. "We Refuse to Be Enemies" is more than a slogan at his Tent of Nations ministry.[7] Even some of the Israeli settlers who once tried to evict the family are beginning to believe it.

My mind was stretched as I listen to Jewish believers in *Yeshu'a* (what some call Messianic Jews) struggle to find reconciliation with Palestinian Christians, with whom they often disagree politically. "We need to believe that our shared faith is greater than our differences," said Salim Munayer, who runs Musalaha, a respected ministry of reconciliation between Israelis and Palestinians.[8]

These people and many more challenged my skepticism and made me examine my own beliefs. Jesus preached peace and reconciliation, and many of these Israelis and Palestinians practice his principles in the face of great obstacles. Their lives are not easy, and yet they have hope. Who am I to have less faith than they do?

As I thought about other places in the world that have seemed irreparably broken, like South Africa and Northern Ireland, I was reminded that we believe in a God of reconciliation; a Lord of healing. Sometimes when situations are most desperate, he has surprised us by bringing people together in ways that are truly miraculous. Nelson Mandela, a man who knew something about peace, said, "It always seems impossible until it's done."

There are many reasons to be cynical about peace in the Holy Land. But as a Christian I have the advantage of trusting in a God who works in mysterious ways. Having seen the remarkable faith of many men and women in the region, I choose to support them through prayer and hope. I don't think about the politicians but the individuals who are faithfully working for peace day after day. I continue to listen and learn. For their sake, and for everyone living in the Holy Land, I pray for a miracle.

---

6. Bethlehem Bible College.
7. Tent of Nations.
8. Musalaha.

Bibliography

Bethlehem Bible College. Accessed July 7, 2015. http://www.bethbc.org.
Holy Land Trust. Accessed July 7, 2015. http://www.holylandtrust.org.
House of Grace. Accessed July 7, 2015. http://www.house-grace.org.
Musalaha. Accessed July 7, 2015. https://www.musalaha.org/home/.
Nazareth Trust. "Nazareth Hospital." Accessed July 7, 2015. http://www.nazarethtrust.org/nazareth-hospital.
———. "Serve Nazareth." Accessed July 7, 2015. http://www.nazarethtrust.org/SERVE.
Parents Circle. Accessed July 7, 2015. www.parentscircle.com.
Tent of Nations. Accessed July 7, 2015. http://www.tentofnations.org.

2

"We Need One More Common Friend"

David Neff

THIS CHAPTER IS PAINFUL for me to write because I have friends who are deeply invested on opposing sides of the Israel-Palestine conflict. Friends who, because of their deep commitments and their public and private advocacy, would find it difficult to be friends with each other.

I hasten to add that these friends are not might-makes-right folk who do not care about the suffering, the aspirations, or the justice claims of the other side. Some of them advocate nonviolence. All affirm the rule of law. Yet, because of the way their personal and ethnic narratives have shaped them, it seems that they cannot find a common language.

What is a Christ follower to do? I usually take the coward's path and listen well to both sets of friends, but rarely challenge them. Shameful but true.

On my visits to Israel-Palestine, I was warmly received and experienced wonderful hospitality on both sides of the divide. I left the country feeling I had established new friendships. But I never tried to bring those friends together.

My first encounter with Palestinian liberation theologian Naim Ateek was far more than the journalist's interview I had sought. At the time, he was pastor to the Arabic-speaking congregation at St. George's Cathedral in East Jerusalem. Naim invited me to play the cathedral's wonderful new pipe organ, and after church, he and his wife fed me dinner in their apartment. Afterwards, we listened to their sons play hymns, and she taught me to make Middle Eastern style coffee. I still have the *ibrik* I purchased on that trip so I could brew it at home.

But I have also received wonderful hospitality from Jews who live in Israel or have family there. My friendship with one well-connected American Jew has allowed me access to places and people American Christians wouldn't normally expect to see. One of my more colorful memories is of a visit to the barracks of young Israeli soldiers near the Lebanon border. I haven't seen such a mess since I lived in a college dormitory in the 1960s. I enjoyed their tales of life together, and we laughed heartily as one of them described his desperate retreat from the battlefield when his armored personnel carrier got stuck in reverse. Unable to turn around and drive normally, he covered that twenty or so miles to safety while looking in his rearview mirror.

Having friends on both sides of the festering issues between Israel and Palestine is not unlike trying to maintain friendships with both parties in a divorce. Shared experience and a concern for their well-being makes it hard to end those friendships even when you know you won't ever share their lives as a couple again.

Perhaps you, like I, have been able to keep alive good relationships with both members of a former marriage. But it requires work and wisdom. The more the parties to a divorce draw their identity from what went wrong in their relationship, the more difficult it is to maintain dual friendships. If one or both parties need you to constantly reaffirm their version of events, it will likely poison your relationship with the other party.

Couples who move on with new lives and new partners, however—those who draw their sense of identity from what is new, who live in the present and for the future—those folk make it possible to maintain parallel friendships.

Much of the time, the Israeli-Palestinian conflict feels like a divorcing couple who aren't ready to move on, to live in the present and to live for the future. Therein lies a problem.

I became interested in Israel-Palestine and its challenges through Evangelicals for Middle East Understanding (EMEU). The affable provocateur Don Wagner pulled me in, and engagement with that organization opened my eyes to an entirely new world.

I liked EMEU's fundamental purpose: to raise American Christian consciousness of the lives, history, contributions, and challenges of Middle Eastern Christians.

The historic churches of the region have rich traditions of spiritual practice and worship. Their theologies are, for the most part, far deeper than those the average evangelical church in America. In places like Egypt, Syria, and Iraq, Christians have had to live as minorities in societies that granted them very limited freedoms. There was no overt evangelism—a fact which made American evangelicals wonder whether perhaps they were not truly Christian. But in this constrained mode of existence, Middle Eastern Christians were far more like early believers living under Roman domination.

Palestinian Christians, however, posed a particular problem for Jewish-Christian friendship. As displaced persons, Palestinians could rightly point to the events of 1948 when, in the tumult that accompanied the creation of the state of Israel, many thousands fled their homes and villages in fear. Others who didn't flee lost not only their homes but their lives. This crisis is the fundamental fact that has shaped several generations of Palestinian life.

But just as you aren't likely to get the full story from only one party in a failing marriage, you aren't likely to get the full story from listening to certain Palestinian Christian leaders. I realize that advocates are not expected to tell both sides of a story. That is what journalists and scholars are for. But unfortunately, some of the most charismatic and winsome spokespersons for the Palestinian cause have indulged in anti-Israel rhetoric that smacks of classic anti-Semitism. Frankly, when you talk about Israel "crucifying" Palestine, you echo some of the worst medieval Christian anti-Semitism.

It is perhaps an unavoidable hazard of EMEU's mission: to present Christians from Palestine to American believers means presenting their perspectives, and not somebody else's, on their most pressing issues.

Nevertheless, I experienced notable moments when the stories rose above victimhood. In the early 1990s, shortly after the First Intifada ended, Palestinian human rights lawyer Jonathan Kuttab spoke of the opportunity Palestinians would soon have to move from a victim identity to something more constructive, namely building the institutions of civil society. He was clearly living in the present and living for the future, and he challenged his fellow Palestinians to do the same.

Similarly, I heard Father (later Archbishop) Elias Chacour speak movingly of interfaith and interethnic cooperation in his northern Israel town of Ibillin in Galilee. His inspiring stories were sometimes met by skepticism. On one occasion, representatives from the Egyptian Christian community called him naïve for trying to work with Muslims toward reconciliation. But he didn't live in Egypt, and he had worked marvelously with Jews and Muslims to educate youth and build civil society together.

Fr. Chacour shares my concern for the one-sidedness that can result from listening to compelling stories of injustice and victimhood. Speaking at Emory University in 2001, Fr. Chacour called on his audience to be friends of Israel, but to "stop interpreting that friendship as automatic antipathy against me, the Palestinian who is paying the bill for what others have done against my beloved Jewish brothers and sisters in the Holocaust and elsewhere." And if his listeners wanted to take the side of the Palestinians, he said, they should not become "one-sided against my Jewish brothers and sisters."

"We do not need such friendship," he continued. "We need one more common friend. We do not need one more enemy, for God's sake."

For me, that statement is the key to the future. Palestinians and Israelis need more common friends, not more enemies of the other side.

And so I try to be a friend to Palestinian Christians and to do my very small part to help them realize their hopes and aspirations. But I cannot do that by becoming an enemy of Israel. I genuinely believe in the right of the Jewish people to a home in at least part of their ancient lands. I believe this, in part, because of God's promises to them (though, I hasten to add, not in the way that dispensationalist Christians do). I believe this also because it is healthy for the Middle East to have a liberal democracy in their midst (and I say that despite the reservations I have about the actions of Israel's right-wing governments). I believe this also because Israel's democratic system has been kinder to its resident Christians than many other governments in the region (again, despite Israel's failure to allow American-style religious freedom).

So how does one stand with Israel and with Palestinian Christians at the same time? First, by making friends in both communities. This requires us to take some initiative.

On the Jewish side of the equation, it is a fact that American Jews and evangelical Protestants, the constituency I served for so long at *Christianity Today* magazine, do not live and work in the same places. This demographic fact is the result of history. Immigrant Jews settled in New York and then spread to other urban areas that facilitated the creation of ethnic enclaves. Evangelicals have a history attached to the American South and Midwest. They are more attracted to smaller cities and rural areas.

Intentional conversations about relationships between Jews and evangelicals have only recently begun. Jews have been in dialogue with Catholics and Mainline Protestants far longer, but because evangelicals are decentralized, with no authoritative head, it has been harder for Jews to know whom to engage. Despite the high profile Zionist apologetics of people like John Hagee and Rabbi Yechiel Eckstein, there has not been much genuine conversation. Indeed, their Zionist apologetics creates a sense of suspicion among evangelical leaders, and their close association with evangelicals creates caution on the part of both Jewish leaders.

Making personal friendships is also important. One of my Palestinian-American friends recently made a Jewish friend. About 80 percent of his frequent Facebook posts are about reports of brutality or other injustices committed by the Israeli Defense Force in the West Bank. But a few weeks ago he wrote of making friends with a Lubavitcher, a member of a Hasidic community founded in the 1700s, from Atlanta while attending a conference in New York. He asked whether he could join him for evening prayers at a *Chabad Shul*, and he found himself deeply impressed "by the enthusiasm of the men praying at the service and by the intensity of the worship." He found the readings and prayers were "focused on God in a way [he] fully recognized and agreed with." "How very sad," he concluded, "that Zionism has separated me from many of these devout and faithful people."

Mutual hospitality is difficult between Christians and observant Jews because of kosher laws, but despite those limits, developing deep friendships is possible. We share so much Scripture that mutual Bible study offers wonderful opportunities to learn from and about each other. One rabbi friend of mine meets regularly with a New Testament professor just to learn the Christian Scriptures better.

To prepare for mutual encounters with Scripture, I highly recommend that Christians read *The Jewish Annotated New Testament*, a study Bible with notes written by contemporary Jewish scholars who read the New Testament authors in light of the rabbinic Judaism that was developing at the same time as these authors were writing.

Making friends with Palestinians will also require some effort. If you travel to the Holy Land, you must make a point of meeting Palestinian Christians. The security barrier adds delays and difficulty, of course. And if you take one of the standard Holy Land bus tours, it will take you to Bethlehem, but you will be marshaled in lockstep through the Church of the Nativity and then deposited briefly at a Palestinian souvenir shop where you can buy carved olive wood nativity sets.

Learning about the lives of Palestinians requires alternative tour planning. Years ago that was hard to do. Now there are many touring options that can put you in touch with the living Christian community in Palestine. Just Google "Tour Palestine" to find alternative, multi-perspective tours that may even get you involved in olive picking in the West Bank or visiting a refugee camp.

For my first visit to Israel-Palestine, I asked Americans who were well networked in each community to suggest people I might talk with to gain perspective. In those days before email, I had to get up in the wee morning hours in Chicago to contact various Palestinians and Israeli Jews whose conversations promised to enlighten me. Because I was representing an influential Christian magazine, I was able to connect with some very significant people on each side. I had decided to travel independently, and that meant a certain amount of risk, I suppose. But I never really felt threatened. It just required careful planning.

As a journalist, I wanted to meet one of my Palestinian counterparts. And so I arranged to meet Daoud Kuttab at the East Jerusalem offices of the Arabic newspaper *Al-Quds*. Getting there was a problem, because Israeli taxi drivers did not want to take me into East Jerusalem. But I was persistent and persuasive, and I finally got a ride. Daoud has a long record as a hard-nosed but fair journalist, and was a critic of Yasser Arafat as much as he was of Israeli leadership. In the years that followed our meeting, he went on to teach at Princeton University, Al-Quds University in Ramallah. He then relocated to Jordan where he was able to found a censorship-free news service (amin.org).

I connected with Daoud's brother, Jonathan, in the American Colony Hotel's legendary cellar bar. The place is a historic favorite meeting place for journalists, so Jonathan knew I'd feel at home. Jonathan, a human rights lawyer, filled me in on the ways in which Israeli law allows West Bank Palestinians to be detained and held without charges up for to six months—a much longer period than would legally be possible in the US or other western countries.[1]

These were just a few of the very helpful Christians who opened my eyes to the difficulties their people faced on a regular basis.

I also sought out Israeli leaders who helped me see things most tourists did not.

One of the most memorable was Itzik Yaacobi, a Holocaust survivor who assisted Jerusalem Mayor Teddy Kollek in the administration of the Old City. He showed me wonderful hospitality, taking me to archaeological digs (a personal interest of mine) and introducing me to old city residents of both Arab and Jewish backgrounds. I reconnected with Itzik several years later when my wife accompanied me to Jerusalem. I wanted to introduce her to Itzik, and I think she fell in love with this charming man when the three of us drank tea with a Palestinian Jerusalemite near the entrance to Hezekiah's Tunnel.

Another helpful conversation partner was the minister of religious affairs (one of the last who held that specific office) who met me at a Chinese restaurant to explain the dynamics and the historical forces that shaped

---

1. Administrative detention allows Palestinians and others threatening the security of Israel to be detained on the basis of an administrative order, without either indictment or trial.

Christian, Jewish, Muslim, and Druze relationships. Going out of my way to arrange meetings with these and others paid off.

It is vitally important to diversify your sources of news from Israel-Palestine. You should definitely read the Middle East news in major American newspapers like *The New York Times*, *The Washington Post*, and *The Wall Street Journal*. But you should also pay attention to Middle East sources.

Use Wikipedia to find lists of appropriate media. Type "Category: Palestinian Media," "Category: Israeli Media," and "Category: Jewish Media" into Wikipedia's search window to find extensive lists of options.

Using those category lists and following links will acquaint you with hundreds of incidents the American press has probably overlooked. Check out, for example, the Israeli alternative blog/magazine +972 (972mag.com) and the Palestinian Electronic Intifada (electronicintifada.net). Watch out for loaded language on these sites: "Israeli apartheid" and "ethnic cleansing," for example. As you read these sources, be aware of their commitments, and you will learn how to evaluate the mainstream news about the ongoing conflict.

Read both Jewish and Arab opinion writers who are not afraid to criticize the actions of their leaders. I could list some of my favorites, but someone would object to their bias. It is better, I think, to explore for yourself the varied sources of information. Just keep in mind that Israeli opinion writers who criticize Israeli leaders and Palestinian writers who try to hold their leaders accountable are just doing what American opinion writers do with our president and Congress. Constructive criticism doesn't make them less American, nor does it make Israelis less Israeli or Palestinians less Palestinian.

Reading such opinion columnists from time to time helps me realize that Israel is not a monolith any more than America is, and that I can love and support Israel without loving and supporting the politicians and bureaucrats whose actions put a drag on any movement toward reconciliation and eventual peace between the two sides. And when I talk with friends from either side of the conflict about things that are not going well, I try to be specific about who has said or done what, and not to generalize about either Israel or Palestine.

It is also important to follow those who work for peace. The Jewish human rights organization B'tselem (btselem.org) is one such source. So is Jeremy Ben Ami's J Street advocacy organization (JStreet.org). On the Palestinian side, Sami Awad's Holy Land Trust (holylandtrust.org) provides training in nonviolent resistance, and the Palestine Centre for Human Rights (pchrgaza.org) documents human rights violations so that peace can be pursued in the context of truth.

Whether or not you adopt the viewpoints of these media, it is important to build relationships with both Palestinians and Israelis to acknowledge the injustice and the violence suffered by both sides. If you don't keep up with the news from the region, you can't express sympathy or concern when tragedies happen. Yet it is exactly such expressions of concern that build friendship. You can be concerned without advocating particular solutions.

Eventually, your friendships may yield confidential information. One Jewish source recently shared several stories with me—off the record—that document good things Israelis and American Jews are doing for the well-being of Palestinians. I've told my source that I would desperately love to share these stories, but that I believe Jesus would agree that he should keep those good deeds hidden (Matt 6:1–4).

Listening to the narratives of the various parties in the conflict is vital.

Some years ago I participated in a series of meetings with faith leaders from various Christian denominations as well as Muslim and Jewish organizations. The goal was to develop a consensus statement on the issues of Israel and Palestine, and given the wide range of the participants, we had to set our sights pretty low. We aimed at nothing daring or radical, just the so-called Road Map to Peace in the Middle East that had already been endorsed by the George W. Bush administration and the other members of the "Quartet"—Russia, the United Nations, and the European Union. The essential elements of that Road Map (look up Road Map for Peace on Wikipedia) were largely commonsensical, if indeed the goal was peace and a two-state solution.

At what I believe was our third meeting, I was surprised to find us going back to square one. Jewish and Muslim participants both said they could not discuss our proposed consensus statement until they had told their stories. I was baffled. Hadn't these same participants told their stories, shared their national and ethnic narratives of how the current crisis came to be, at previous meetings? Indeed they had. But reciting these narratives was an important foundation for every conversation. The painful legacies of European anti-Semitism and of the violent displacement experienced by many Palestinian families needed to be articulated, and not merely assumed.

Our Israeli and Palestinian friends find that their identity is tightly tied to the particularity of a land and the painful events of recent history. One Palestinian friend, for example, still has his father's pre-1948 passport (one that says Palestine and lists his place of residence as Jerusalem, which puts the lie to claims that there was no political entity called Palestine before the founding of the state of Israel). He tells of watching his father during the violence of 1948 go out into the street waving a white flag, only to be felled by an Israeli bullet. That narrative—those events—indelibly shapes his identity. He is who he is because of what happened then.

It is important to note that not every Israeli Jew tells the same story, nor does every Palestinian. Wartime atrocities were once omitted from the standard accounts. Now a new historiography has emerged which deals with the evidence head on. This puts Israel in the same position as the United States. Both countries gained much of their territory at the expense of native suffering.

With such honest talk, we can begin to talk about prudential steps toward peace. As long as our stories are ideological and our claims are maximalist, we will not approach either reconciliation or peace. But if our stories are nuanced and true to history, we can begin to aim at realistic solutions and reconciled relationships.

Years ago, I had an experience working with a professional Christian arbitrator. Two Christian ministries were engaged in a public dispute, and I was asked to observe as the arbitrator met with the parties. He met with them separately, and he was very clear with them that what had been done could not be undone. They could not ask the other party to somehow create the situation that existed before the fight erupted. There were tarnished reputations. There were hurt feelings. And there were economic losses as well.

But if the clock could not be turned back, what could be done? That was the question posed by the arbitrator. You would like a lot of compensation and public apologies. But that is not going to happen. What would you actually settle for? He was asking the parties to be realistic.

I learned from observing that process how important it is to recognize present reality as the starting point for whatever comes next. Yes, we must not forget the narratives that have made us who we are, but we must live in the present and live for the future. Those of us who live in the West can listen to the founding narratives our Israeli and Palestinian friends tell and then ask realistic questions that will help move us all toward peace. Friends help friends get real.

3

How Should Christians Relate to the State of Israel?

Rich Nathan

IN 1894 A WOMAN named Maria Bastian was cleaning the German Embassy in Paris, France. She was a spy on the payroll of French counter-intelligence. In one of the waste paper baskets in the German Embassy she discovered a hand-written list offering French military secrets to the Germans. Suspicion immediately focused on a French artillery officer named Alfred Dreyfus.

Dreyfus was a Jewish captain in the French army. Despite testimony by handwriting experts who said that Dreyfus did not write the list, the army rushed to prosecute Dreyfus. By the time the trial came, the army became aware of the fact that there was a significant amount of evidence exonerating Dreyfus from guilt. But by then, it was politically impossible to withdraw the charges without creating a major scandal for the army.

The charges against Dreyfus provided an opportunity for ever-present anti-Semitism to come to the surface. Many French newspapers demanded that Dreyfus be punished. Horrible cartoon caricatures of Jews were distributed with the suggestion that Jews were always lurking in the shadows conspiring to sell France out to the Germans.

The Roman Catholic Church in France joined in the condemnation of Dreyfus. In a public ceremony in Paris, Dreyfus was stripped of his military ribbons, his sword was broken in two, and he was exiled to the notorious French prison on Devil's Island.

Finally, exonerating evidence made its way to a brilliant French novelist named Emile Zola. In an open letter to the French president, the novelist

HOW SHOULD CHRISTIANS RELATE TO THE STATE OF ISRAEL?

detailed Dreyfus's unjust conviction and the French army's cover-up. Zola's attack was published in a front-page story about the case under the headline "J'Accuse!" (I accuse!). More than 300,000 copies of the newspaper were sold and French public sentiment began swinging to Dreyfus's side. Eventually, Dreyfus, after a second guilty verdict, was found innocent of all charges and returned to the army where he was awarded the French Legion of Honor.

Why is the Dreyfus Affair so important in the history of our world? While Dreyfus was being publicly humiliated at his first trial, a French crowd surrounded the courtyard where Dreyfus was being stripped of all of his ribbons. The crowd began screaming "Death to the Jews! Death to all Jews!" In the crowd there happened to be a journalist named Theodor Herzl, who was covering the trial for an Austrian newspaper. Herzl was also a Jew. As he heard the shouts of the crowds crying out "Death to all Jews!" and watched the public humiliation of this innocent soldier, he realized that Jews would never be treated fairly in Europe. Even in liberal France, crowds were screaming for Jewish blood. Herzl came to the conviction that it was impossible to ever root anti-Semitism out of the European soul. So in 1896, Herzl founded The World Zionist Organization, which called for the creation of a Jewish state in the Jews' historic homeland—Palestine.

Eventually Herzl's dream became a reality. Following the shocking discovery of the extent of the Nazi slaughter of Jews during WWII, the state of Israel was formally recognized in 1948 by the newly formed United Nations. Many Christians around the world saw the creation of the State of Israel as the clearest sign of the present day fulfillment of prophecies written in the Bible thousands of years ago. This belief holds even today with many Christians.

The issue of Israel is not just academic to me. I was raised in a Jewish family. In terms of my personal identity, I consider myself to be a Jew who believes that Jesus is the Jewish Messiah, the one promised by the God of Abraham, Isaac, and Jacob.

As a child, I went to a synagogue in which the prayers were all said in Hebrew. I wore the skull cap known as the yarmulke and a prayer shawl known as a tallis each week as I attended synagogue—and I attended weekly. I went to Hebrew school and Hebrew high school. I was bar mitzvahed, which is a rite of passage for Jewish boys at age thirteen. Growing up I had a deep attachment to Israel. I gave money as a child to plant trees in Israel. At Jewish holidays we always greeted each other with the Hebrew greeting, "L'shana habaa biyerushalayim," which means "Next year in Jerusalem." I even considered leaving college during my freshman year and joining the Israeli army when the Yom Kippur Day War broke out in 1973. I would have been able to do this as a Jew. Six months after this, I came to faith in Jesus as my Messiah and Savior.

As a Jewish believer in Jesus, as a man who prays to the God of Abraham, Isaac, and Jacob every day of my life, as a person who grew up praying "next year in Jerusalem," and as a Jew who loves my own people and knows our history, I have a deep commitment to a Jewish state of Israel. But as a believer in Jesus, my Messiah and Lord, I have struggled with the idea that the hopes, aspirations, homes, families, safety, and the very lives of millions of Arabs don't seem to matter to many of my fellow Christians. As a Jew, I understand what it feels like to have a history of being victimized by enemies too strong for you. I deeply empathize with Arabs whose homes and lives have been taken because the Israeli army, backed by the United States, is too strong for them.

When Christians cavalierly say that the Bible gives the land to the Jews, then what the Arab, and the broader Muslim community, hears is: "We Christians care nothing about you, or your family at all. You mean nothing to us as an Arab, whether you are a fellow Christian or a Muslim." Muslims may legitimately conclude, "I suppose I mean nothing to your God. Your Bible is not worth reading."

Why should an Arab or a Muslim embrace a message that tells that person that their families, their history, their homes, and their lives don't matter? I grieve when I hear Christian radio hosts and TV evangelists speak as if every Arab is a terrorist and the Bible has nothing but bad news for Palestinians. I question if the people who say these things have spent even thirty seconds walking in the shoes of an Arab?

Jesus and the apostles, especially the Apostle Paul, reinterpreted all the promises given to Abraham in light of Jesus' coming. Because Jesus of Nazareth is the Messiah, because the Christ of God has come, every single promise in the Old Testament, every single statement, every command and ritual and symbol is seen in an entirely new light. The coming of Christ changes our vision of everything. It is the difference of what your skin or hair color looks like in a dimly lit room and what it looks like in the sunlight. It is the difference of what your couch looks like in your dimly lit living room and what it looks like when you move it outside and realize, "Oh my goodness, this couch is faded."

The coming of Jesus sheds an entirely new light on the whole Old Testament and all of its promises. For example: in light of the coming of Jesus into the world, who are the children of Abraham today?

Who can say today according to the New Testament, "I am a descendent of Abraham. I am one of Abraham's kids"? Listen to what the first New

Testament prophet, John the Baptist, said to the Jewish people living in his day.

> John said to the crowds coming out to be baptized by him, "You brood of vipers! Who warned you to flee from the coming wrath? Produce fruit in keeping with repentance. And do not begin to say to yourselves, 'We have Abraham as our father.' For *I tell you that out of these stones God can raise up children for Abraham.* The ax is already at the root of the trees, and every tree that does not produce good fruit will be cut down and thrown into the fire." (Luke 3:7–9, NIV, emphasis mine)

And on a more positive note, consider what the Apostle Paul wrote to Gentiles about who the true children of Abraham are today.

> So in Christ Jesus you are all children of God through faith, for all of you who were baptized into Christ have clothed yourselves with Christ. There is neither Jew nor Gentile, neither slave nor free, neither male nor female, for you are all one in Christ Jesus. If you belong to Christ, then *you are Abraham's seed*, and heirs according to the promise. (Gal 3:26–29, NIV)

What do non-Jews, who become children of Abraham through faith in Messiah Jesus, inherit? What is the promise given to everyone—Jews and Gentiles who trust in Christ and become sons and daughters of God?

Is it a piece of ground in the Middle East? Is it the West Bank? The Gaza Strip? The Sinai Peninsula? Listen to the Apostle Paul's answer in Romans 4:13, "It was not through the law that Abraham and his offspring received the promise that he would be *heir of the world*, but through the righteousness that comes by faith" (NIV, emphasis mine).

Jesus says in Matthew 8:10–12 that our inheritance is not merely the world. The children of Abraham inherit the *kingdom of God*.

> When Jesus heard this, he was amazed and said to those following him, "Truly I tell you, I have not found anyone in Israel with such great faith. I say to you that many will come from the east and the west, and will take their places at the feast with Abraham, Isaac and Jacob in the *kingdom of heaven*. But the subjects of the kingdom will be thrown outside, into the darkness, where there will be weeping and gnashing of teeth." (NIV, emphasis mine)

The return from exile and the re-gathering of Abraham's children from the four corners of the world was not fulfilled according to Jesus in 1948 with the Israeli declaration of independence. The re-gathering of the people of

Israel occurs when Jews and Gentiles place their faith in Jesus as Savior and Lord and join his movement as his followers.

The question that divides Christians today—and let me put it as starkly as I can—is this: Did Jesus and the Apostle Paul properly interpret the Old Testament regarding who God's people are today, what the covenant promise is, and how we should think about the promised land? The bottom line is that nowhere in any New Testament writing does Jesus or Paul or the Apostle John or Peter or any other New Testament writer reaffirm the promise of a piece of land to the Jewish people. The Old Testament promises have been extended and furthered beyond the Old Testament horizon to include not just the Middle East, but the world and not only the world, but the kingdom of God. The children of Abraham include not only people who are Jews by way of natural descent, like me, but include you who are Jews by spiritual descent through our shared faith in Jesus the Messiah.

In other words, can we trust Jesus and the Apostle Paul as Old Testament scholars? Are Jesus and the Apostle Paul our authorities for interpreting various passages from the Old Testament so that we read the Old Testament in light of the New Testament? Or, and I write this with all affection and respect, should we instead trust Tim LaHaye, Hal Lindsey, Pat Robertson, John Hagee, and all the other folks, who write books in the biblical prophecy section of the bookstores, and read the Old Testament as if the Messiah had never come and the New Testament had never been written?

This is the great divide. When we read the promises in the Old Testament, especially about the land, do we read them the way that Jesus and Paul read them, or do we read them as if the coming of Jesus did not radically reinterpret everything, shedding entirely new light, and new understanding on all that we see in the Old Testament?

Here is where I'm at as a Jewish believer in Jesus, as a person who has come to trust Jesus as my authority in life and my ultimate interpreter of God's Word found in the Old Testament: Jesus is my supreme, infallible interpreter of the Bible. I do not believe that it is right for any Christian, whether you became a Christian from a Gentile background, or whether like me, you became a Christian from a Jewish background, to resolve the current political dispute between the Israelis and the Palestinians by quoting a few verses from the Old Testament about the promise of the Holy Land to the Jewish people.

Does this mean that the Jews have no claim to their historic homeland? I didn't say that. I said you can't base Jewish claims to the land on promises made by God 4,000 years ago to the descendants of Abraham. I do believe, *as a matter of biblical justice*—not the promise of God to Abraham, but as a matter of justice—that the Jewish people do have a claim to a portion of the land between the Jordan River and the Mediterranean Sea.

Why do I say this? I believe that the world owes the Jewish people a secure nation in their historic homeland in light of 2,000 years of the world's treatment of the Jewish people. The history of the twentieth century and the Holocaust, with its systematic slaughter of six million Jews tells us of the participation of many countries in that slaughter, including the United States. We Americans shut our borders to Jewish refugees. We sent Jews back to Nazi Germany to be exterminated. We cannot read the history of the world without coming to the conclusion that Jews have never been secure in a nation ruled by others—whether ruled by the Germans, the French, the Russians, the Americans, or the Arabs. As a matter of biblical justice, Jews must have a nation in their own historic homeland.

But biblical justice cuts in two directions. It also cuts in the direction of the Palestinians. When Palestinians—who can trace their ancestry back 1,300 years in the land—are pushed off of their land, when Palestinian children are murdered in Israeli bombing raids, when houses are knocked down and men, women, and children are systematically humiliated and abused, biblical justice stands up for the victim and says, "This must not continue!" We must have justice for both Jews and Palestinians. Biblical justice is not easy to achieve. There are many unresolved problems—terrorism, political complications, water rights, outside interference by other nations—but the God of the Bible cares for all people, not just Jews. The God of the Bible works justice for *all of the oppressed*, not just Jews.

So what is the way forward? How can there be peace in the Middle East?

Peace in any relationship begins when two unreconciled people are willing to listen to the hurt and pain of the other person and not just their own hurt and pain. If you are married and you are distant from your spouse, the only way you will ever be brought together is if, at some point, you open yourself up to hear the hurt, the wounds, and the pain that you caused to your spouse. If you simply insist that your spouse understand your hurt and pain, and you are not willing to ever listen to the pain and hurt that you have caused, there is no possibility of true reconciliation. People have to get past simply telling their own stories. We have to listen to the story of the other person. We can't have peace unless we walk in the other person's shoes.

What is true at a personal level is also true at a national level. Palestinians must acknowledge that the Jewish Holocaust changed everything for the Jewish people. The pain experienced through the Holocaust and subsequent terrorist attacks deeply affect Israelis' perceived need for security. And Israelis must acknowledge that the discrimination, the bombing, and displacement of hundreds of thousands of Palestinians deeply affect the way Palestinians relate to the State of Israel today. Here is where I think Christians have an opportunity to be bridge-builders and peace-wagers.

If we Jewish Christians and Gentile Christians become just arbiters, if we stop communicating to Palestinians that none of their claims are legitimate, that they are all terrorists, that Christ has nothing good to say to them, that the blessing of God is only for the Jewish people—if we Christians repent of our biases and our prejudices and sacrificially offer ourselves as possible bridge people—I think that in Jesus' name we could assist in this process of reconciliation and peace. I have hope for us as Christians. I believe we can change. I believe that if we do change, if we become people who love justice and love peace, there is hope for peace in the Middle East.

———————— 4 ————————

Speech at the Presidential Palace with Palestinian Authorities in Bethlehem[1]

———— Address of His Holiness Pope Francis ————

Bethlehem
Sunday, May 25, 2014
Mr. President,
Dear Friends,
Dear Brothers and Sisters,

I thank President Mahmoud Abbas for his kind welcome and I offer cordial greetings to the representatives of the government and the entire Palestinian people. I thank the Lord for the opportunity to be here with you today in the birthplace of Jesus, the Prince of Peace. I thank all of you for your warm reception.

For decades the Middle East has known the tragic consequences of a protracted conflict which has inflicted many wounds so difficult to heal. Even in the absence of violence, the climate of instability and a lack of mutual understanding have produced insecurity, the violation of rights, isolation, and the flight of entire communities, conflicts, shortages, and sufferings of every sort.

---

1. Pope Francis, "Meeting with Palestinian Authorities" (speech, Bethlehem, May 25, 2014), The Vatican, Accessed June 29, 2016. https://w2.vatican.va/content/francesco/en/speeches/2014/may/documents/papa-francesco_20140525_terra-santa-autorita-palestinesi.html.

In expressing my closeness to those who suffer most from this conflict, I wish to state my heartfelt conviction that the time has come to put an end to this situation which has become increasingly unacceptable. For the good of all, there is a need to intensify efforts and initiatives aimed at creating the conditions for a stable peace based on justice, on the recognition of the rights of every individual, and on mutual security. The time has come for everyone to find the courage to be generous and creative in the service of the common good, the courage to forge a peace which rests on the acknowledgment by all of the right of two states to exist and to live in peace and security within internationally recognized borders.

To this end, I can only express my profound hope that all will refrain from initiatives and actions which contradict the stated desire to reach a true agreement, and that peace will be pursued with tireless determination and tenacity. Peace will bring countless benefits for the peoples of this region and for the world as a whole. And so it must resolutely be pursued, even if each side has to make certain sacrifices.

I pray that the Palestinian and Israeli peoples and their respective leaders will undertake this promising journey of peace with the same courage and steadfastness needed for every journey. Peace in security and mutual trust will become the stable frame of reference for confronting and resolving every other problem, and thus provide an opportunity for a balanced development, one which can serve as a model for other crisis areas.

Here I would like to say a word about the active Christian community which contributes significantly to the common good of society, sharing in the joys and sufferings of the whole people. Christians desire to continue in this role as full citizens, along with their fellow citizens, whom they regard as their brothers and sisters.

Mr. President, you are known as a man of peace and a peacemaker. Our recent meeting in the Vatican and my presence today in Palestine attest to the good relations existing between the Holy See and the State of Palestine. I trust that these relations can further develop for the good of all. In this regard, I express my appreciation for the efforts being made to draft an agreement between the parties regarding various aspects of the life of the Catholic community in this country, with particular attention to religious freedom. Respect for this fundamental human right is, in fact, one of the essential conditions for peace, fraternity, and harmony. It tells the world that it is possible and necessary to build harmony and understanding between different cultures and religions. It also testifies to the fact that, since the important things we share are so many, it is possible to find a means of serene, ordered, and peaceful coexistence, accepting our differences and rejoicing that, as children of the one God, we are all brothers and sisters.

Mr. President, dear brothers and sisters gathered here in Bethlehem: may Almighty God bless you, protect you, and grant you the wisdom and strength needed to continue courageously along the path to peace, so that swords will be turned into ploughshares and this land will once more flourish in prosperity and concord. Salaam!

Part II

God's Chosen People and the Family of Abraham

©stellalevi. IStockPhoto.com. Photo ID: 71370987. Aug 14, 2015.
Downloaded June 26, 2016.

"I will bless those who bless you, and whoever curses you I will curse; and all peoples on earth will be blessed through you."
Genesis 12:3 (NIV)

5

I am Jewish: Reflections on Jewish Identity in the Holy Land

Dr. Judith Mendelsohn Rood

I'M JEWISH. BOTH OF my parents are Jews, as were their parents, and theirs before them back into the obscurity of a forgotten past. I was raised in the conservative synagogue, where my parents were members of the Tree of Life in Pittsburgh and B'nai Brith and Adas Israel in Washington, DC, where I was bat mitzvahed in 1971, and confirmed in 1974. This is the same synagogue that President Obama spoke at in 2015, where he talked about his relationship to the Jewish people. Today the congregation's position on Israel and the Middle East is much like the one I had forty years ago, when I left as a pro-Palestinian renegade, never to return.

    I first went to Israel on a United Synagogue Youth Pilgrimage that year, 1974, as a reward for my continued Hebrew studies. Adas Israel had a big impact on me—I preferred Hebrew school to my public schools because the level of scholarship was so much higher. I loved studying Hebrew—one of my earliest memories is of studying the Hebrew text of Exodus as an eight year old. I remember praying as a young girl, asking God to help me understand the meaning of the words I was reading. I did not mean translation—what the Hebrew words meant in Hebrew—but what the words really meant. The Bible was always my favorite book—so complex and profound, mysterious and ancient, somehow just beyond my understanding. It spoke to me of marvelous things, holy things, about which I knew I knew nothing. It was MY book, my heritage, THE book of my people's history. It was beautiful, savage, tragic, perplexing, and filled with yearning and hope. It was about a distant place, my homeland, where my people were once free. I daydreamed about life in the desert as a nomad, sleeping in tents under skies filled with stars.

During those years of elementary school, the Arab-Israel Conflict dominated the news. Also as an eight year old, I read Marguerite Henry's wonderful children's book, *King of the Wind*. I was one of those horse-crazy girls and I loved the story, set in Morocco. The book was lavishly illustrated. One of the plates pictured an old man with a flowing white beard standing atop a minaret, blowing a shofar! The illustrator's confusion of Muslims and Jews was innocent and sweet, and I, not knowing the facts, thought Arabs and Muslims were Jews! I wanted to understand, then, from the very earliest years of my life as a student of the world, why did Arabs and Jews hate one another?

In Hebrew school, the rabbi would sometimes assemble all of the classes to teach us about Israel and her Arab neighbors. He'd put up a map of the Middle East, point to the little Jewish state, and show us all of the surrounding countries threatening Israel. The first war I experienced with understanding was the Yom Kippur War, a war that outraged my elders because it was secretly launched while Jews were in synagogue on our holiest day! I also remember at Rosh Hashanah and Yom Kippur services, worship was overshadowed by fundraising for Israel. My friends, bored and tired from standing up and praying for hours at a time, would escape into little cliques to talk and fool around, thinking about anything BUT God. I thought we ought to be taking the Torah seriously, and was confused about why God didn't punish everyone for not obeying Him. I began to test Him, to see if he'd punish me if I sinned. I then learned Jews no longer believe in sin, just good works. I was troubled by this discovery, and pondered its meaning deeply in my heart.

My bat mitzvah was tremendously important to me. My grandmother, my father's mother, was given the honor of being the first woman in my synagogue to have an *Aliyah*—to go up on the *bimah*, the raised platform in front of the *aharon ha-kodesh*, the ark, to bless the Torah. I then read the *haftarah*—girls didn't get to read the *maftir*, or portion from the *Chumash*, the Pentateuch, in those days. My portion was from Samuel, and dealt with the Amalekites. My bat mitzvah was on the Shabbat before Purim. My reading was the backstory, telling us the roots of our archenemy Haman, the prototype of all of my people's enemies. The Amalekites were evil because they attacked the rear of the column of Hebrews fleeing Egypt in the desert. Our people's enemies were merciless—attacking the weak and the helpless. In the story, his descendants are cursed for all time. They are the family of Haman. On Purim, every time this villain's name is mentioned in the Scroll of Esther, the *Megillah*—the "Telling"—we grind a *gregor* (noisemaker) to drown out the sound of his name. May his name be blotted out, erased forever. The Jews, one day, will triumph over our enemies. This should be the hope and prayer of all of us, for the men of violence are the scourge of our times, too. Purim is a lot of fun—all the kids dress up in costumes and parade around the sanctuary and then eat treats and party at the special *oneg*, when everyone shares the joy of the Sabbath meal together. Jews laugh through their tears. Somehow the laughter and the tears have hidden God, as Jews decided it was up to them to try to live in this world of endless enmity in our own strength.

I noticed my friends weren't too interested in any of these issues. I discovered that I was different—shy and studious and definitely not cool. I tried to hang out with my friends but I didn't really understand them. They were interested in worldly things, while I was interested in spiritual things. I liked my teachers, but as I was growing up many of them betrayed my trust. I began to doubt authority. And I began to believe that God had removed himself from history, leaving humanity alone to rely on our own resources. I later discovered, much later, that this is exactly what the rabbis had decided after the destruction of the Second Temple. God proposed, it was up to us to dispose.

This idea began to take a strong hold on my mind because my father and his family had escaped from the Holocaust—just barely. The key point in our education was to assure Jewish survival—both from destruction and assimilation. But the idea that God had abandoned us was powerful and led me to leave the synagogue in 1975, after I went to Israel because the idea that the only real point to life was the survival of the Jewish people was not enough for me. I felt that my rabbis and the Jewish leadership had led us astray. I was angry at the state of confusion among the Jewish people about law—no one could even agree whether or not we could eat peas during *Pesach*. It seemed no one could agree upon anything, except supporting Israel, achieving social justice through our own efforts, and ensuring Jewish survival. Above all else, God was irrelevant to *Tikkun Olam*—the repair of the world. Everyone seemed hypocritical to me. I felt betrayed. And, most of all, I wondered why God had allowed the enmity between my people and the Arabs, my cousins, as we continued to spill each other's blood.

I learned about the Palestinians during my first visit to Israel, and I could not understand why my family's tragedy led to the suffering of the Arabs there. Or how they, my noble cousins, could justify murdering school children to terrify the innocent. I met the survivors of the 1974 Ma'alot massacre at the hands of Palestinian terrorists. Were they the Amalekites?

Why weren't we—Arabs and Jews—united against the Christians, the Jews' enemy since time immemorial? Weren't the Arabs Semites like us, hated by the Christians? Shouldn't we build up the Middle East together, and turn the world back to God?

In college, I ploughed through the library, looking for any books I could find on the Arabs. I discovered Islam and read the thoughts of many European Jewish scholars who'd asked the same questions. The Arabs didn't accuse the Jews of killing God—only the Christians did that. While Christians were slaughtering Jews during the Crusades, Jewish warriors were fighting with Muslims against them. One even became the commander of a Muslim army! To me, this was astounding! I read books that are now dismissed as "Orientalist" because they were written by Westerners about Islam, it was said, in order to control it. For that reason, no one reads them today, least of all Muslims. These scholars had not encountered Salafist Islam in the way that we have; instead, their scholarship focused on philosophy and literature, art and architecture, poetry and knowledge. This was the House of Wisdom, and I wanted to enter it.

I decided to go to Hebrew University for my sophomore year. I loved studying Hebrew and Middle East history and politics there from 1977–78. I studied the history of the Israeli-Palestinian conflict and fell in love with a quiet Palestinian student working on his PhD on the transfer policies of the founders of Israel. I went to the first *Yom al-Ard*—Day of the Land—demonstration in March 1978. In the 1970s, my friends were all secular and hoping to achieve peace between equals as we fought for freedom and equality. It seemed possible, if only the superpowers would allow the Israelis and Palestinians to work it out. We were pragmatists. My Palestinian friends, when asked, told me they would stay in Israel, as long as there was a Palestinian state to which the refugees could return. My friends understood the freedoms they enjoyed in Israel and hated the Arab regimes that had betrayed them. I understood Palestinian identity, because it mirrored my own, shaped by hatred and injustice, and a longing for dignity and honor.

I returned to the US to write my thesis on Ibn Khaldun, a fourteenth-century Maliki judge from Andalusia who'd served as a political advisor and diplomat, who'd been imprisoned as a political enemy, and who'd been captured and interrogated by the great warrior Tamerlane in Damascus. Ibn Khaldun is best known for the translation of the introduction to his great history of the world, the *Muqaddimah*—in summer 2015, this was the eleventh book on Facebook CEO Mark Zuckerberg's Year of Books Club. In it the Sunni philosopher of history systematically analyzes the rise and fall of states, focusing upon the phenomenon of religion to inspire the *espirit de corps* that motivates desert warriors to attack the civilized world to set up caliphates. My study of Ibn Khaldun awakened in me an understanding of the role of philosophy in the religion in the Middle East. I would later discover that this topic was not being studied at the best programs on the Modern Middle East—like the ones I enrolled in at Georgetown University and the University of Chicago. There the focus was secular—culture and society, politics and economics.

What had moved me most about Ibn Khaldun's Aristotelian understanding of Sunni Islam was its strong proclamation of faith in the God of Israel! In college, I was unaware of the development of Qur'anic hermeneutics and, especially, I did not understand the importance of Salafism and the importance of the Saudi Arabian *da'wah*—the Muslim missionary movement. All I knew was that the Quran interpreted biblical history—Jewish history—and pointed the way to obedience, thereby guaranteeing the believer admission into heaven through works. My texts did not include essays on gender. No mention of the hijab or female genital mutilation. Instead, they were historical accounts of the Muslim philosophers who created a fragile, ephemeral world where Jews, Christians, and Muslims studied God and free will, creation and the cosmos. In this world I resonated with Ibn Khaldun's idea that law establishes justice, and that without Divine Law, society will cannibalize itself as it descends into depravity. I dwelled on these ideas, tempting as they are, but eventually realized that men are too depraved, too treacherous to establish just laws without humility before our Creator, especially when they declare that they are the arbitrators of divinity. My suspicion of authority kept me from becoming a Muslim.

No one had been paying attention to the Iranians in those days—the Shiites had no power, but they had the Shah, and he'd been a friend to the US and Israel. Now that the Shah was disgraced and abandoned, the Islamic world teetered on the edge of a new, volatile age. I would never go to my dream cities of Isfahan and Shiraz, now that they were enemy territory, and my country was named "The Great Satan" and Israel "The Little Satan" by the Westoxified anti-imperialist revolutionary regime. For the rest of my life, Iran would solidify terrorism into its global policy, inexorably expanding its power into the Arab world, despite the enormous and tragically misguided sacrifices of my country to prevent it. Today, as the ancient Christians of the Middle East have lost favor as the Arabist regimes that used to protect them crumbled under Iranian pressure, it seems that the judgment of the ages has come. Now these Christians are being scattered, and are returning to first things. Their Muslim neighbors, horrified by the excesses of the anti-Shiite militias, are also turning back to the God of Abraham and Ishmael. No one prepared for this. Back in the '80s no one thought about what would happen if we armed the Salafists to fight the Communists. Now we do.

I had decided to pursue my studies of the Middle East. I took an internship at the Egypt Desk at the State Department, where, among other things, I read dozens of letters from Copts begging for help to escape from the fanaticism of their Muslim compatriots. I admit I had little sympathy for these Christians. I had a low view of Christianity, and my hopes for a Muslim-Jewish détente led me to disregard the very real issues brewing just below the surface of Sadat's Egypt. I thought that since Muslims believed in God, they were capable of creating a virtuous society. I did not understand the depth of popular Egyptian antagonism to the West, even though I recognized the deceits of the Nazi-allied Palestinian anti-Zionist jihad, a struggle which Middle East Christians had embraced as they sought acceptance and safety in the dream-palaces of Arab nationalism.

I had rejected Conservative Judaism (also known as *Masorti* Judaism), because it accepts both the Torah and Talmud as authoritative. I could never live under rabbinic law—I was a feminist, after all. I was living "outside the camp" but never lost my strong Jewish identity—an identity that tied me to my people and my God. My love of the Jewish prayer book, the *Siddur*, and the *Tanakh*, by which I mean the Hebrew Scriptures in their entirety, allowed me and my husband to create our family's little egalitarian house synagogue, much later in my life. But all through college into grad school I didn't know anyone like me, who believed in God, and who was mortified by our rebellion from him. I did not know how to bridge the gap, and my belief spiraled into a state of spiritual depression. I could find no meaning for my life, for my survival. When so many millions perished, and were perishing still, what justification could there be for my useless presence in this world? I'd read all of the existentialists and philosophers and I could not think myself out of the pit that I'd dug for myself. I didn't know it was a commandment to be joyous despite the tears.

And then God began to answer my prayers. Long before, while I was in Israel, I'd gone with a friend to Galilee, where we read the New Testament. I knew that this was a Jewish book, and that Jesus was a rabbi. I thought to myself that if I'd lived in Israel during his time, I probably would have become a follower and then betrayed him along with all the rest. All of the centuries of Christian anti-Semitism kept me from ever considering him as the true Messiah of Israel, and I certainly was not equipped to understand Him as the Son of God. I stayed outside the camp, alone.

Now, at the University of Chicago, seven years after leaving the synagogue, I met a group of Jewish Christians who shared their faith in Yeshu'a with me, and, after a brief battle, I surrendered myself to him as my Lord and God. Everything that I'd read now came into focus. I understood profound truths as the biblical story became clear to me, and even today, as I continue to study, new depths of understanding come, strengthening my faith, enabling me to keep moving forward, knowing that the arc of history is towards justice and mercy. What was important then was that I understood the outlines of the whole story, even the parts that remain unwritten. At first, I worried that my self-identity as a Jewish woman would become meaningless if I accepted Jesus. But God has redeemed that identity and has given me my voice as a Jewish woman.

When my parents named me after my paternal great-grandmother, Jenny Moses, they decided to call me Judith. They probably didn't understand the power and the problems that come with that name. It is the same name as Judah—a Judean. The root of the word is praise, and the name means "s/he who praises Yahweh." My name means "Jew" or "Jewess." In Arabic, too. Everywhere I go, I'm the Jew, who praises God. I couldn't get around it. The Lord is with me; I am His witness.

So, in the miraculous way that God arranged my life, I went to Jerusalem to study at the Islamic Court archives as a Jewish Christian. The congregational Messianic Jewish movement was still in its infancy then. The Christian world was utterly gentile, a foreign faith, a faith that needed translation. There was no indigenous, Hebrew-speaking church (although there were Anglicans, Catholics, Lutherans, Presbyterians, and Baptists with Jewish congregants). Israeli congregations were heavily expat. American Messianic congregations lacked authenticity for me.

I was still outside the camp, but I found that there were others who were beginning to build communities of believers, and, as we raised our family, we began to see the fruits of the spirit as more and more Jews like me, raised in Conservative and Orthodox homes, began to fellowship together with others drawn to the God of Israel. People who loved the Bible and for that reason still loved the Jews. People like the ones during the Holocaust era who did the right thing because they read the Bible and knew that faith was meaningless without good works. I began to see myself as a bridge between the church and the Jewish people. I sought out other evangelicals interested in the Middle East. I was not received well. I discovered the depth of evangelical animosity towards Israel. Very few Christian intellectuals whom I encountered during this period of my life believed that God has a purpose and a plan for Israel. They believed that the church had replaced Israel, and that, being unjust, Israel will be judged and exiled, the land restored to its rightful inhabitants, the Palestinian Christians, as the Christians claimed, or the Muslims, as the Muslims claimed.

Over the past several years, I've written about these developments, and I don't want to write about that here. What I want to write about is my Jewish identity, because for years I was focused on Palestinian identity, defending the Palestinian right to self-determination. Forty years ago such a position was derided as left-wing nonsense. Today even most Conservative Jews believe as I did, but now it's too late. The secular Palestinian nationalism of the '70s and '80s has been overthrown by Islamist jihadism, which rejects me as a Jew, as a Christian, as a woman. The past forty years of warfare has created an apocalypticism amongst my people, amongst Muslims, and amongst Christians, with the result that religions are viewed as extremist—feared and hated for creating fear and hatred. Without God, religion only divides, creating perpetual enmity. Only the God of love can break the power of hate.

And now, I am returning to the texts that have empowered me all of my life—not as an individual, but as a member of my community. The Messianic Jewish community is maturing. Praying in community for the sake of the world, as a Jewish follower of Yeshu'a, as a member of the *Ekklesia*, the "called out ones"—the church, not in my head, not in my house, but aloud, with others, in the presence of the Lord among us, together. Without the Jewish presence in the church, there will be no church. Ephesians 3:6 makes this crystal clear.

In the years of my engagement with Palestinian evangelicals, I have never felt accepted for who I am: a Zionist Jew. I have recognized that I could become a useful weapon against Israel, but have carefully guarded my words and my actions to prevent that. I have found conditional acceptance as a Jewish Christian, so long as my strong Jewish voice does not assert privilege. Jesus does not ask that we reject our identity: he redeems it. My people have a homeland. It is a strategic land bridge, the site of endless warfare. History has shaped it, and many peoples have sought God there, claiming him—and the Land, *Eretz Yisrael*—for themselves, in his name. They are part of my story, which is also the story of the church. I am in that great cloud of witnesses, along with all of the others who've accepted Yeshu'a as Lord, from all tongues, tribes, nations. Only when Israel recognizes the legitimacy of God's work in history among non-Jews will peace come for the Jewish people. Only when the church accepts Israel as a legitimate nation will peace come. Like Jacob and Esau, Israel and the Arabs will one day recognize the Lord in one another, and embrace.

Without the Jewish presence in the church, the people Israel cannot be redeemed. Without those who have sought to follow the God of Israel there, the Jewish people cannot fulfill its destiny to serve humanity. Barrels of ink have been spilled writing about Jewish nationalism and Zionism, the conflict, the ways to solve it, justifying it, perpetuating it. Only the presence of the Lord among us will empower us to love our enemies and break the power of Satan over the region.

We must accept one another on God's terms, not our own. Unconditionally. In this time of jihad, we must fight the good fight together, in the name of the Merciful, the Compassionate. In him we have the power to forgive, and the desire to love. We must recognize the humanity of our enemies and love them as we have been commanded to by he who possesses real wisdom.

To my Palestinian brothers, who've told me that I would not be welcomed to live among them in their state, I say, without the presence of Jews, your state will perpetuate the evils that have destroyed you. I accept your identity as a fact of history. You must recognize mine as a witness to the dependability of God's promises. You must share the gospel with your enemies—the Jewish people—in order to redeem them from hatred. We, together, must show Muslims the power of our faith in the God of Israel. Until we do that, we bring shame to the name of our Lord in the eyes of his enemies.

Many Muslims have realized that the Allah of the Salafists is not the Allah of Abraham, Ishmael, Isaac, and Jacob. Let us begin there. Let us testify to them: we must together worship him in Christ, praying for forgiveness, for mercy, for a good future together under God.

6

The Holy Land and the Larger Family of Abraham

Dr. Tony Maalouf

WHILE OBSERVING THE FAILURE of an indigenous population in Ethiopia to discern the picture of an animal foreign to their tribal culture, environmentalist Paul Hawken notes, "What we already know frames what we see, and what we see frames what we understand."[1] This observation from anthropology applies also in our doing of theology, since we often let our understanding of the Bible limit what we see in it. Consequently, our prior knowledge may become a hindrance to the process of discovering new truths. For long years I reflected this reality in my reading of the Patriarchal narratives. Having been largely exposed to an exclusive reading of texts related to the covenant community of old, I reasoned: God elected Sarah, but not Hagar; Isaac, but not Ishmael; Israel, but not Arabia. I followed a common stereotype that assumed that non-election implies automatic rejection—both on a national and a personal level!

However, after a long journey of tedious research I realized that this simplistic and restrictive reading is largely unsupported by an honest and objective scrutiny of Scriptures.[2] To begin with, it fails to reflect God's loving heart for the larger family of Abraham, but it fails also in "rightly dividing the word of truth" (2 Tim 2:15, KJV). While redemptive roles are clearly assigned to a special elect line in biblical history, non-election to

---

1. Hawken, *Blessed Unrest*, 15.
2. For a full discussion of my findings, see Maalouf, *Arabs*.

THE HOLY LAND AND THE LARGER FAMILY OF ABRAHAM   57

those roles does not preclude personal salvation and divine favor. It is more natural when a special line is assigned pulpit ministry, to see others sitting in the pews rather than placed outside the sanctuary! Accordingly, I am arguing that while God elected Sarah, Isaac, and Israel to a redemptive role, he placed Hagar, Ishmael, and his Arabian line inside the Abrahamic circle, allowing their *participation* in covenantal blessings.[3] Highlighting only the Arabian elements in this short essay will allow us to draw conclusions that may indirectly serve the peace cause in the Holy Land today. I also hope to lead Christians to read Scriptures in a way that encourages outreach rather than exclusion, healing rather than strife, and to offer a biblical ground for reconciliation rather than alienation in the context of Arab-Israeli relationships.

The Case for Hagar's Participation!

Though the Hagar story in Genesis 16:7-13 is loaded with comforting messages, Christian pulpiteers rarely preach on texts related to Hagar. When the slave woman is brought up, it is often done in the context of her "infamous" liaison with Abraham (Gen 16:3) that resulted in the "unfortunate" birth of Ishmael (Gen 16:4-6, 15), whose line supposedly only brought "trouble" to Israel (Gen 16:12)! However, while Sarah is clearly presented in Scriptures as a blessed matriarch both in the Old Testament (Gen 17:15-16) and the New Testament (Heb 11:11), Hagar is not without her own share of divine favor either. In fact, God dealt in a very special way with the slave woman as a believer in Yahweh. Thus she became the only woman in the Bible who was the subject of two divine appearances—theophanies (Gen 16:7-13; 21:17), in which the Lord revealed himself to her as the "God who listens." In the first, he promised her a son whose God-given name Ishmael (meaning, "God listens") will always remind her of God's gracious attention to her (Gen 16:11). In the second, she is reminded that she and her son will not become a scapegoat for God's unique plan for Isaac. Instead they will be

---

3. My use of the term Arabian and/or Arabs is done exclusively with reference to the nomadic tribes related to Abraham through Hagar and Keturah (Gen 16; 25:1-6), whom the Patriarch dismissed to the Arabian desert in the East (Heb., *qedem*) away from his son Isaac (Gen 25:6). Some Arabs today are related to these tribes in blood relationship. However, those who do not, they associate with them either by geographical or theological associations. Furthermore, Ishmael and his children in this chapter are not to be equated with Islam and Muslims that came some 2,600 years later, though the study bears implications on both groups. For a fuller treatment of this point, see Maalouf, *Arabs*, 44-49.

blessed, and her son will become "a great nation" under the direct care of the Lord (Gen 17:18, 20; 21:17–18, 20).

Furthermore, Genesis 16:10–11 makes Hagar the only woman in the Bible to receive a direct promise of multiplication of descendants. Whether linked to the Abrahamic promises (Gen 12:1–3; 13:14–17; 17:4–6; 22:16–18), or a self-standing pledge given by God to her, this promise is a sign of a great blessing God only bestows on those who find favor in his eyes (Ps 37:28). Consequently, Hagar names God saying, "You are El Roi"—the God who Sees (Gen 16:13), and becomes also the only person in the Bible to give God a name that reveals a character by which he will be later identified. No wonder Jewish rabbis in the Genesis Midrash considered this Egyptian theologian the first in a list of nine women proselytes in the history of Israel.[4]

It is true that Hagar was just a simple Egyptian maid in the service of an upper social class. However, the "God who Sees" (*El Roi*), and delights in reviving the heart of the lowly (Isa 57:15), chose to listen to her misery and to compensate the so-called "non-elect" with an extra measure of his presence in her life. Abraham was called to be the first missionary in Israel's history (Gen 12:1–3), in whom "all the families of the earth" were to receive blessing. Therefore, it is more natural to see his secondary wife and immediate members of his household included in the larger covenant community by faith, rather than excluded from it. To argue against this defeats the evangelistic purpose of the Abrahamic calling and narrative!

The Case for Ishmael's Participation!

At the end of the Genesis 16 account, we see that it is Abraham who gives his firstborn the name *Ishmael*, and thus appropriates him as a legitimate heir (Gen 16:15). Obviously, Hagar, who obeyed the Lord's command and returned to her mistress (Gen 16:9), must have recounted to Abraham all the details of her divine encounter and the promises she had received at the well (Gen 16:7–13). As a result, Abraham likely concluded for thirteen years that Ishmael was after all the "son of promise" (See: Gen 16:15; 17:1, 18, 25). Yet God revealed to the Patriarch that it was through Isaac—the son born the supernatural way—that his "seed shall be called" (Gen 17:16–17; 18:10–15; 21:12). Thus it became clear that the Lord elected Isaac—whose birth fits the symbolism of the supernatural redemption of Christ—to a special role in redemptive history, from which Ishmael was to a certain degree excluded.

4. See Kasher, *Genesis*, 2:219.

However, what is clear as well is that God did not automatically alienate Ishmael from him. When he appointed Isaac for pulpit ministry, he did not automatically drive Ishmael out of the sanctuary. Rather Ishmael was to sit in the pews and potentially receive blessings by faith from the ministry entrusted to Isaac and his line. There is plenty of evidence pointing in this direction, and the burden of proof falls upon those who argue against that conclusion.

To start with, Hagar's son was named directly by God and received a theophoric name, Ishmael (meaning, *God listens*), revealing one of the beautiful traits of God. It is also noteworthy in biblical narratives that God never personally names evil characters before their birth—much less gives them names reflecting a divine attribute. There is also no instance of God directly announcing to parents the birth of an evil person (cf. Judg 16:3–21; Luke 1:11–20; 26–37). Ishmael received both favors from the Lord!

Furthermore, God's listening to Hagar's affliction under slavery, announced in Genesis 16:11, unfolds in the verse that follows. As a reversal of Hagar's *lack of freedom* and power under slavery, her son is predicted to be *free* and untamable like a wild donkey in the desert (v. 12a). While many have mistakenly interpreted this prediction as a negative characterization, this trait is in perfect harmony with the context of comfort and listening, and with the use of animal bynames in nomadic culture. In fact, five of Jacob's children receive animal bynames (Gen 49). What determines whether the animal imagery is meant in a negative or a positive way is the type of animal being identified. That the wild donkey is envied and praised as a freely roaming animal in the desert is clarified in Bedouin literature and in the Bible (cf. Job 39:5–8; Jer 2:24; Hos 8:9). Thus the prediction describes the free nomadic lifestyle that characterized Ishmael and his line in history (Gen 16:12a), with all the struggle it involves for survival in the wilderness (Gen 16:12b). Thus an *enslaved* and *helpless* Hagar, fleeing from the harsh subjection of her mistress, receives the promise of a son who will be *free* and *strong* as a nomad in the neighboring desert. Such free living and power has resulted throughout history in the survival until today of Arabian nomadic tribes related to Abraham.

Additionally, Ishmael is also predicted to dwell *al-pené*, with all his brethren (Gen 16:12c). Contextual evidence favors a meaning of geographical proximity to the Abrahamic circle of the Hebrew expression *al-pené*. It is unfortunate that a prominent Bible translation like the NIV fails to render the true meaning of the Ishmael text in Genesis 16:12c, and rather prescribes enmity between the line of Ishmael and the line of Israel throughout generations.⁵ Needless to say, this lapse in translation accuracy may contribute to racial antagonism today, whether in the Arab-Israeli context or in the raging tension between Islam and the West.

A correct rendering of the Hebrew expression rather serves the healing cause on both ends. Fortunately, Jews of old, and modern day Jews give *al-pené* in Genesis 16:12c a more positive nuance. Accordingly, Targumic and modern Jewish translations of Genesis 16:12c tell us that Ishmael will dwell *alongside of* and will *intermingle with* all of his brethren.⁶ These translations catch the inclusive nature of God's blessings in the Abrahamic narrative. For while Isaac's line of faith will perpetuate the Abrahamic Covenant throughout history, Ishmael will nevertheless stay close to the Abrahamic circle of blessings. From a divine perspective, this geographical proximity will serve a double purpose. *First*, it will be a potential for Ishmael to be blessed by faith through the pulpit ministry entrusted to the elect line (Jer 12:16). *Second*, it will be a constant reminder for Israel that faith, and not mere blood relationship, is the way to enjoying the Abrahamic promised blessings.

A clear favor given to Ishmael is uttered by Yahweh in Genesis 17, where the plan for Isaac is revealed (Gen 17:15–17, 19). Abraham pleaded before the Lord that Ishmael might live "before" him (Gen 17:18), and God told him that Isaac's line would be the one fulfilling the covenantal promises in history (Gen 17:19). Nevertheless, the Lord listened to Abraham's intercession on behalf of his firstborn (Gen 17:20). As a result, Ishmael will be blessed by God, multiplied exceedingly, and made a "great nation." "He too is to walk [before the Lord] as one of Yahweh's children."⁷ To remove any doubt as to his inclusion in the covenant community, the narrator of Genesis shows how both Abraham and Ishmael obeyed the divine command for the sign of the covenant (Gen 17:23–25).

Finally, though Ishmael and his mother had to exit Abraham's home to pursue God's prescribed plan for him in the neighboring wilderness (Gen 21:12–13), several details point to his continued favor in the eyes of the Lord. *First*, the Lord allowed Ishmael to be reared by Abraham for almost seventeen years (Gen 17:25; 21:8) before he was to pursue his own destiny in a neighboring land. As a result he sat under the godly instruction of his

---

5. *The NIV Study Bible* generalizes this misinterpretation further in its comments on verse 12c making an unwarranted statement, "the hostility between Sarah and Hagar (see vv. 4–6) was passed on to their descendants (see 25:18)." See Barker, *The NIV Study Bible*, 30.

6. See Maher, *Targum Pseudo-Jonathan*; also, Grossfeld, *The Targum Onkelos*; and *The Torah, The Five Books of Moses.*

7. See Hamilton, *The Book of Genesis*, 480.

father Abraham until he matured and was able to "keep the way of the Lord" on his own (Gen 18:19). *Second*, it's true Ishmael was out of Abraham's sight, but he was definitely not out of the Lord's sight. In fact, while he was almost dying from thirst, the "God who listens" heard his voice and called his mother Hagar from heaven (Gen 21:17). He calmed her fears, showed her a water spring nearby, and instructed her to help her son Ishmael since he would be made by the Lord "a great nation" (Gen 21:18). *Lastly*, as "the Lord was with Joseph, and he was a successful man," (Gen 39:2), "God was with the lad (Ishmael)," and he grew up, and dwelt in the wilderness of Paran, where he became an archer (Gen 21:20–21, KJV). It is interesting to note that this is the land Yahweh came from to meet the Israelites coming out of Egypt to lead them into the land promised to Abraham (Hab 3:3, 7).

Against what many are predisposed to think, Scripture evidence does not support that Ishmael was a sworn enemy of Israel throughout biblical history. In fact, Isaac dwelt at Beir Lahai Roi, the sacred well of the Ishmaelites (Gen 25:11), and both brothers later buried their father Abraham together (Gen 25:9). After the calling of Israel to the land of Canaan for a mediatorial ministry among the nations and to act as "light to the Gentiles" (Exod 19:6; Isa 42:6; 49:6), Ishmael and his descendants were among the first people to benefit spiritually from Israel's testimony. Despite two brief periods of conflict (Judg 6–8; 1 Chr 5:9–22) the time span stretching from Abraham to Solomon witnessed an integration of Ishmaelites into Israel's socioreligious life.[8]

Two of Ishmael's tribes, Mibsam and Mishma, apparently merged under the tribe of Simeon (1 Chr 4:25).[9] Biblical Arabs, like Obil the Ishmaelite and Jaziz the Hagarite, participated in David's cabinet rule (1 Chr 27:30–31). Also David's sister married Jether the Ishmaelite, whose son Amasa was appointed by David as the leader of Israel's army supposed to replace Joab (cf. 2 Sam 20:4–13; 1 Chr 2:17). During Solomon's rule, while many vassal kingdoms paid him tributes, all the kings of the Arabs visited Israel, offering gifts of gold to the king of Israel as friendly nations rather do (Ps 72:10, 15; 1 Kings 10:15; 2 Chr 9:14). Among these, the Queen of Sheba stands out as the one that brought to Israel an amount of spices unmatched in all of its history (1 Kgs 10:10). She was declared by Jesus as a believer in Yahweh who joined the community of faith (Luke 11:31). Thus Ishmael appears to have dwelt *alongside* (*al-pené*) all of his brethren and *intermixed* with them rather than lived *in hostility with* them as proposed by some. He became part of the

---

8. For a detailed treatment of this claim, see Maalouf, *Arabs*, 109–45.

9. See Dussaud, *La pénétration*, 175; also Musil, *Arabia Deserta*, 479; Eph'al, *The Ancient Arabs*, 238–39; Sarna, *The JPS Torah Commentary: Genesis*, 122.

people of God, and his children were to sit in the pews and potentially benefit by faith from the ministry of the missionary line in the Old Testament! However, as Israel struggled with idolatry during the prophetic period, her pulpit ministry was jeopardized, and those in the pews dipped into spiritual darkness. Both parties harvested divine chastisement (Mic 1:1–7; Jer 25:1–26), but both were promised restoration of a faithful remnant that will exalt God at the end (Isa 42:1–10; 60:1–7).

The Case for Arabia's Participation.

In anticipation of the blessings of the kingdom to come, Isaiah reflects a beautiful picture of universal worship, when God will call Egypt "my people," Assyria (modern-day Iraq) "the work of my hands," and Israel "my inheritance" (Gen 19:23–25). However, this eschatological worship featuring the nations is also forecast in the typological development of redemptive history. Thus we see a recurring pattern in redemptive narratives consisting of a blindness within the covenant community with regard to God's redemptive program, and a survival of God's anointed one among neighboring nations. Of those nations, Egypt is consistently used with the motif of power for the protection of God's "messiah." In his sovereignty the Lord endowed Egypt both with political stability and military might (Isa 30:1–3; 31:1), and he uses that endowment for the survival of his appointed "savior." Hence, Egypt appears in Joseph's life (Gen 37–50), in Moses's life (Exod 2:1–15), and in Jesus' life (Matt 2:13–15). Furthermore, the nation Israel develops inside Egypt's womb and is born out of it (Exod 1–12; Hos 11:1). This role gives God's anointed one and the salvation he brings a universal dimension, allowing Gentile elements to be grafted in the Covenant community by faith (Gen 41:45; 46:20; Exod 12:38)!

However, while Egypt is used with the motif of power, indirectly *protecting* God's anointed one, Arabia is used with the motif of wealth, somehow *providing* for Him. In fact, Arabia is often portrayed in Scriptures as a land blessed by God with a coveted wealth of gold, incense, and aromatics (Ps 72:10–15; 1 Kgs 10:10), and a land of divine revelation and Abrahamic legacy (cf. Gen 25:6; Exod 2:1–4; 19–24; Deut 6–8; 33:1–2; Hab 3:3, 7; Gal 4:25). In Joseph's case, the Arabian element is exemplified by the involvement of nomadic caravan traders who were instrumental in rescuing Joseph from the sure death he was facing in the pit (Gen 37:25–30; Acts 7:9). They purchased him with incense money, while on their way to sell spices and aromatic goods in Egypt. In Moses's case, Arabia appears in his flight to the incense trading land of Midian where God provided for him through

Arabian Midianites. It is in Arabia that God prepared Moses spiritually for forty years, after he was rejected by his own and Pharaoh sought to kill him (Exod 2:15–22; Acts 7:29).

It is during his sojourn in Arabia that Moses met the Lord on Mount Sinai (Exod 3:1–10; Hab 3:3, 7) after marrying one of the daughters of Jethro, the priest of Midian (Exod 2:21). Interestingly, Jethro—whose by-name Reuel means, "friend of God" (Num 10:29)—was the first to utter a national prayer in Israel. He was also the first to offer national sacrifices before the Lord with all the elders of Israel participating in the sacrificial feast he prepared before God (Exod 18:8–12). His priesthood is most likely after the order of Melchizedek.[10] Furthermore, Jethro organized the first judicial system in Israel by instructing Moses to delegate God-fearing secondary judges to deal with minor disputes and leave only the major disputes for him to settle (Exod 2:13–26).

As a result of the sojourn of Moses in Arabia, Arabian elements entered into the makeup of "the people of God." In fact, the Kenites who descended from Jethro (Judg 1:16) eventually joined the covenant community (Num 10:29–32), and became part of Israel. Among them, Jael is greatly blessed by Deborah for killing Israel's enemy Sisera (Judg 5:24–27). Amazingly, scriptural evidence reveals that the families of the scribes in Yahweh's temple were from the line of Moses's father-in-law, Jethro (1 Chr 2:55). There is a great likelihood that the phrase, "the Kenites who came from Hammath, the father of the house of Rechab," refers to a branch of the Kenites, namely the Rechabites, who assumed the office of scribes (Jer 35:1–11). This very likely inference makes a beautiful fulfillment of the blessing uttered by the Lord upon Jonadab son of Rechab, predicting that he "shall not lack a man standing before" the Lord forever (Jer 35:18–19). So while it was true that Israel's line would assume the pulpit ministry, it seems that God entrusted the recording of Hebrew messages to an Arabian line descended from Abraham as well (Gen 25:2)!

The recurring element of threat on the life of God's anointed one is found also in the account of Christ's infancy (Matt 2:3, 16–18). However, before Jesus was sent to Egypt for protection, Arabia had to provide for his trip there! As someone said, our God is not only the Lord of history, but the Lord of geography too! Therefore, he symbolically moves the natural resources of Arabia—the biblical land of the East, to the feet of the newborn Messiah, prompting magi from the East to come and offer their expensive gifts of gold, frankincense and myrrh (Matt 2:11). In doing so, these Arabian visitors fulfilled what was prophesied about them by Isaiah (60:6), and

---

10. See Sailhamer, *The Pentateuch as Narrative*, 280–81.

provided for the poor family of Joseph (cf. Luke 2:24) to spend on the expensive sojourn in Egypt. Once again, Arabian wealth that carried Joseph to Egypt for preservation, provided through the gifts of the magi for Jesus's protection down there as well. Geographical reference to the East (Heb., *qedem*), the earliest church fathers' position, prophetical expectations (Isa 42:1–10; 60:1–7), and the above-mentioned typological pattern in redemptive history, all point to an Arabian origin of the magi who visited the Jewish Messiah to worship him![11] Thus Arabia, endowed with Abrahamic legacy, seems to have played an important role in redemptive history. No wonder Paul visited it first in his journeys to preach the gospel among the Gentiles (Gal 1:15–17; 2 Cor 11:32), and end-time prophecy seems to forecast for it a role of sheltering a remnant of believers in the Messiah (Rev 12:6, 14).

Concluding Remarks

In the present chapter, I focused mostly on the often-overlooked inclusion by faith of "non-elect" Abrahamic elements in covenantal blessings, and in the makeup of the larger people of God. Individuals like Job "the easterner" (Job 1:3), Caleb the Kenezzite (Josh 14:6, 14), Agur ben Yaqeh the Massa'ite (Prov 30:1), Lemuel, king of Massa, and his mother (Prov 31:1), and many others, could also be considered if time and space permitted.[12] However, what have been discussed so far helps us establish the following theological and practical points.

First, biblical history yields no evidence of a sustained pattern of enmity between the line of Ishmael (and biblical Arabs associated with him) and that of Israel. Biblical Arabs were not sworn enemies of biblical Israel! Integration of Ishmael in the socioreligious life of the Hebrew nation was at times evident instead.[13] Sporadic conflicts in biblical and post-biblical history were the exceptions rather than the norm.[14] Therefore, the present conflict in the Middle East over Abrahamic material blessings reveals a crisis in interpretation of history and theology. Uninformed Christians should stop spreading the idea that this conflict is unavoidable since it is deeply rooted in biblical history and prophecy. This unfounded premise does not offer hope to any of the antagonists in the land. Instead, as "Children of

---

11. For a detailed study of the Arabian origin of the magi, see Maalouf, *Arabs*, 183–218.

12. See the study on Job, Agur, and Lemuel in Maalouf, *Arabs*, 109–45.

13. For a fuller treatment of those relationships in the period called "Light of Israel," see Maalouf, *Arabs*, 109–45.

14. See Goitein, *Arabs and Jews*.

God," Christians should evenhandedly examine the related Scriptures, biblical history, and secular history as well, looking for reconciliation grounds in line with their calling to be peacemakers (Matt 5:9).

Second, in biblical times, Israel was not a homogeneous ethnic entity and Yahwistic faith rather than mere ethnicity was supposed to be her distinction. As the nation developed in the womb of Egypt, and was born out of it, Egyptian elements were inserted in it (Gen 41:45-50; Exod 12:38; Deut 26:5). As she learned how to walk under the Lord in Arabia (Deut 6-8; Hos 11:1-4), Arabian elements were grafted in as well (Num 10:29-32; Judg 1:16). In Patriarchal times and in later history, several non-Israelite entities related to Abraham joined the covenant community by faith, and some held prominent roles even in Jewish sacred services (1 Chr 2:55; Job 1-42; Prov 30-31). This establishes the fact that Israel's calling is not primarily an ethnic one, but first and foremost a faith calling, and a spiritual and moral one (Luke 3:8; Rom 9:6-9). Therefore, Christians should refrain from supporting controversial political agendas, and uphold justice and righteousness in the Land, while praying for a spiritual awakening among Jews and Arabs. After all the Abrahamic blessings can only be enjoyed by faith in the Messiah (Gal 3:6-9).

Finally, while Scriptures seem to forecast a spiritual restoration of a remnant of the Jews (Rom 11:25-32), prophecy includes also a divine visitation of a larger remnant among Arabs (Isa 42:6, 11; 60:1-7). Arabian elements in the larger family of Abraham were potentially put under covenantal blessings through circumcision (Gen 17:23-25; 25:1-6), and therefore were given priority in God's visitation program to the Gentiles (Gal 1:15-17). The visit of magi to Jerusalem to express loyalty to the Messiah is a foreshadowing of a greater future visitation of Arabs (Isa 19:23-25; 60:6-7). This mutual eschatological prospect should awaken among various parties a future and eternal perspective that would put the land in a subsidiary place. When called to inherit the land, Abraham sojourned in that land dwelling in tents, because his heart was set on the Landlord (Heb 11:9-10)! Only when those who claim Abraham as ancestor follow his moral example, and sacrifice the temporal for the sake of the eternal that they will be able to love instead of hate, and forgive instead of retaliate, in a land that is deeply yearning for a display of these spiritual virtues.

Bibliography

Baker, Kenneth, ed. *The NIV Study Bible, New International Version*. Grand Rapids: Zondervan Bible, 1985.
Dussaud, Rene. *La Pénétration Des Arabes*, Beirut: Ifpo, 1955

Eph'al, Israel. *The Ancient Arabs: Nomads on the Border of the Fertile Crescent 9th–5th Centuries, B.C.* London: Brill, 1982.

Goitein, S. D. *Arabs and Jews: Their Contact through the Ages.* New York: Schocken, 1974.

Grossfeld, Bernard, tr. *The Targum: Onkelos to Genesis.* The Aramaic Bible—The Targums, edited by Martin McNamara. Wilmington, DE: Michael Glazier, 1988.

Hamilton, Victor. *The Book of Genesis: Chapters 1–17*, NICOT, edited by R. K. Harrison. Grand Rapids: Eerdmans, 1990.

Hawken, Paul. *Blessed Unrest: How the Largest Social Movement in History is Restoring Grace, Justice and Beauty to the World.* New York: Penguin, 2008.

Kasher, Menahem M. *Genesis.* Encyclopedia of Biblical Interpretation, edited by Harry Freedman. New York: American Biblical Encyclopedia Society, 1955.

Maalouf, Tony. *Arabs in the Shadow of Israel: The Unfolding of God's Prophetic Plan for Ishmael's Line.* Grand Rapids: Kregel, 2003.

Maher, Michael, tr. *Targum Pseudo-Jonathan: Genesis.* The Aramaic Bible—The Targums, edited by Martin McNamara. Collegeville, MN: Liturgical, 1992.

Musil, Alois. *Arabia Deserta: A Topographial Itinerary.* New York: American Geographical Society, 1927.

Sailhamer, John H. *The Pentateuch as Narrative.* Grand Rapids: Zondervan, 1992.

Sarna, Nahum M. *The JPS Torah Commentary: Genesis.* Jerusalem: The Jewish Publication Society, 1989.

The Torah, The Five Books of Moses: A New Translation of the Holy Scriptures According to the Masoretic Text. Philadelphia: The Jewish Publication Society of America, 1962.

7

Will God Really Bless Those Who Bless Israel Today?

Dr. Michael L. Brown

ROUGHLY 4,000 YEARS AGO, God promised to make Abram into a great nation and then said, "I will bless those who bless you, and him who dishonors you I will curse, and in you all the families of the earth shall be blessed" (Gen 12:3, ESV). Does this apply to Abraham's descendants today, meaning, to Jewish people worldwide and, in particular, to the State of Israel? If so, what are the implications of that promise, in particular, as to how America should treat Israel and how Christians worldwide should treat Israel?

Christian Zionists are absolutely convinced that God *will* bless the nation that blesses Israel and curse the nation that curses Israel. Some even argue that, for example, the British Empire went into decline when it began to stand against the national aspirations of the Jewish people living in Palestine in the early twentieth century. They would also argue that one reason America is still strong, despite our decadence and sin, is because of our historic solidarity with the modern State of Israel. Accordingly, they would advocate for staunchly pro-Israel policies. These Christian Zionists believe it is spiritually expedient to support Israel. They also believe Israel's cause is right, even to the point of neglecting the plight of the Palestinians.

Non-Zionist Christians take issue with this viewpoint. They do so primarily on two levels, the first exegetical and the second practical. Exegetically, they feel that it is a gratuitous and even fallacious jump to connect Genesis 12:3 with Israel today. Practically, they feel that Christian Zionism contributes to inequality and injustice, most particularly towards the Palestinians, since Israel is viewed unfairly as God's chosen people, to be backed and supported no matter what, even at the cost of Palestinian suffering.

How do we sort this out? We do so exegetically and practically, beginning with the exegesis of the relevant texts and then with the practical application of our conclusions, but always in the context of the larger biblical call to justice.

Focusing first on Genesis 12:2–3: it is undeniable from an Old Testament context that the "great nation" God made out of Abram was the nation of Israel (e.g., Isa 51:1–2; Ps 105:6–11), and it would be logical to assume that the word "you" in v. 3 ("I will bless those who bless *you*, and him who dishonors *you* I will curse, and in *you* all the families of the earth shall be blessed," ESV) would refer to Abram's posterity and not just to him alone. The promises of Genesis 12:2–3 are reaffirmed to Abraham in 18:18 and 22:17–18 (for the promise to Sarah, see 17:16), while a distinct and very different set of promises are given to his son Ishmael in 17:20.

Turning now to Abraham's chosen son Isaac, God gives him a significant word in Genesis 26:3–5, this time explicitly connecting the promise of what would become the land of Israel to the divine blessing:

> Sojourn in this land, and I will be with you and will bless you, for to you and to your offspring I will give all these lands, and I will establish the oath that I swore to Abraham your father. I will multiply your offspring as the stars of heaven and will give to your offspring all these lands. And in your offspring all the nations of the earth shall be blessed, because Abraham obeyed my voice and kept my charge, my commandments, my statutes, and my laws. (Gen 26:3–5, ESV)

Although the Lord does not repeat here the promise that "I will bless those who bless you, and him who dishonors you I will curse," he does repeat other parts of the promises given to Abraham, one of which he refers to as an oath that he swore, and, as stated, it ties in directly with the promised land, a constant theme in the patriarchal narratives (e.g., Gen 13:14–17) which then continues into the exodus and conquest accounts (e.g., Exod 6:1–9; Josh 1:1–6).

It is now Isaac himself who pronounces an important blessing over Jacob—although gained deceitfully it was nonetheless irrevocable (see Gen 27:33)—saying to his son, "Let peoples serve you, and nations bow down to you. Be lord over your brothers, and may your mother's sons bow down to you. Cursed be everyone who curses you, and blessed be everyone who blesses you!" (Gen 27:29, ESV). And before Isaac sent Jacob away to find a wife, he said, "God Almighty bless you and make you fruitful and multiply you, that you may become a company of peoples. May He give the blessing of Abraham to you and to your offspring with you, that you may take possession of the land of your sojournings that God gave to Abraham!" (Gen 28:3–4, ESV).

So, once again we have: 1) the continuation of the blessing from Abraham to Isaac to Jacob; and 2) the direct connection of the blessing to the possession of the land of Israel. Those trying to argue that these words can somehow be transferred to the church—Abraham's spiritual seed (see Galatians 3:28)—have to overcome a mountain of exegetical obstacles, including: 1) nowhere in the New Testament are believers referred to as spiritual Jacob, yet "Jacob" is frequently used as a title for the nation of Israel in the Old Testament; 2) nowhere in the New Testament are believers referred to as the children of Abraham, Isaac, and Jacob, yet the promises here come to Abraham, Isaac, and Jacob; 3) throughout the Old Testament, the land of Israel is described as the land promised to the patriarchs, as in Psalm 105:

> Remember the wondrous works that he has done, his miracles, and the judgments he uttered,
>
> O offspring of Abraham, his servant, children of Jacob, his chosen ones!
>
> He is the LORD our God; his judgments are in all the earth.
>
> He remembers his covenant forever, the word that he commanded, for a thousand generations, the covenant that he made with Abraham, his sworn promise to Isaac,
>
> which he confirmed to Jacob as a statute, to Israel as an everlasting covenant,
>
> saying, "To you I will give the land of Canaan as your portion for an inheritance." (Ps 105:5–11 ESV)

It would be difficult to have stated this any more clearly, emphatically, or dogmatically, yet it simply summarizes what many other Old Testament texts also say.

Some non-Zionist Christians object at this point, with reference to Paul's words in Romans 9:6–8, where he explains that, "not all who are descended from Israel belong to Israel, and not all are children of Abraham because they are his offspring, but 'through Isaac shall your offspring be named.' This means that it is not the children of the flesh who are the children of God, but the children of the promise are counted as offspring" (Rom 9:6–8, ESV). But Paul is not denying the scores of Old Testament verses that speak of the land-related promises belonging to the people as a whole—in fact, he does not have the land promises in view at all here—and he is not denying that God's promises to the nation as a whole remain intact.

We can see this first from Paul's use of the word "Israel" or "Israelites" in the verses that follow in this very important section of Scripture, namely, Romans 9–11. Simply stated, every time he speaks of Israel after Romans 9:6, he is referring to the nation as a whole, often with an emphasis on Israel's disobedience. (See Romans 9:27 (2x), 31; 10:19, 21; 11:1–2, 7, 11, 25–26.) Notice that v. 26 speaks of Jacob as well—and then note Paul's important statement in 11:28–29: "As regards the gospel, they [speaking of the people of Israel] are enemies for your sake. But as regards election, they are beloved for the sake of their forefathers. For the gifts and the calling of God are irrevocable" (Rom 11:28–29, ESV). That's why numerous contemporary, evangelical Romans scholars understand Paul's words in 11:26, namely, that "all Israel will be saved," to refer to the Jewish people as a whole at the end of this age, not to the accumulation of the remnant of Israel through the generations and not to the church as a whole. In fact, the immediate context of 11:25–26 makes it virtually impossible to separate the Israel of v. 25, which is hardened in part, according to Paul and is distinct from the "fullness of the Gentiles," from the "all Israel" of v. 26. In the words of F. F. Bruce, one of the most acclaimed evangelical New Testament scholars of the last generation, "it is impossible to entertain an exegesis which takes 'Israel' here in a different sense from 'Israel' in v 25 ('blindness in part is happened to Israel')." He continues, "Temporarily alienated for the advantage of the Gentiles, they are eternally the object of God's electing love because his promises, once made to the patriarchs, will never be revoked."[1]

Paul's point in 9:6–8, then, is not to deny the ongoing existence of Israel as a chosen nation in God's sight but rather to explain that it is only the remnant—the children of the promise—who have been loyal to God in every generation and have been recipients of his spiritual blessings, culminating in the Jewish remnant in Paul's day who embraced Jesus as Messiah. They are the Israel within Israel, the Jewish believers within the larger nation (certainly not the church as a whole), and it is the larger nation that he continues to speak of as "Israel" throughout Romans 9–11.

Confirmation for this comes from the book of Numbers, where the promise of Genesis 12:3 is repeated once more, this time by the pagan prophet Balaam, speaking words inspired by the Lord. And note over whom he speaks these words: over the people of Israel as a whole, the undeniable subject of Numbers 22–24. See, for example, 22:12, "God said to Balaam, 'You shall not go with them. You shall not curse the people, for they are

---

1. Rom 11:26, 28–29.

blessed'" (ESV). And then note the response of Balak, king of Moab, to Balaam, once Balaam was hired to curse Israel: "And Balak said to Balaam, 'What have you done to me? I took you to curse my enemies, and behold, you have done nothing but bless them.'" (Gen 23:1, ESV). Balaam's inspired response is blunt: "Behold, I received a command to bless: he has blessed, and I cannot revoke it" (Gen 23:20, ESV; see also 23:25; 24:1, 10). And then, as Balaam looks at the tribes of Israel from his vantage point on the mountains, he speaks these critically important words over the people as a whole, not just the remnant: "God brings him out of Egypt and is for him like the horns of the wild ox; he shall eat up the nations, his adversaries, and shall break their bones in pieces and pierce them through with his arrows. He crouched, he lay down like a lion and like a lioness; who will rouse him up? *Blessed are those who bless you, and cursed are those who curse you*" (Gen 24:8–9, ESV).

These verses substantiate that the divine promises of Genesis 12:2–3 apply not only to Abraham but to his physical descendants through Isaac and Jacob, the twelve tribes of Israel. They cannot be restricted to the Israel within Israel, nor can they be transferred in full to Abraham's spiritual seed, something the New Testament never does. In other words, nowhere does the New Testament transfer the land promise to the church as a whole, and nowhere does the New Testament state that the land promised to Israel has been revoked. Quite the contrary. It reiterates the ongoing nature of the promises (see again, Romans 11:28–29); it speaks of the scattering of the Jewish people from Jerusalem and of their regathering (Luke 21:24); it speaks of a future restoration of the nation of Israel (Matt 19:28; Acts 1:6–7); it states that all that the prophets have spoken concerning Israel's restoration—which certainly includes a glorious resettling in the land—will come to pass (Acts 3:19–21). As for the church's physical inheritance, the whole world belongs to the people of God (Matt 5:5; 1 Cor 3:21–23).

It could be argued, of course, that there *will* be a future restoration of Israel, both to the land and to the Messiah, but just as the spiritual restoration remains future, so also the physical restoration remains future. And so, even if one believes that God has miraculously preserved his ancient people (at times under severe discipline), he has not brought them back to the land at present. Rather, this is the result of human effort and human decisions, of colonialism and political nation-making, not the result of the Lord's powerful hand.

But this too can be easily rebutted. First, are we to say that God's sovereignty somehow ceased in the twentieth century and that the massive, world-shaking events that took place, including two world wars, the Holocaust (which included the slaughter of two-thirds of Europe's Jewish population), and the regathering of the Jewish people to their ancient homeland, took place primarily (or, worse still, exclusively) through human machinations? It is one thing to acknowledge the agonizing mystery of the Holocaust in terms of divine presence or absence; it is another thing to say that the Jewish people were almost exterminated, then regathered against all odds to their ancient homeland, and the Lord had nothing to do this deliverance from death and this merciful restoration. Second, no people in history, other than the Jewish people, has been exiled from its homeland for a period of many centuries and still managed to preserve its national identity, let alone return to its homeland almost 2,000 years later, let alone revive its ancestral tongue, let alone have much of this laid out in Scripture in advance—some of this is clearly included in chapters like Ezekiel 36, which did not reach its fulfillment with the return from Babylonian captivity. Third, there are prophetic passages yet to be fulfilled that require the Jewish people to be back in the land with Jerusalem under their control—note in particular Zechariah 12; 14; Jesus' words in Matthew 23:37–39 presuppose this as well. And according to the best evangelical exegesis of these passages, this points to a time before Israel has turned to the Messiah, hence a Jewish presence in the land but not in full belief.

Fourth, and most importantly, the Word makes clear that when God blesses no one can curse and when he curses, no one can bless—see especially Leviticus 26 and Deuteronomy 28. In the same way, when he wounds no one can heal and when he heals no one can wound, and when he opens a door no one can shut it and when he shuts a door no one can open it (see Deut 32:39; Rev 3:7). So, if the Jewish people have been scattered by God in judgment, no one—most of all the Jewish people themselves—can regather them. To claim otherwise is to claim that the divine edict is meaningless and can be overthrown by mere mortals. And since the Bible is explicit that the exile from the land was a divine judgment (among many Scriptures, see 2 Chr 7:17–22), the only explanation for the regathering to the land is that God himself did it. As declared through the prophet Jeremiah, "Hear the word of the LORD, O nations, and declare it in the coastlands far away; say, 'He who scattered Israel will gather him, and will keep him as a shepherd keeps his flock'" (Jer 31:10, ESV). And, "For I am with you to save you, declares the LORD; I will make a full end of all the nations among whom I scattered you, but of you I will not make a full end. I will discipline you in just measure, and I will by no means leave you unpunished" (Jer 30:11, ESV). These words of regathering cannot be limited to the return from the Babylonian exile any more than the promise to scatter disobedient Israel and Judah can be limited to the exile into Babylon, and before that, Assyria.

This is not to say that there may not be an even more supernatural, climactic, final gathering of scattered, future Jewry in times to come (e.g., Isa 35). But it is to say that the current regathering can only be attributed to the hand of God, and, consequently, the irrevocable promises given to Abraham, Isaac, Jacob, and the twelve tribes of Israel still apply: God *will* bless those who bless Israel and curse those who curse Israel. Those ancient words have not lost their power.

How then should these truths be applied? While whole books could be written on this subject, let me offer some simple, closing reflections.

First, the fact that God still has corporate purposes for the people of Israel does not mean that everything Israel does is right or righteous. To the contrary, to whom much is given much is required (Luke 12:48), and chosenness carries with it responsibility (e.g., Amos 3:2). Even if we can debate where Israel stands with God today in theological terms (is Israel still under the Sinai Covenant?) we can agree that it does not follow that just because the Lord has preserved his ancient people, Christians should back everything Israel does. To the contrary, of all nations on the planet, Israel should be called to heed the ethics of the Torah, something that most of the nation's leadership would readily embrace, since Israel prides itself on ethical conduct, despite being a largely secular nation. A corollary is that the Palestinians do best when they cease trying to destroy Israel and agree to live harmoniously with them, even under Israeli sovereignty. Whenever this has occurred, and whenever it does occur today, the quality of Palestinian life has increased dramatically.

Second, once we recognize that it is God himself who established the modern State of Israel, our perspective changes dramatically. Not only do we recognize his providential hand in history, including the Six-Day War, which was rightly called miraculous in many ways—God being for Israel—but we also realize the diabolical nature of the attempts to destroy Israel: Satan being against Israel. From Hitler to Hamas, we find a common, and, indeed, ancient, thread, and we can better understand the irrational hatred towards the Jewish people from a completely disparate and unrelated group of enemies ranging from black supremacists to white supremacists, from Stalin's atheism to ISIL's Islam, from anti-Zionists in Japan to the latest believers in the *Protocols of the Elders of Zion*, from medieval popes to Martin Luther.

On a practical level, this means that we are hesitant to buy into a narrative which demonizes the Jews lest we follow the example of many church leaders (and others) in the past. It also means that we recognize that any proposed solution to the Middle East conflict must take into account the intense spiritual conflict as well as the intense political conflict, understanding that there is often more going on than meets the eye. To give one case in point, we cannot look at the battle for control of Jerusalem through natural eyes alone, since behind the natural conflict is a deeply spiritual one. Why else does the whole world care about what happens to this city? And what other city is singled out in Scripture as the place of the final world battle (Zech 12, 14) or is mentioned as the city to be prayed for until it becomes the praise of all the earth (Isa 62; also Ps 122) and the city to which Jesus will return when his Jewish people welcome him back (Acts 1:9–11; Matt 23:37–39; Acts 3:19–21)? This does not mean that we trample the needs of the Palestinians under foot—God forbid—but it does mean that we look at this difficult conflict with our eyes wide open.

In light of these considerations, we can safely say reject the judgment of a respected New Testament scholar that Christians must side with justice rather than prophecy. I say that, to stand with God, we must stand with both justice and prophecy—and that means standing with Israel today.

8

The Land of Israel and the Problem of Supersessionism

Rev. Dr. John E. Phelan Jr.

> One has got either to be a Jew or stop reading the Bible. The Bible cannot make sense to anyone who is not "spiritually a Semite." The spiritual sense of the Old Testament is not and cannot be a simple emptying out of its Israelite content. Quite the contrary! The New Testament is the fulfillment of that spiritual content, the fulfillment of the promise made to Abraham, the promise that Abraham believed in. It is never therefore a denial of Judaism, but is affirmation. Those who consider it a denial have not understood it.
>
> —Thomas Merton, *Conjectures of a Guilty Bystander*[1]

The Problem of Supersessionism

RABBI JONATHAN SACKS, THE former Chief Rabbi of the United Hebrew Congregations of the Commonwealth, once wrote that Paul was "the architect of a Christian theology which deemed the covenant between God and his people was now broken. Pauline theology," he continues, "demonstrates to the full how remote from and catastrophic to Judaism is the doctrine of

---

1. Merton, *Conjectures of a Guilty Bystander*, 5–6.

the second choice, a new election. No doctrine has cost more Jewish lives."[2] I will try to demonstrate later in this chapter that Rabbi Sacks is wrong about Paul. Sadly, he is undoubtedly right about the brutal effects of what he calls "the doctrine of the second choice." In Christian circles this is often known as "supersessionism" or "replacement theory." It is, in simple terms, the assertion that God's covenant with Israel is abrogated and that the church is now the new Israel, the new people of God.

For many church fathers this meant the Jews had been assigned to the scrap heap of history, worthy only of scorn. Most infamous was John Chrysostom, whose *Discourses Against the Jews* have been called "the most horrible and violent denunciations of Judaism to be found in the writings of a Christian theologian." As David Nirenberg laconically comments, "Certainly they are not friendly."[3] In addition to common Christian attacks on Judaism (e.g., Jews are obstinate, stiff-necked, murderous, always rebellious against God, etc.), John Chrysostom "presented the Jews as the antitype, not just of Christians but of humans. 'Their condition is not better than that of pigs or goats.'"[4] Why was Chrysostom so exercised?

Within Chrysostom's memory was the reign of the so-called Julian the Apostate. Raised a Christian, the emperor had turned against the faith and even gone to far as to promise the Jews that they could rebuild the temple in Jerusalem. Julian was well aware that permitting the Jews to return to their holy city and rebuild their temple would strike at the heart of Christian views of history and theology. Generations of Christians had looked with satisfaction at the rubble of the temple as proof that God had abandoned the Jews in favor of the Christian church. A renewed temple would call all that into question. Julian died after less than two years as emperor and "according to John the construction site was destroyed by earthquake and the laborers devoured by fire. Once again," Nirenberg comments, "the defeat of the Jews provided the best evidence, 'clear and obvious even to the very young,' that Christ, not Caesar Julian and his Jews, was king."[5]

Chrysostom was not the only opponent of the Jews in the earliest days of the church. Nirenberg goes on to cover the writings and opinions of such major figures as St. Ambrose of Milan, that notable theological crank St. Jerome, and perhaps most important the hugely influential St. Augustine. The latter's approach to the Jews assigned them the status of Cain. The Jews were not to be killed, but rather, like Cain, condemned to bear the mark

---

2. Levine, *The Jewish Annotated New Testament*, 586.
3. Nirenberg, *Anti-Judaism*, 113.
4. Ibid., 113–14.
5. Ibid., 116.

of their murder (Gen 4:15). "Not by bodily death shall the ungodly race of carnal Jews perish.... So to the end of the seven days of time the continued preservation of the Jews will be proof to believing Christians of the subjection merited by those who... put the Lord to death."[6] The marginalization of the Jews, their landless wandering, and brutal oppression were clear demonstrations of the superiority of Christianity and the defeat of the "enemies of God."

Modern Supersessionism

Many modern Christians rightly find this history an embarrassment. That towering figures like Chrysostom, Ambrose, and Augustine could speak and write so vilely of the Jews is shocking. The impact of their words upon the Jews within the Christian empire was horrendous, leaving an indelible stain on the Christian church. But these same modern Christians should not forget that these negative attitudes were (and are) very much alive and well in our own era. It was only in the wake of the *Shoah* (Holocaust) that many Christians in the West, at least, were confronted with the cruel effects of anti-Judaism. Tragically, a straight line can be drawn from Chrysostom and Augustine through Martin Luther and his virulent *On the Jews and their Lies* to European anti-Semitism and the murder of six million. This is not to discount the rise of secular and anti-religious anti-Semitism, particularly in the late nineteenth century. But it is to insist that this secular anti-Semitism grew in European soil already well plowed and sown with anti-Jewish seed planted and nurtured by Christians.

It is tempting to excise the early examples of Christian anti-Judaism from our collective memories. But modern examples are close at hand. To cite one from my own church, The Evangelical Covenant Church, G. F. Hedstrand wrote to *The Christian Century* in response to an editorial recounting anti-Jewish activities during the early days of Hitler's Third Reich. "The Jew," Hedstrand wrote:

> ... can squeal much without meaning much by it, and he does not need to be hurt very much in order to squeal much. And it seems to me that *The Christian Century* should know it and think before it runs to the defense of the 'defenseless and persecuted Jew'.... The Jews are not persecuted in Germany because of their religion, but because of their political and economic activities. They are Communists, many of them and 'persecuted' the nationalists before they came to power.... They are

---

6. Ibid., 130.

children—reminding one of the colored race—in their mental makeup. They need to spoken to with authority, or they will not believe you. That is what the nationalists are doing. They are not persecuting the Jews—they are talking to them in the only language they know.[7]

Letters and attitudes like these were depressingly common in the prewar period and led far too many people to ignore the warning signs and deny the realities of murderous oppression until it was too late.

The Christian Century during those prewar years was itself ambivalent about the state of the Jews in Europe and particularly concerned with their national aspirations. In Hertzel Fishman's *American Protestantism and a Jewish State*, he argues that *The Christian Century*, as the representative of mainline, liberal American Protestantism "did not understand the unique nature of American Jewry." During the 1930s, it vigorously upheld the melting pot theory, and the principle target of its indignation was the Jews. When the Jews exercised their distinctive patterns of faith and culture outside the purview of the majority populace, they were, in the magazine's view, violating a cardinal democratic principle of "majority rule."[8]

This was not simply a matter of the Jews' cultural adjustment to the realities of life in the American democracy. Editors had a *theological* point to make as well. "When the doctrine of cultural pluralism is taken to mean religious pluralism—'Judaism is true for the Jew and Christianity is true for the Christian'—it sets itself in direct opposition to the Christian faith which cannot exist at all except on the presumption of its universality."[9] Not only were the Jews viewed as a cultural irritant, with their refusal to join the American cultural mainstream, they were seen as a *theological* irritant refusing, once again, to recognize the superiority and finality of Christianity. The editors even went to far as to warn the Jews that their stubborn refusal to leave their distinctive characteristics behind was the breeding ground for growing American anti-Semitism. The Jews were culpable, in other words, for their own oppression.[10]

The Christian Century was also exercised over Jewish nationalism. Throughout the early decades of the twentieth century the magazine editorialized against the aspirations of the Jews for a homeland. Jewish members of the Congress of the United States have often been charged with having

---

7. Ross, *So it Was True*, 26–27.
8. Fishman, *American Protestantism*, 31.
9. Ibid., 33.
10. Ibid.

"divided loyalties" between the United States and Israel. This is not a new charge. In 1944 the editors wrote:

> No single factor has done more to render insecure the position of the modern Jew than the charge that he is not completely, whole-heartedly, first, last and all the time a citizen of the country in which he resides, but that he attempts to hold a dual citizenship, which in actuality works out in a divided loyalty, with his primary loyalty given to an allegiance other than the land in which he lives.[11]

By 1944 it should have been clear to the editors of *The Christian Century* that Jewish loyalty to Germany, Poland, and France, to mention only a few, had actually served them poorly. Even the most sophisticated and assimilated Jews had been slaughtered along with their more orthodox sisters and brothers.

This was only the latest of a series of editorials fulminating against Jewish national aspirations. And as with the Jewish resistance to assimilation, the editors had a theological point as well as a nationalistic and cultural one. They encouraged their readers as early as 1933 to distinguish between "Jews as Jews and Jews as nationalists." It reminded its Christian readers that it was *nationalistic* Jews that had crucified Jesus:

> He was crucified because he had a program for Israel which ran counter to the cherished nationalism of Israel's leaders— political and priestly. He opposed their nationalism with the universalism of God's love and God's kingdom . . . . In the eyes of the Jewish rulers, he was a seditious person, a menace to their fantastic nationalism and to their vested rights and prestige . . . . It was nationalism that crucified Jesus . . . . It was because he threatened by his teaching to upset their cherished ambition to make Israel and Israel's God the dominant power of the world that he came into collision with Israel's rulers.[12]

The editors of *The Christian Century* here manifest the same nervousness as those fourth-century Christians horrified by Julian's efforts to rebuild the temple. For these mainline leaders of the '30s and '40s, a Jewish state was as great a threat to the theological superiority of the Christian faith as a rebuilt Jewish temple had been to their forebears.

Fishman notes that the magazine "carried little criticism" of other nationalist groups. "American nationalism is applauded, and the nationalist

11. Ibid., 36.
12. Ibid., 37–38.

aspirations of colonially held societies are respected. Only Nazi nationalism and Jewish nationalism are put in the same category."[13] Shockingly, in the wake of the war, in 1945 *The Christian Century* "expressed the hope that the German people would not develop a martyr complex and 'become another Jewry; they have not lived long enough with their ideology of a unique and privileged race.' The implication [is] that the Jews have a 'privileged race' mentality analogous to the Nazi superior race ideology."[14] The ovens of Auschwitz were barely cool and *The Christian Century* was warning the Germans not to be like the Jews.

The shadow of Christian supersessionism is long. The current question of whether the Jews have a right to a national existence in their ancient homeland cannot be separated from 2,000 years of Christian theologizing. It has served the interests of Christian apologetics for the Jews to be marginalized, ghettoized, and left without political, military, cultural, and even economic power. Jewish marginalization was facilitated not only by the likes of Chrysostom and Augustine, but by a reading of the Jewish Scriptures that not only invalidated the covenant God made with Israel, but spiritualized the very physical and national hopes of the Jewish people or assigned them to Christians. In what follows, I will briefly review Paul's understanding of the enduring validity of the covenant with Israel. I will suggest that supersessionist readings of Paul are misreadings that, as Rabbi Sacks suggests, have led to the shedding of much Jewish blood. I will finally argue that the eschatological hopes of both Israel and the church are connected with the land of Israel and that the Old and New Testaments understand God's future to entail a Jewish state in their ancient homeland.

Paul and Israel

Over the last forty years, New Testament scholars have called into question the "Lutheran" readings of Paul—readings that suggested God had rejected both the Jews and their Law. As John Gager pointed out in his recent *Who Made Early Christianity?*, Paul's letters can be read in an anti-Jewish or pro-Jewish manner. Paul makes statements, sometimes in the same letter, that appear to be contradictory: "Circumcision is of great value; *it counts for nothing. The Law is holy; it places its followers under a curse and cannot justify them before God.* All Israel will be saved; *they are enemies of God and have failed to fulfill their own law.*"[15] This means, "Paul was lost in a hopeless

13. Ibid., 38.
14. Ibid., 37.
15. Gager, *Who Made Early Christianity*, 15.

quagmire of intellectual and emotional inconsistency," or the reader is missing something!¹⁶ Gager insists that what many ancient and contemporary readers have missed is that Paul's concern was with the attempt to apply the "works of the Law," specifically the "boundary markers" that set Jews apart from Gentiles, to his *Gentile* converts. He never imagined that the law was passé or that God's covenant with Israel was abrogated. Gager's views are supported by many recent Jewish readers of Paul as well as by the so-called "New Perspective" Pauline scholars.¹⁷ Paul was *not* anti-Jewish or "supersessionist"—quite the contrary.

In Romans 11, Paul asks, "Did God reject his people?" and responds with his strongest negation: "By no means!" A bit later he insists, "the gifts and calling of God are irrevocable" (11:29, HCSB). He finally and famously insists: "All Israel will be saved" (11:26, HCSB). Paul certainly longed for his fellow Jews to follow Messiah Jesus (see Rom 9). But he never seems to imagine that the conversion of the Gentiles meant the rejection of Israel. He also never imagined that he was founding a new religion—Christianity. He thought what he was doing in preaching the gospel of Messiah Jesus was consistent with his Judaism and not a departure from the law and the prophets. Israel's "hardening," Paul thought, was only temporary. When the "full number" of the Gentiles had come in, as noted before, "all Israel" would be saved.

A Jewish professor once told one of my colleagues that all Christians, if they are honest, are at least a bit supersessionist. Even if the "hard supersessionism" of rejection is itself rejected, it is hard to escape Paul's insistence on the finality of Jesus. But this, for Paul, certainly did *not* mean the rejection of the Jews *as Jews* or the spiritualizing or elimination of their expectations. The habits of Christendom are hard to break even when Christendom itself is shattered. When a Christian emperor ruled a Christian empire and Christian kings were enthroned across Christian Europe it was easy to imagine that the prophets' promises were already fulfilled. It was easy to transfer Christian hopes from the earthly rule of God to immortality in heaven. But as Jurgen Moltmann has argued:

> The promises given to Israel are as yet only fulfilled in principle in the coming of Messiah Jesus . . . and the outpouring of the Spirit "on all flesh" [is] as yet realized only partially. . . . Through the gospel and the Holy Spirit the divine promises given to Israel are extended to all nations . . . [Christianity] can only remain true to its own hope if it recognizes Israel as the older

---

16. Ibid.
17. Phelan, "(Re)reading Paul."

community of hope alongside itself. In its hope for the nations the church also preserves the "surplus of hope" in Israel's prophets, and therefore waits for the fulfillment of Israel's hopes too.[18]

The hope of Israel in the Hebrews Scriptures is inextricably linked with the land. It is earthy, tactile. As N. T. Wright has pointed out, the *Christian* hope is equally earthy and tactile. Christians hope not "to go to heaven when they die," but for the "new heavens and the new earth."[19] At the center of this expectation is Jerusalem—not an idealized state of communal bliss— but the actual city in the actual land of Israel in its old or new form, having descended from heaven (Rev 21). In fact, as generations of Jews and Christians have expected, the Bible insists that great final assize will be in Jerusalem. And in the end all the Gentiles "will go up [to Jerusalem] year after year to worship the King, the Lord Almighty" (Zech 14:16, NIV). "Spiritualizing" these and scores of other texts will simply not do.[20] So, what does this all have to do with the more recent Jewish return to the land and the current state of Israel?

The Current State of Israel

It is fair to say that many if not most Jews, and certainly many, if not most, Israelis, are not particularly interested in theological arguments for the existence of the State of Israel. Their concerns are much more personal and practical. The Jews, scattered throughout a hostile world, far from their homeland, have seldom been safe from oppression and violence. The State of Israel represented for many of its founders not the fulfillment of biblical expectations, but a place where the Jews could be at home and defend themselves. While there are certainly Jews (and even more Christians!) who saw (and see) the State of Israel as part of the fulfillment of the prophets, for many it is simply their homeland.

The current nation-state, in spite of the claims of some Christian dispensationalists, is a state like any other. It deserves, like any other state, scrutiny and criticism when it acts in ways that violate its foundational commitments. Ironically, both Israel's most rabid supporters and severest critics sometimes seem to expect Israel to act in ways that suggest it has a unique status in the world! Seldom have the actions of a state been so closely scrutinized and critiqued by both friends and enemies! Israel is a tiny state

---

18. Moltmann. *The Coming of God*, 197.
19. Wright, *Surprised by Hope*, and Phelan, *Essential Eschatology*.
20. Phelan, *Essential Eschatology*, 15–29, 153–69.

and the Jewish population of the world amounts to only 13,000,000—small enough to fit comfortably in some of the world's largest cities with room to spare. And yet both the Jews and Israel seem to draw inordinate attention from the world. The Muslim and Christian worlds, in fact, still seem obsessed with the Jews, in spite of their tiny population and minuscule state.

For Christians, at least, this obsession has very deep roots. Throughout Christian history Jews, as argued above, have represented both an irritant and an object lesson. Their unwillingness to acknowledge the superiority of Christianity frustrated Christian leaders over the centuries. Their miserable and marginal existence, however, was a satisfying mark of that superiority. For most Christian leaders throughout history, Jewish return to the land would represent a violation of a cherished narrative of superiority. It would call into question, especially, the doctrine of supersessionism. I fear that supersessionist orientations still undergird Christian opposition to the state of Israel. Against this supersessionism and the continuing marginalization of the Jews I would argue the following:

1. The Bible, as argued above, uniformly asserts that the land of Israel and the city of Jerusalem remain at the center of God's plans for the redemption and restoration of the world. To strip the land of Israel and the Jews out of the story of God's redeeming work is an act of Christian supersessionism unsupported by both the Hebrew Scriptures and the New Testament. "For Zion's sake not keep silent," declares the prophet. "For Jerusalem's sake I will not remain quiet, till her vindication shines out like the dawn, her salvation like a blazing torch" (Isa 62:1, NIV). In both Zechariah and the book of Revelation, the Gentiles stream into the holy city to worship God (Zech 14, Rev 21) and the water of life and the trees of life are there, as John puts it, "for the healing of the nations" (Rev 22:1-2, NIV).

2. Neither Jesus nor Paul imagined that the new thing that God was doing in the death of resurrection of Jesus meant the final and complete rejection of the Jewish people or the invalidation of their very physical hopes. In fact, it meant, as Moltmann argued above, their fulfillment and inclusion. The Jews, according to Paul, had not "stumbled beyond recovery" (Rom 11:11) and were capable of being "regrafted" into the old "olive tree" that remained as much theirs as the Gentiles (Rom 11:17ff).

3. To say, then, that the Jews have no right to a state in their ancient homeland is not only a statement of Christian supersessionism, but also an assertion of anti-Semitism. It is to single out the Jews as the

only people unworthy of a place in their own native land and to deny that their aspirations are as valid as those of any other displaced and marginalized persons, including the Palestinians.

4. To say that the land of Israel remains in the plan of God and that the Jews have a right to a state in their ancient homeland is *not* to place the State of Israel beyond criticism or deny that the Palestinians have often been oppressed and abused by the State. Not only the laws of the nation-state, but the Law and Prophets in fact, demand justice for the Palestinians. What this justice entails is certainly a complex and distressing question—but not an insoluble one.

Conclusion

The Bible is a rigorously *physical* book. Both Judaism and Christianity are *earthy* traditions. Torah is filled with earthy concerns: what the Jews eat, how and when they work, with whom and when they may have sex. Torah is very *tactile*! And though it is not so often noted, Christianity is also earthy. At the center of Christian faith is the *incarnation*. Jesus did not come as a spirit or ghostly apparition, as some of the Gnostics imagined, but as a human being. When Christians celebrate their salvation they remember a man who rose from the dead—again, not as a ghostly apparition, but as a human being who could be seen and touched. The New Testament anticipates the new heavens and the new earth and God's rule from the "New Jerusalem" (see Rev 21, 22 and Isa 65:17–25). This too is neither ghostly nor vaguely "spiritual," but concrete, tactile, earthy. Christians and Jews hold this hope in common even though their expectations of how and by whom it will be fulfilled differ! However one does and should critique the current State of Israel, the presence of Jews in their ancient homeland bears witness to this hope.

Bibliography

Fishman, Hertzel. *American Protestantism and a Jewish State*. Detroit: Wayne State University Press, 1973.

Gager, John. *Who Made Early Christianity? The Jewish Lives of the Apostle Paul*. New York: Columbia University Press, 2015.

Levine, Amy-Jill, and Marc Zvi Brettler. *The Jewish Annotated New Testament*. Oxford: Oxford University Press, 2011.

Merton, Thomas. *Conjectures of a Guilty Bystander*. New York: Doubleday & Company, 1966.

Moltmann, Jurgen. *The Coming of God*. Translated by Margaret Kohl. Minneapolis: Fortress, 1996.

Nirenberg, David. *Anti-Judaism: The Western Tradition*. New York: W. W. Norton, 2013.

Phelan, John E., Jr. *Essential Eschatology: Our Present and Future Hope*. Downers Grove, IL: InterVarsity, 2013.

———. "(Re)reading Paul: Jewish Reappraisals of the Apostle to the Gentiles." In *Doing Theology for the Church: Essays in Honor of Klyne Snodgrass*, edited by Rebekah A. Eklund and John E. Phelan Jr., 79–93. Eugene, OR: Wipf and Stock, 2014.

Ross, Robert W. *So it Was True: The American Protestant Press and the Nazi Persecution of the Jew*. Minneapolis: The University of Minnesota Press, 1980.

Wright, N. T. *Surprised by Hope: Rethinking Heaven, the Resurrection, and the Mission of the Church*. New York: HarperOne, 2008.

Part III

Intersections of History

©duncan1890. IStockPhoto.com. Photo ID: 78080305. Nov 2, 2015.
Downloaded June 26, 2016.
Historical Illustration of Mt. Zion in Jerusalem

9

Land & People

Dr. Andrea Lee Smith

WHEN I WAS YOUNGER, I uncritically supported the State of Israel and never even considered the well-being of Palestinian peoples. I related the State of Israel to the Cherokee nation. I thought, just as the Cherokee people should have the right to regain their lands in Georgia and should never lose that right, so too do the Jewish peoples have the unconditional right to their lands in Israel. My position was further bolstered by my strong biblical belief that God had given Israel to the Jewish peoples. Since, my views have changed, but not so much in terms of questioning the relationship between Jewish peoples and Israel. Instead, I began to question the assumed relationship between peoples and lands as well as the assumption that the goal for any liberation struggle is the attainment of a nation-state.

Many evangelicals often equate supporting Jewish people with supporting the modern nation-state of Israel. It is understandable how these two become equated. Given the history of oppression and genocide faced by Jewish peoples, it makes sense to see the State of Israel as something that can help liberate Jewish peoples from this history. Certainly, many Native peoples have often called for the formation of indigenous nation-states as a means of decolonizing Native nations from settler colonial rule. However, increasingly more Native organizers and scholars have called this assumption into question. They have argued that it is possible to have a nation without a nation-state based on different principles of governance. Native women activists in particular have visions of indigenous nationhood and sovereignty that are separate from nation-states. Whereas nation-states are governed through domination and coercion, indigenous sovereignty and nationhood is predicated on interrelatedness and responsibility. This interconnectedness exists not only among the nation's members but also among all creation—human and nonhuman. As Native organizer Ingrid Washinawatok once stated:

> Our spirituality and our responsibilities define our duties. We understand the concept of sovereignty as woven through a fabric that encompasses our spirituality and responsibility. This is a cyclical view of sovereignty, incorporating it into our traditional philosophy and view of our responsibilities. There it differs greatly from the concept of western sovereignty which is based upon absolute power. For us absolute power is in the Creator and the natural order of all living things; not only in human beings.... Our sovereignty is related to our connections to the earth and is inherent.[1]

Lakota Harden has described how indigenous sovereignty is based on freedom for all peoples. Indigenous sovereignty rests on the idea that "if the system doesn't work for one of us, it doesn't work for any of us." When I first learned the definition of sovereignty, I believed, "none of us are free unless all of us our free.... We're all in this together. We can't—we won't turn anyone away."[2]

These visions question the assumption that the endpoint of a national struggle should be a nation-state. Rather than nation-states based on exclusivist control of land, it is possible to build nations that are inclusive and understand themselves as fundamentally connected to all other nations.

This distinction actually also had a biblical basis. In 1 Samuel, when the Israelites ask for a king, they essentially are asking for a nation-state instead of a nation. God tells the people when they ask for a king, they are asking for a system of governance based on oppression. God should be the only sovereign because God is the only just sovereign. As described in 1 Samuel 8:11–18:

> This is what the king who will reign over you will claim as his rights: He will take your sons and make them serve with his chariots and horses, and they will run in front of his chariots. Some he will assign to be commanders of thousands and commanders of fifties, and others to plow his ground and reap his harvest, and still others to make weapons of war and equipment for his chariots. He will take your daughters to be perfumers and

1. Washinawatok, "Sovereignty as a Birthright," 12.
2. Harden, Interview.

cooks and bakers. He will take the best of your fields and vineyards and olive groves and give them to his attendants. He will take a tenth of your grain and of your vintage and give it to his officials and attendants. Your male and female servants and the best of your cattle and donkeys he will take for his own use. He will take a tenth of your flocks, and you yourselves will become his slaves. When that day comes, you will cry out for relief from the king you have chosen, but the Lord will not answer you in that day.

But the people refused to listen to Samuel. "No!" they said. "We want a king over us. Then we will be like all the other nations, with a king to lead us and to go out before us and fight our battles." (NIV)

Thus, what Jesus' pronounced in Matthew 23:8–12 can be read as a reversal of 1 Samuel:

But you are not to be called 'Rabbi,' for you have one Teacher, and you are all brothers. And do not call anyone on earth 'father,' for you have one Father, and He is in heaven. Nor are you to be called instructors, for you have one Instructor, the Messiah. The greatest among you will be your servant. For those who exalt themselves will be humbled, and those who humble themselves will be exalted. (NIV)

Jesus is essentially announcing an end to kingship, proclaiming the restoration of God as the only true sovereign, and calling for a new form of governance based on principles of equality. And as many biblical scholars have noted, the early church was in fact based on these principles of equality until the church began to connect itself to empire.

Frequently, critics of Israel often rely on an Israeli exceptionalism that can be anti-Semitic. That is, Israel is portrayed as qualitatively worse than any other nation-state. But in fact, Israel is the rule rather than the exception: when any oppressed peoples seek liberation through a nation-state, their liberation is based on principles of the right to self-determination at the expense of other nations. That is why many Indigenous peoples have argued that indigenous self-determination must be based on different principles that recognize the right of all nations to exist. One such example would be the statements issued by Indigenous peoples' organizations at the 2008 World Social Forum. They contended that the goal of indigenous struggle was not simply to fight for the survival of their particular peoples, but to transform the world so that it is governed through principles of participatory democracy rather than through nation-states. The nation-state has not worked for the last 500 years, they argued, so it is probably not going to start working now. Their vision of nationhood required a radical re-orientation toward land. All are welcome to live on the land, they asserted, but we must all live in a different relationship to the land. We must understand ourselves as peoples who must care for the land rather than those who control it.

These principles of indigenous governance can inform how we interpret, the proclamation that there "is neither Jew, nor Greek."

> Therefore, remember that formerly you who are Gentiles by birth and called "uncircumcised" by those who call themselves "the circumcision" (which is done in the body by human hands)—remember that at that time you were separate from Christ, excluded from citizenship in Israel and foreigners to the covenants of the promise, without hope and without God in the world. But now in Christ Jesus you who once were far away have been brought near by the blood of Christ.
>
> For he himself is our peace, who has made the two groups one and has destroyed the barrier, the dividing wall of hostility, by setting aside in his flesh the law with its commands and regulations. His purpose was to create in himself one new humanity out of the two, thus making peace, and in one body to reconcile both of them to God through the cross, by which he put to death their hostility. He came and preached peace to you who were far away and peace to those who were near. For through him we both have access to the Father by one Spirit.
>
> Consequently, you are no longer foreigners and strangers, but fellow citizens with God's people and also members of his household, built on the foundation of the apostles and prophets, with Christ Jesus himself as the chief cornerstone. In him the whole building is joined together and rises to become a holy temple in the Lord. And in him you too are being built together to become a dwelling in which God lives by his Spirit. (Eph 2:11–22, NIV)

As many Christian Zionists have pointed out, these passages have been often interpreted historically through an anti-Semitic framework: Jesus has abandoned the Jewish peoples and now embraces Christians (perceived as mutually exclusive from Jews) as the true people of God. But read in conjunction with 1 Samuel, we can also interpret these passages to be calling for a different kind of self-determination. When the Israelites were invested in kingship, their path to self-determination was exclusivity (the Canaanites must be destroyed to make way for the Israelites). But Jesus announces the end to self-determination through kingship. Self-determination for a peoples cannot exist at the expense of self-determination for another peoples. It is possible to have a nationhood for one people (in this case Jewish people) that exists through its relationship with all other nations. God's promises to Israel do not have to be the expense of God's promises for all other peoples. This different understanding of nationhood requires a different understanding of the relationship between peoples and land. Within Native organizing, many organizers/thinkers note that this exclusivist understanding of nation-states are based on a commodification of land. That is, land—and for the matter, the rest of creation—is something that can be owned, bought, sold, and controlled by one group of people. Thus under our current Western legal system, the only response to colonial encroachment on land is to say "It's not your land; it's our land." The question you cannot ask is, "Why should anyone get to own and control a piece of land?" As Mohawk scholar Patricia Monture-Angus once explained:

> Although Aboriginal Peoples maintain a close relationship with the land . . . it is not about control of the land . . . . Earth is mother and she nurtures us all . . . it is the human race that is dependent on the earth and not vice versa . . . .
> Sovereignty, when defined as my right to be responsible . . . requires a relationship with territory (and not a relationship based on control of that territory) . . . . What must be understood then is that Aboriginal request to have our sovereignty respected is really a request to be responsible. I do not know of anywhere else in history where a group of people have had to fight so hard just to be responsible.[3]

Ella Shohat, who is an Iraqi Jew, has made a similar argument about the assumption that the Israel and Palestine can only be exclusively owned by either Jewish or Arab peoples in her germinal essay "Israel from the Point of View of its Jewish Victims."[4] She argues that this assumption ignores the fact that both Jewish and Arab peoples lived together on the land historically without major conflict for centuries. However, the creation of a Jewish-only state not only led to the displacement of Palestinians from Israel, but the displacement of Arab Jews (including her family) from surrounding countries. Thus, rather than assume that supporting the right of all peoples to be on the land necessarily means that Jewish people should *not* be there, we could rearticulate the assumption that land should ever be under the

---

3. Monture-Angus, *Journeying Forward*, 36.
4. Shohat, "Separdim in Israel."

exclusive control over one group of people. To do so necessarily results in the creation of apartheid systems because anyone who is not part of that group that is supposedly entitled to land necessarily does not have equality under that system. That is why the Indigenous peoples stated at the World Social Form, that when they called for the restoration of indigenous governance, that this form of governance was not exclusivist. They said that their goal was not to tell everyone else to "go home." Rather, they said we could all be on this land if we all understood ourselves differently. They articulated an expansive notion of indigeneity by stating that all are welcome to their lands if they live in good way with the land. Of course, these kinds of statements can be troubling in the New Age context in North America where they might be heard as "everyone can be indigenous by doing a pipe ceremony, sweat lodge, etc." Essentially, this expansive understanding of indigeneity could be understood to erase the specificity of indigenous peoples and their struggles today.

But in this context, while this is a call for a complete transformation of subjectivity and humanity, it is also a call to decolonize epistemology.

That is, as Denise Da Silva has noted in important work *Toward a Global Idea of Race*, the western subject sees itself as self-determining by positioning itself over and against other subjects that are not self-determining. The divide between subjects that are self-determining and those that are not is racialized (if we understand racialization as fundamentally the divide between those that are deemed fully human and those that are not). In other words, I know who I am because I am not you. But Indigenous epistemologies understand the self as being in radical relationality to all other selves: I know who I am because of my relationships with all humanity and all of creation. When you have a self-determined self, then the nation you build from that sense of nation will be exclusivist. But when your sense of self is conceptualized in radical relationality to all other selves, then one's sense of nationhood will be in relationship to all other nations and will be inclusive rather than exclusive.

This framework allows us to reread Galatians 3:38: "There is neither Jew nor Gentile, neither slave nor free, nor is there male and female, for you are all one in Christ Jesus" (NIV), to signify that not only should the body of Christ not be divided, but that the body is all fundamentally interconnected. Similarly, Leviticus 19:33–34 states: "When a foreigner resides among you in your land, do not mistreat them. The foreigner residing among you must be treated as your native-born. Love them as yourself, for you were foreigners in Egypt. I am the Lord your God" (NIV). This is not simply a call to be kind to "foreigners" but to no longer see foreigners as such. The well-being of the peoples of a land relies on the well-being of all peoples.

A biblical approach toward the Holy Land then requires us to frame the issue not as one of Jewish peoples vs. Palestinian peoples, but the well-being of both peoples mutually interconnected. Furthermore, the well-being of Palestinian peoples is necessary for the well-being of the world because it is about rejecting the idea that some peoples can be expendable and disposable. Benny Morris, an Israeli historian, once justified the expulsion of Palestinians in 1948 through the logic of disposability:

> I feel sympathy for the Palestinian people, which truly underwent a hard tragedy. I feel sympathy for the refugees themselves. But if the desire to establish a Jewish state here is legitimate, there was no other choice but to expel the Palestinian population. To uproot it in the course of war . . . .
>
> Even the great American democracy could not have been created without the annihilation of the Indians. There are cases in which the overall, final good justifies harsh and cruel acts that are committed in the course of history . . . . There are circumstances in history that justify ethnic cleansing.[5]

This quote by Morris points again to the importance of rejecting an Israeli exceptionalism to explore how nation-states are built on the expendability of some peoples. Many peoples will critique Israeli atrocities committed against Palestinian peoples and completely ignore the historical and continuing atrocities committed against Native peoples (that currently include everything from the theft of water, the disposal of radioactive wastes on Native lands, the refusal of the US legal system to prosecute rape against Native women, the theft of Native children, and rampant sterilization abuse). For instance, Max Blumenthal, who routinely critiques the policies of Israel, once stated:

> When people ask me, "Why are you as an American covering this situation and focusing on it 5,000 miles away? Isn't the United States a settler colonialist state and what are you doing about that?" That's a legitimate question, it's a legitimate challenge. Of course I have written about abuses of indigenous rights and immigrant rights in this country but I feel like I'm not doing enough.
>
> One of the issues though is that the process of settler colonialism that brought the United States and Canada into being is largely a completed project which has left the First Nations, the Aboriginal people, the Native Americans, on reservations— the kind which Palestinian population centers increasingly

---

5. Morris, "Survival of the Fittest."

> resemble.... It's a reflection of the fact that they have been disappeared from the lives and the view of the white man.
>
> The Jewish population of Israel... still considers the Palestinians to be a major threat to their existence. Palestinian resistance is ongoing and the process of settler colonialism is ongoing....
>
> If I were a journalist in the 1880s, I would hope that I would have been in the American West documenting these final massacres of the Lakota Sioux.[6]

Thus, Blumenthal (and many critics like him) based their solidarity with Palestinians on the assumption that Native peoples in the United States have already "vanished" and the injustice of Indigenous genocide in the United States no longer needs to be undone. Such critics accept the expendability of Native peoples in the United States in their Israeli exceptionalist paradigm of solidarity with Palestinian peoples.

But Native scholar Robert Warrior's germinal essay "Canaanites, Cowboys, and Indians" points the importance of going beyond solidarity with any one group of peoples to ask the larger question—why do we feel it is acceptable to frame deliverance of oppressed peoples at the expense of others? In his critique of how Exodus is typically narrated, Warrior argues that this narrative was foundational to the European conquest of the Americas because of how it conceptualizes a God of deliverance. In that case, God was going to create a "New Israel" in the Americas for European peoples. Unfortunately, the peoples already in the Americas have to be disappeared to make way for this new Israel. Warrior contends that "as long as people believe in the Yahweh of deliverance, the world will not be safe from the Yahweh the conqueror." That is, by conceptualizing ourselves as oppressed peoples who are to be delivered at all costs, we necessarily become complicit in oppressing those who stand in the way of our deliverance. Instead, Warrior argues, we need to reconceptualize ourselves as "a society of people delivered from oppression who are not so afraid of becoming victims again that they become oppressors themselves."[7]

This is why so many Native scholars and organizers are contending that liberation for Native peoples must challenge the manner in which we understand liberation. That is, liberation for one group of peoples necessitates the liberation of all peoples. As Native scholar Scott Lyons states:

> A... pressing danger in my view is the use of Native nations and indigenous sovereignty for purposes that can be just as harmful

---

6. "Process of settler colonialism."
7. Warrior, "Canaanites, Cowboys, and Indians," 99.

and retrograde as anyone else's oppression. When . . . anyone [is] in the name of tribal sovereignty, then discourses other than nationalism are called for in the name of justice . . . . [We must] look also at racism, political and economic oppression, sexism, supremacism, and the needless and wasteful exploitation of land and people, *no matter who perpetuates the injustice*.[8]

It has certainly been my experience in my involvement in Native liberation struggles in the United States that many injustices have been perpetuated by Native peoples in the name of sovereignty. I and many others who have been involved in this work have engaged in self-critique of our movements to ask ourselves, what is liberation anyway? It becomes clear that liberation and decolonization requires not only the decolonization of land and resources, but a decolonization of our imaginations. Part of colonization is that it colonizes what we think can even be possible. Colonization is thus an act of idolatry whereby we believe the world's systems are more powerful that God. When I reread 1 Samuel, we see this colonization of our imaginations. We no longer trust in God as sovereign. Instead, we invest sovereignty within nation-states that we value more than God. We believe in the God of expedience rather than a God of justice. We no longer dare to imagine that we could work with God to create a world based on principles of respect, interconnectedness, and justice. We accept instead the world as it is now. Thus liberation struggles become confined to getting a bigger piece of the pie for the group with which we belong or sympathize rather than ask why we cannot create governance and economic systems that promote justice for all.

Thus, my consciousness about Israel and Palestine has changed because my understanding of what liberation means has changed. It is not about now supporting Palestinians instead of Israelis; it is rejecting the paradigm that liberation is a zero-sum game. It is about decolonizing our imaginations to envision not what the world considers to be justice, but what God considers to be justice. It is about believing in a God of the (im)possible. As scholar Dylan Rodriquez puts it: "Our job is to think the unthinkable, imagine the unimaginable and make the impossible a reality."

Bibliography

Harden, Lakota. Interview with the author. Rapid City, South Dakota, June 13, 2001.
Lyons, Scott. *X-Marks*. Minneapolis: University of Minnesota Press, 2010.
Monture-Angus, Patricia. *Journeying Forward*. Halifax: Fernwood, 1999.

8. Lyons, *X-Marks*, 163.

Morris, Benny. "Survival of the Fittest." *Haaretz*, January 8, 2004. http://www.haaretz.com/survival-of-the-fittest-cont-1.61341.

"Process Of Settler Colonialism In The US Is Largely Completed. In Palestine It's Ongoing." Rania Khalek.com. Accessed May 29, 2014. http://raniakhalek.com/2014/05/29/process-of-settler-colonialism-in-the-us-is-largely completed-in-palestine-its-ongoing/.

Shohat, Ella. "Separdim in Israel: Zionism from the Standpoint of Its Jewish Victims." In *Dangerous Liaisons*, edited by Anne McClintock, Aamir Mufti, and Ella Shohat, 39–68. Minneapolis: University of Minnesota Press, 1997.

Warrior, Robert. "Canaanites, Cowboys, and Indians." In *Natives and Christians*, edited by James Treat, 93–104. New York: Routledge, 1996.

Washinawatok, Ingrid. "Sovereignty as a Birthright." In *Indigenous Women Address the World*, edited by Indigenous Women's Network. Austin, TX: Indigenous Women's Network, 1995.

10

Martin Luther King, Jr.'s Hope for a Better Israel

Dr. Clayborne Carson
(with Rev. Dr. Troy Jackson)

IN MARCH 1959 DR. Martin Luther King, Jr. visited Jerusalem and other communities west of the Jordan River but never entered Israel. He was attracted to the biblical "holy sites" that were in the Jordanian sector of the divided city and knew that obtaining an Israeli visa would have barred him from traveling in an Arab nation. Like the many other Christian tourists he would see during his short stay, King focused his attention on the ancient sites that had been preserved in Jerusalem, Bethlehem, Hebron. When he later recounted his visit to his congregation at Montgomery's Dexter Avenue Baptist Church, he referred only fleetingly to the 1948 and 1956 wars that had left Jerusalem "divided and split up and partitioned." Rather than taking sides in the ongoing Arab-Israeli political conflict, King merely mentioned his "strange" feeling of going to "the ancient city of God" and witnessing "the tragedies of man's hate and his evil, which causes him to fight and live in conflict."[1]

King's reflections on his 1959 visit to East Jerusalem and the surrounding Jordanian-controlled areas offer only slight guidance regarding how he would have viewed the extension of Israeli-controlled areas that resulted from the 1967 Six-Day War. King certainly felt a deep affinity toward Jews in Europe as well as America, believing their long struggle against bigotry

---

1. King, "A Walk Through the Holy Land."

paralleled that of black Americans. His prophetic Christianity was rooted in the Jewish prophetic tradition of Amos, Hosea, Ezekiel, Isaiah, and Jeremiah. King also sympathized with oppressed people throughout the world who were breaking free from European colonialism. After the successful conclusion of the Montgomery bus boycott in 1956, he had spoken of "the deep rumblings of discontent, the uprisings in Africa, the nationalist longings of Egypt" as indications of the birth of "a new world order," as liberation "from the Egypt of Colonialism and Imperialism."[2] Even as he preached about his 1959 walk through the Holy Land, he predicted that "all the lands of Africa will be free one day" and that "there will not be a colonial power existing anywhere in this world." King's affirmation of black-Jewish unity in the cause of equal rights and his opposition to anti-Semitism were consistent throughout his life, but so too were his anti-colonial sentiments and his belief, expressed in his 1963 Letter from Birmingham Jail: "Injustice anywhere is a threat to justice everywhere."

On May 15, 1967, King announced plans to lead a November 1967 pilgrimage to the Holy Land. He had worked with friend and fellow pastor Sandy Ray to develop and promote the opportunity to possible participants. In announcing the planned trip, King stressed that people should not infer any political implications or connections to his work for nonviolence in his decision to lead this voyage. Instead he emphasized his desire focus on spiritual concerns noting, "I must always remind people that I am first a minister of the Gospel."[3] The fall out from the June 1967 Six-Day War, during which Israel seized control of Gaza, East Jerusalem, and the West Bank, caused King to reconsider the pilgrimage. He decided he could not reassure participants regarding their safety and that the trip could not avoid political overtones. Despite his intentions to avoid the divisions and conflict and rather focus on his role as a "minister of the Gospel," King could not avoid the divisions and tensions that far too often define the region.

Just ten days before his assassination on March 25, 1968, King attended and addressed the Rabbinical Assembly as they celebrated the sixtieth birthday of Rabbi Abraham Heschel. During the session, King addressed the controversy: "in SCLC we have consistently condemned anti-Semitism. We have made it clear that we cannot be the victims of the notion that you deal with one evil in society by substituting another evil. We cannot substitute one tyranny for another, and for the black man to be struggling for justice and then turn around and be anti-Semitic is not only a very irrational course but it is a very immoral course, and wherever we have seen

---

2. King, "Facing the Challenge of a New Age," 453–54.
3. "Dr. King to Lead Fall Pilgrimage."

anti-Semitism we have condemned it with all of our might." King intentionally distanced himself from the charged statements by SNCC and others.

King went on to address the tensions around the Middle East:

> I think it is necessary to say that what is basic and what is needed in the Middle East is peace. Peace for Israel is one thing. Peace for the Arab side of that world is another thing. Peace for Israel means security, and we must stand with all of our might to protect its right to exist, its territorial integrity. I see Israel, and never mind saying it, as one of the great outposts of democracy in the world, and a marvelous example of what can be done, how desert land almost can be transformed into an oasis of brotherhood and democracy. Peace for Israel means security and that security must be a reality. On the other hand, we must see what peace for the Arabs means in a real sense of security on another level. Peace for the Arabs means the kind of economic security that they so desperately need. These nations, as you know, are part of that third world of hunger, of disease, of illiteracy. I think that as long as these conditions exist there will be tensions, there will be the endless quest to find scapegoats. So there is a need for a Marshall Plan for the Middle East, where we lift those who are at the bottom of the economic ladder and bring them into the mainstream of economic security.[4]

Because of his strong ties to Jewish-American leaders, King became an enduring symbol of the Black-Jewish civil rights coalition. He understood the Zionist impulse that led to the creation of Israel and objected to the anti-Semitism that was occasionally evident in the Black Power militancy that erupted during this, but he did not live long enough to learn about the gradual Israeli settlement and partial annexation of the predominantly Palestinian West Bank and Gaza. Had he lived longer, he doubtless would have been ensnared in the Black-Jewish controversies that erupted during the last decades of the twentieth century. Since Coretta Scott King asked me in 1985 to edit her late husband's papers, I have often been asked how he would have responded to Louis Farrakhan's inflammatory statements about Jews or to the emergence of a Palestinian resistance movement against Israeli occupation policies. It was my search for answers to the latter question that led me to visit many of the same places King had seen more than three decades earlier.

I first traveled to the Holy Land in 1991 as part of a delegation of African American leaders who were sponsored by Project Interchange and

---

4. Gendler, "Interview with Martin Luther King Jr.," 1–19.

the American Jewish Committee. I spent most of my time in Israel. More recently, in February 2010, I had the opportunity to return to Israel and Palestine for a four-day visit at the invitation of the US State Department and the US Consulate in Jerusalem. On my return visit, my focus was on discussions with Palestinian advocates of nonviolent resistance in Bethlehem, Ramallah, Hebron, East Jerusalem, and Gaza (via video conference). Like King, I noticed the signs of division at nearly every turn. A meeting with the Consul General, Michael Ratney, included a briefing by a security officer who gave a clear warning against becoming involved in the frequent West Bank protests. Later in the morning, through a link with Al-zhar University, I participated in the Gaza video conference (the State Department officially "urges U.S. citizens to avoid all travel to the Gaza Strip, which is under the control of Hamas, a terrorist organization"). Although physically separated from the approximately fifteen Gaza students, professors, and activists, the discussion was cordial as well as frank. As in subsequent sessions, I briefly outlined my personal involvement in the African American freedom struggle and explained my scholarly emphasis on bottom-up organizing rather than top-down leadership. I mentioned that, although I am closely associated with the King legacy through my editorship of *The Papers of Martin Luther King, Jr.*, I still greatly admire the grassroots perspective of the Student Nonviolent Coordinating Committee (SNCC, pronounced "snick"), the brash, youthful group that challenged the system of white supremacy by mobilizing black residents of communities where segregation was most entrenched. The group in Gaza seemed receptive to suggestions based on my experience in and study of the African American freedom struggle.

I spent that afternoon in Bethlehem, where I noticed the dramatic changes that had occurred there since my 1991 visit. The Israeli security wall can hardly be ignored, although I heard that most international visitors were limited by Israeli regulations from getting a close-up view. The moment I arrived at the offices of Zoughbi Zoughbi,[5] founder and director of the Palestinian Conflict Resolution Centre Wi'am,[6] it was difficult for me to avoid staring at the wall while trying to understand its significance. Although it was justified as a security wall, I quickly noted that it was placed far from the Israeli settlements that surrounded Bethlehem's Palestinian areas, separating its residents from the orchards where I was told Palestinians once went for family picnics and farmed their historic family lands. Land that once had been part of Bethlehem now was part of the Israeli hilltop settlements that had expanded since my previous visit. From the balcony

5. Zoughbi, "Zoughbi Zoughbi."
6. Wi'am.

of Zoughbi's office, I could see the pastoral setting that was now accessible only from the settlements and noted the contrast with the nearby crowded Palestinian neighborhoods in Bethlehem. As I talked with Zoughbi, we watched a group of young students who walked beside the wall and began throwing rocks at the guard tower. "We have to offer them better alternatives," Zoughbi commented.

After a discussion with the nonviolent activists invited by Zoughbi, I talked with youthful camp leaders and a visiting group of Argentineans that included a young woman who had been born in Palestine but grew up in Argentina. The group then toured the Aida Refugee Camp for young people whose families were displaced by the 1967 war, but my visit was cut short by the next event on my schedule. As I walked beside the wall to the camp, I noted the graffiti expressing antiwar sentiments and especially the misspelled message, "We Have Dreem." During my 1991 visit, a tour of Yad Vashem, the Israeli Holocaust Museum, set a somber tone for the entire visit; this time, my first view of the wall served as a context for everything that followed.

Following the visit to the refugee camp, I joined a session with Palestinians brought together by Sami Awad, Director of Holy Land Trust[7] (established in 1998). Awad is one of the most prominent Palestinian proponents of nonviolent resistance to the Israeli occupation of the West Bank. Holy Land Trust has its roots in the work of Mubarak Awad, who in 1984 established the Palestinian Center for the Study of Nonviolence and was expelled by Israel in 1988. Sami Awad, nephew of Mubarak, studied international peace and conflict resolution at American University in Washington, DC. He often lectures in the United States and was recommended to me by Dr. Mary King,[8] a SNCC veteran, former Peace Corps administrator, and an internationally recognized expert on nonviolence principles and strategies. I had a productive exchange of ideas with Awad and his colleagues but regretted not being able to spend more time with them and not being able to observe the nonviolent Palestinian protest that was occurring nearby that day. In this discussion as well as others, I was often made aware of the sense of urgency felt by Palestinians as they observe more and more of the West Bank coming under Israeli control through settlements, the construction of the wall and highways for use by settlers, and the continued confiscation or demolitions of Palestinian homes.

On the second day of my visit, we traveled to the offices of the Palestinian Center for the Dissemination of Democracy and Community

---

7. Holy Land Trust .
8. King, "Mary Elizabeth King."

Development (PANORAMA[9]) in Ramallah, the city where the Palestinian Authority has its headquarters. Established in 1991, PANORAMA has a wide range of programs, and my visit to its office enabled me to meet with staff members as well as other prominent figures in the Palestinian nonviolent movement. The roundtable discussion gave me a chance to share ideas with a variety of activists seeking, through different means, to bringing about a peaceful resolution of the Israeli-Palestinian conflict. I talked briefly with a man who had spent ten years in Israeli jails yet remained committed to nonviolent resistance. But I also noted the expressions of frustration among the Palestinians with the lack of progress and with the failure of the United States to act in an even-handed manner in the Middle East or act effectively to prevent Israeli violations of international law.

We left the Ramallah area for the Ambassador Hotel in East Jerusalem to attend a session of the Palestinian-Israeli Peace NGO Forum. The meeting was intended to bring together Palestinians with representatives of Israeli Peace NGOs, but nearly all of the attendees were Palestinian. Even the presence of a few Israelis, however, was enough to make the discussion more contentious than my previous meetings involving only Palestinians. When one of the Palestinians expressed his grievances, a self-described ultra-orthodox rabbi, who had been invited by one of the regular Israeli participants, responded by saying that 80 percent of Israelis were willing to give up land for peace but that 80 percent also did not believe that peace would result from giving up land. Therefore, he suggested, it was up to the Palestinians to demonstrate that peace would be the result of the establishment of a Palestinian state. The Palestinian, who mentioned he had spent time in Israeli jails, was far from satisfied with this response, insisting that it was not the task of Palestinians to provide sufficient assurance to satisfy Israelis. After the meeting broke up, the two talked briefly, but there was no indication they found common ground.

The third and final day of my visit began with a drive to Hebron where an extended meeting with nonviolent activists had been organized by Library on Wheels for Nonviolence and Peace[10] (LOWNP), another offshoot of the Palestinian Center for the Study of Nonviolence. The library's founder is sociologist Nafez Assaily,[11] who had worked with Mubarak Awad before the latter's expulsion from Israel. The discussions followed the general pattern of those elsewhere, although some participants expressed particularly intense resentment against vicious Israeli settlement activities in the Hebron

9. Panorama.
10. The Library on Wheels.
11. Assaily, "Nafez Assaily's page."

area. I was encouraged to observe these activities for myself, although time limitations and other restrictions of my visit prevented me from doing so. I saw some possibilities for future collaboration with the library regarding the dissemination of educational materials and left behind several books (unfortunately nothing in Arabic).

Overall, my visit was as productive as possible, given its brevity. This was due to the careful preparations of Cynthia, Suzan, and their Palestinian organizational contacts who invited a wide range of representative activists to my sessions. This produced a crowded three-day schedule that never gave me the sense that I was wasting any time. With few exceptions, I was able to meet all of the Palestinian nonviolence proponents that I had heard about or read about. The audiences were attentive and cordial, welcoming my insights derived from experience and research, while also occasionally advising me that their struggle was different from the African American struggle or the South African struggle. While accepting that all struggles are unique, I think I was able to present a persuasive argument, using the example of Gandhi's impact on King and the African American struggle, that each sustained freedom struggle has learned valuable lessons from proceeding ones.

I admire the steadfast commitment to nonviolence displayed by my hosts and the other nonviolent groups with which I had contact, but I wondered how widely that commitment is shared by other Palestinians, especially Muslims, who were under-represented in groups with whom I met (Mubarak Awad is a Christian, as are many of his closest associates). Nonetheless, I left with some hopeful impressions of the Palestinian nonviolent movement. First, it is a broad-based movement rather than simply a collection of individual advocates of nonviolence. I was encouraged that Palestinians have formed a variety of organizations that are exploring different paths to nonviolent solutions to the conflict with Israel. Second, many of the activists I met stressed that progress will require changes within Palestinian communities as well as changes in relations with Israel, and they have focused much of their attention on reducing the level of internal violence within Palestinian communities. Third, although many activists mentioned the need for a Gandhi-like figure to serve as the international symbol of their movement, most shared my belief that an effective movement needs to be built from the grassroots rather than through reliance on a single charismatic leader comparable to King, Gandhi, or Mandela.

Indeed, the likelihood that emergent leaders would face expulsion or imprisonment by Israel may provide another reason for Palestinians to avoid reliance on top-down models of struggle. The diversity of grassroots leadership is a strong point of the Palestinian resistance movement; yet I believe that at least one spokesperson with international visibility and local credibility will emerge from grassroots activism that he or she did not create.

Despite these reasons for optimism, I recognize that the Palestinian movement faces many challenges. A military occupation is difficult to overcome through nonviolent means, since military forces can severely restrict the press coverage on which nonviolent resistance relies and can equate nonviolent resistance with violence, thereby further fueling a violent response. Moreover, many of the Palestinian activists are convinced that their appeals to global public opinion are frustrated by a double standard that ignores or downplays Israeli violations of Palestinian human rights. Whether this is due to Western guilt about the Holocaust or Western fear of Islamic terrorism, the result has been that Israel's invasion of Gaza prompted no protests in Western nations comparable to the outrage that resulted from the South African apartheid regime's suppression of black South African protesters. Although the emergence of a charismatic Palestinian advocate of nonviolent resistance might attract more international support, I believe that the immediate need for Palestinians is to develop dramatic tactics that will attract popular support in Palestine and then take advantage of new communications technologies, such as the Internet, to reach a global audience of sympathizers and potential supporters. Palestinians will probably develop their own King-like figure only after the appearance of a figure comparable to Rosa Parks, who in 1955 initiated a sustained boycott movement by acting on her own. Given the recent upsurge of Palestinian protest activity, it seems likely that Palestinian activists are in the process of adapting traditional nonviolent strategies to develop innovative tactics that are appropriate to their circumstances, capable of attracting international attention, and able to provide a powerful expression of the Palestinian aspiration for enduring peace and reconciliation with Israel.

Over the past few years, many have rightly seized upon Dr. King's strong rejection of anti-Semitism and the strong ties between Jewish leaders and the civil rights movement, particularly during the march from Selma to Montgomery. Some have gone further, however, claiming King was unambiguously pro-Israel and leave it at that. The implication is that King would fully endorse the positions and actions of Israel no matter what, including the wall, regulations that restrict and control the movement of Palestinians, the expansion of settlements, and strong military responses to Palestinian violence or threats of violence. These attempts to cast King as unambiguously pro-Israel fail to realize King's heartfelt concern for the economic and racial injustices that plague the Palestinian people. Just as the wall defined my visit to Israel in 2010, it is hard to imagine the wall and all it represents not shaping King's response to injustices facing so many in Israel and Palestine today.

When I reflect on my time in the Holy Land, I am reminded of the divisions, pain, unrest, and hatred King emphasized during his visit over fifty years ago. There is ample reason to be disheartened. That said, I cannot help but imagine King's hope resting in the multi-faith nonviolence movement that seeks to transform the region and fully address injustice. King's hope, and mine, rest in the courage and conviction of those putting their bodies on the line day after day in their nonviolent struggle for peace and justice.

Bibliography

Assaily, Nafez. "Nafez Assaily's Page." *The Gandhi-King Community*. Accessed June 20, 2016. http://gandhiking.ning.com/profile/NafezAssaily.

"Dr. King to Lead Fall Pilgrimage to the Holy Land." *New York Times*, May 16, 1967. http://query.nytimes.com/mem/archive/pdf?res=9A03E7DE123AE63ABC4E52 DF B366838C679EDE.

Gendler, Everett. Interview with Martin Luther King, Jr. *Conservative Judaism* 22.3 (Spring 1968) 1–19. http://www.rabbinicalassembly.org/sites/default/files/assets/public/resources-ideas/cj/classics/1-4-12-civil-rights/conversation-with-martin-luther-king.pdf.

Holy Land Trust. Accessed June 12, 2016.http://www.holylandtrust.org/index.php.

King, Martin Luther, Jr. "A Walk Through the Holy Land, Easter Sunday Sermon Delivered at Dexter Avenue Baptist Church." King Encyclopedia, Stanford University, n.d. Accessed March 12, 2017. Http://kingencyclopedia.stanford.edu/encyclopedia/documentsentry/a_walk_through_the_holy_land_easter_sunday_sermon_delivered_at_dexter_avenu.1.html.

———. "Facing the Challenge of a New Age." Address Delivered at the First Annual Institute on Nonviolent and Social Change. December 3, 1956. In *The Papers of Martin Luther King, Jr., Volume III: Birth of a New Age, December 1955–1956*, edited by Clayborn Carlson et al., 453–54. Oakland: University of California Press, 1997.

King, Mary Elizabeth. "Mary Elizabeth King's Page." *The Gandhi-King Community*. Accessed June 20, 2016. http://gandhiking.ning.com/profile/MaryElizabethKing?xg_ source=profiles_memberList.

Panorama Center. Accessed June 12, 2016. http://www.panoramacenter.org/.

The Library on Wheels for Nonviolence and Peace. Accessed June 20, 2016. http://www.lownp.com/portal/.

Wi'am: Palestinian Conflict Resolution Centre. Accessed June 20, 2016. http://www.alaslah.org/.

Zoughbi, Zoughbi. "Zoughbi Zoughbi on the Palestinian-Israeli Conflict." *Christian Today*, August 1, 2007. http://www.christiantoday.com/article/zoughbi.zoughbi.on.the.palestinianisraeli. conflict/11995.html.

11

A Very Short History of Christian Zionism

Dr. Donald M. Lewis

THE ESSENCE OF CHRISTIAN Zionism across time is the belief held by some Christians that the Jewish people have a theologically based claim to a homeland in Palestine.[1] Today it is used of Christians who hold that the State of Israel's right to exist is based on biblical teachings; before the twentieth century, however, many Christian Zionists envisioned a "Jewish return" and a Jewish "homeland" but not necessarily a Jewish state.[2] Of course, many Christians have believed in Israel's right to exist without being "Christian Zionists" in the way thus defined. In 1948 many Gentiles supported the establishment of the State of Israel by the United Nations without a specifically Christian Zionist motivation. One can be a Christian and favorable toward the notion of a Jewish homeland without being a "Christian Zionist."

To date there exists no comprehensive short history of Christian Zionism that demonstrates a close acquaintance with the nuances of Christian

---

1. The term *Christian Zionism* is problematic in that it appears to have been first used only in 1919 and thus it is anachronistic to use it before that period. Before then Christian advocates of a physical return of the Jews were called "restorationists." Robert O. Smith defines it as "political action, informed by specifically Christian commitments, to promote or preserve Jewish control over the geographic area now comprising Israel and Palestine." Smith, "The Quest to Comprehend," 293. See also Ehle, "Prolegomena," 339.

2. The Balfour Declaration of 1917 pledged the British government's support for a "Jewish homeland," without explicitly promising a Jewish state.

theology; I hope to take on this task as my next writing project but in this short chapter all I can do is attempt a broad brushstroke overview.[3]

This chapter looks at the emergence of Christian Zionism at the time of the Reformation, traces its development in Puritan England and colonial America, then examines the impact of German Pietism on Jewish-Christian relations. It then moves on to the resurgence of Christian Zionism in Victorian England and nineteenth-century America, and closes with a look at the enormous shift in direction that the movement took in the twentieth century and concludes with a few observations about the phenomenon.

The Background

If we are to understand the phenomenon of Christian Zionism, we have to understand where the idea of a Jewish restoration to Palestine fits in the history of Jewish and Christian thinking. The starting place for these theological questions is the call of Abram as recorded in Genesis 12:1-8:

> Now the Lord said to Abram,
> "Go forth from your country,
> And from your relatives
> And from your father's house,
> To the land which I will show you;
> And I will make you a great nation,
> And I will bless you,
> And make your name great;
> And so you shall be a blessing;
> And I will bless those who bless you,
> And the one who curses you I will curse.
> And in you all the families of the earth will be blessed."
> So Abram went forth as the Lord had spoken to him; and Lot went with him . . . thus they came to the land of Canaan . . . . The Lord appeared to Abram and said, "To your descendants I will give this land." (NASB)

This promise, however, was never entirely fulfilled for the Jews; they never occupied all of the area promised to them, and their possession of the "land of Canaan" has not been continuous.

---

3. A British rabbi has written a helpful overview but fails to understand many of the dynamics operating in the Protestant world he is trying to map. See Cohn-Sherbok, *The Politics of Apocalypse.*

In the wake of the Babylonian dispersion of Judah in 587 BC, it was the prophet Nehemiah (d. ca. 413 BC) who articulated a theological explanation for the exile of the Jews from their land that ascribed the exile to God's punishment of the unfaithfulness of Israel.[4] Following the second dispersion of the Jews by the Romans in 70 AD, the Jewish hope was that in the Messianic age to come, the Messiah (literally "anointed one") would, once and for all, secure the settlement of the Jews in the promised land. The conditional nature of the original promise and the interpretation of exile as being divine punishment for Israel's unfaithfulness provided Augustine in the fourth century with the basis for his interpretation of the second expulsion from the promised land as the Jews' punishment for their role in the death of Christ. Neither Augustine nor any of the early church fathers expected a physical return of the Jews to Palestine. David Brown has observed that while the early church was divided on the matter of the timing of the reign of Christ on earth, "the national and territorial restoration of the Jews not only never entered into the controversy at all but seems not to have been believed in by either of the parties."[5]

In the Middle Ages, the general attitude toward the Jews was indebted to Augustine, who held that they served as a negative witness for Christianity, preserving the Old Testament Scriptures for the Christian church while being dispersed throughout the world. He understood the Jews to be "our supporters in their books, our enemies in their hearts, our witnesses in their scrolls."[6] Many of the prophecies related to the Jews were understood to have been accomplished in the return of the people of Israel following the Babylonian exile; passages indicating a glorious future were to be fulfilled in the Christian church. Yet the view (held by Augustine and others) persisted that the Jews would eventually, as a people, turn to Christianity. "'If the Jews were utterly wiped out,' the abbot of Clairvaux asked [in the twelfth century]: 'what will become of our hope for their promised salvation, their eventual conversion?'"[7]

However, in the late Middle Ages, beginning in about the thirteenth century, Christian theologians emphasized that the Jews were "not a people" and had no positive ongoing significance for Christians; the hope for their eventual conversion seems to have faded into the background and their actual return to Palestine was not canvassed except, it seems, by heretical

---

4. See Neh 1.
5. Quoted in Ehle, *Prologomena*, 33.
6. Quoted in Haynes, *Reluctant Witnesses*, 32.
7. Endelman, "Introduction," 3.

proto-Protestants like John Wycliffe and Jan Hus, who both had "interpreted literally the Biblical texts relating to the return of the Jews to Palestine."[8]

Christian Zionism in the Reformation Era

Many Protestants as they examined the Scriptures afresh, came to understand the Apostle Paul to have predicted a mass turning of Jews to the Christian faith at some point in the future—a spiritual "turning" or "return" in the same way that Augustine and some medieval Catholic theologians had formulated their understanding on this matter. The young Luther appears to have held this position and recommended that Christians should, in a friendly way, bear witness to Jews in the expectation that their conversion to Christianity had been promised by Christ himself. But later in life Luther abandoned this hope and, bitterly disappointed with the lack of Jewish response, he became antagonistic to the Jews, thus reverting to a position of late medieval Catholic hostility to them. In the ensuing two centuries Lutherans took little interest in the evangelization of Jews, although belief in their eventual conversion persisted.[9]

With the emergence of Reformed Protestantism, however, attitudes to the Jews came to be profoundly influenced by two separate—but often closely related—understandings of a "Jewish return"—one purely spiritual, the other both spiritual and physical. Very early in Reformed Protestantism a new understanding began to emerge that insisted that the Old Testament promises about the physical return of the Jews to their homeland had not been negated and that this remained to be accomplished. The earliest Protestant proponents of this view appear to have emerged in Strasbourg in 1526 with Martin Borrhaus, a German Hebraic scholar, convincing Wolfgang Capito, the respected provost of St. Thomas Church (and also a reputed Hebrew scholar), of the validity of this interpretation. In turn, Capito incorporated this view in his Latin commentary on Hosea, published in 1528.[10] However, Borrhaus and Capito soon found their ideas firmly rejected by other Reformed Protestant leaders, particularly by Martin Bucer, the leading reformer in Strassbourg, and by Ulrich Zwingli in Zurich.[11]

8. Hill, "Till the Conversion," 14.

9. The concept of a widespread Jewish conversion, however, continued as a tenet of the mainstream "orthodox" Lutheran party until about 1650; thereafter it came under criticism and became associated in the minds of many with the more radical spiritualist writers. Clark, *The Politics of Conversion*, 18.

10. Capito built his argument from Hosea 1:11 and 3:5. See Capito, *In Hoseam*.

11. I am indebted to Dr. Gerald Hobbes for the information on the Stassbourg developments. Hobbes, "Will the Jews Return?"

Puritan Development of Christian Zionism

The expectation of both a spiritual and a physical return—a clear instance of Christian Zionism—that had emerged in the 1520s in Strasbourg and been firmly rejected by key Protestant leaders began to gain traction in late-sixteenth-century England. Robert O. Smith has argued persuasively that during this time it was understood by some that the two major threats to Protestantism were Islam and Roman Catholicism (the "Turk" and the Pope as Antichrist) both of which would be thwarted by the Jews returning to Palestine. The most significant early developer of this theme was John Bale (1495–1563), one of the English Protestants exiled on the continent in the 1550s during the reign of Mary I.[12] The creative phase of this movement occurred between 1585 and 1640; after that date no new themes were developed in the seventeenth century, the old ones were only replayed many times, by many different authors.[13]

During the revolutionary Puritan revolutionary period (ca. 1642–1660), authors such as Thomas Brightman (d. 1607), Sir Henry Fitch, and Joseph Mede were widely read (having long been suppressed by James I and Charles I for their prophetic speculations), and the idea gained popularity that the end was near (probably in 1656): the Jews would convert, the Turk be overthrown, and the Pope brought low.[14] From John Bale through the seventeenth-century Puritans and forward through to the nineteenth century, much of Protestant Christian Zionism would be framed in terms of the twin concerns of helping the Jews, on one hand, and opposing Catholicism, on the other. Following the collapse of the Puritan Commonwealth in England in 1660, the expulsion of Puritan clergy from the Church of England in 1662 and the subsequent crushing of Puritan theology, Christian Zionism went into the background in England as the Puritan hopes for a Jewish spiritual return and their physical return to Palestine were put off into the distant future. Puritan New England, however, remained a place where Christian Zionists hopes were kept alive and in the eighteenth century they became central to the emerging identity of America as a divinely chosen nation where Reformed Protestants could recapitulate the same sort of covenant that Israel experienced with God in the Old Testament. "America's covenantal vocation" involved a special concern for and identification with the Jews.[15]

12. See Smith, *More Desired*, 55–59.
13. I have discussed these themes in Lewis, *Origins of Christian Zionism*, 29–36.
14. Hill, "Till the Conversion," 16–17.
15. See Smith, *More Desired*, chapter 6, which is entitled "Typologizing the Jew: The Judeo-Centric Foundations of America's Covenantal Vocation."

The German Pietist Interest in the Jews

In the period of Puritan decline in England, another movement was emerging on the European Protestant scene, known as German Pietism. Its genesis is commonly dated to 1675 with the publication of a work by a Lutheran pastor, Jakob Spener, known by its Latin title *Pia Desideria*—or "Pious Longings." The book is built around the theme of the anticipated mass conversion of the Jews to Christianity. The evangelization of Jews was in Spener's mind an essential duty of Christians, which had long been neglected. Failure to respond to God's command to evangelize the Jews was a real possibility, but it would incur the judgment of God on faithless Christians. The imperative work of Jewish conversion would require highly skilled workers with specialized knowledge and appropriate financial and communal support. The very future of the Protestant cause depended on it. Its success required a new way of Christians approaching the Jews based on an appreciation of Jewish traditions and sympathy for their plight in a hostile culture. In Spener's view the Pietist mission to the Jews was at the very heart of Protestant identity. As Christopher Clark puts it: "The mission was urgent because God's honour was at stake. It was a question of making amends for the history of human ingratitude in the face of God's grace and favour. In this way, Spener made the conversion of the Jews the keystone in the arch of revealed Christian truth."[16] Spener linked the future of Protestantism to its evangelizing mission to the Jews.

Now, for the first time in the history of Protestantism, the Jews were being focused on as a group to be proselytized by voluntary agency and not by state initiative. For centuries it had been the policy of continental European governments to use more or less nefarious means to induce Jewish conversions. The new mission to the Jews was a voluntary one, a key element of the impressive international outreach of the Pietist institutions in Halle, which the philosopher Leibniz predicted would become the world centre for a general reformation. Two of Pietism's novel emphases were the engagement of Lutherans in cross-cultural missionary work and, flowing out of Spener's new eschatological view, the need to establish missions to the Jewish people, whom Spener regarded as integral to God's sovereign plan for the end of history.

---

16. Clark, *The Politics of Conversion*, 31.

PART III: INTERSECTIONS OF HISTORY

The Crossover: From Germany to Britain

It is important to realize that in the eighteenth century Lutheran Pietism did not embrace Christian Zionism but it is crucial in the wider story for two reasons: the Pietists were strong advocates of the Christian duty to love the Jews even in their unbelief (contributing strongly to the impulse toward philosemitism); and because it contributed to the explosion of interest in the evangelization of the Jews in the English-speaking world beginning in the 1790s, which in turn affected the resurgence of Christian Zionism in Britain and in America. The interest in the evangelization of Jews was introduced into England by a German Jewish convert in the early 1800s who was in London to study to become a missionary in South Africa but ended up founding the first British society to focus on the evangelization of Jews—the London Society for Promoting Christianity Amongst the Jews.

Thus in the period between 1790 and 1850 there was a fusion of two impulses in the English-speaking evangelical world—the new concern to demonstrate Christian love toward the Jewish people while at the same time seeking to evangelize them (from the German Pietist side) and belief in the return of the Jews to a homeland in Palestine (from the Reformed/Calvinistic side) which Victorian evangelicals then sought to operationalize.

The French Revolution proved to be a huge catalyst for change in British society, especially in its religious life. The fear of political revolution did much to stampede people back into the English churches. There is truth in the cliché that "the English became pious as the French became republican." These events led to much speculation as to their significance in terms of the understanding of biblical prophecy. British evangelicals concerned with the evangelization of the Jews began to revive the Puritan hopes for Jewish conversion and for their "return" to Palestine and worked tirelessly to bring about their physical return, even at a time when the cause seemed entirely hopeless from a geopolitical standpoint. Palestine was a neglected backwater under the control of a Muslim empire and was of little interest to anyone in Britain or America except the Christian Zionists.

This new practical concern on the part of convinced Christian Zionists working for the physical return of the Jews raised new questions. How was the anticipated spiritual return related to their physical return? Would the Jews be converted before their return, simultaneously with their return, or after their settlement in Palestine was accomplished? The long-standing consensus that their conversion would precede their physical return was beginning to be set aside. Britain as an "elect nation" was called upon to act as the benefactor of the Jews, to work for their protection, and for their "restoration" to Palestine.

In 1838, Britain established a vice-consulate in Jerusalem, in large measure because of intense Christian Zionist lobbying orchestrated by Anthony Ashley Cooper, the leading Victorian social reformer and evangelical Member of Parliament (in 1851 he became the seventh Earl of Shaftesbury). This move initiated a scramble for power and position in Palestine and other major powers soon followed suit—the French, the Americans, the Russians, and even the Germans soon had a diplomatic presence in Jerusalem, an out-of-the-way, third-rate city in a sleepy backwater of the Ottoman Empire. The big-power scramble for influence that ensued transformed Palestine in the nineteenth century. By 1900 the evangelization of the Jewish people and their "restoration" to Palestine were deeply embedded in the British and American Protestant mind.[17]

Christian Zionism and Prophetic Interpretations

How this embedding took place is related to Christian interpretations of biblical prophecy. In terms of schemes of interpretation of prophecy, the Puritans were by and large postmillennial and convinced that Jewish restoration to Palestine was consistent with their view of Scriptures. In the nineteenth century postmillennialism went into decline and new forms of premillennialism became popular and these premillennial forms were generally strongly Christian Zionist. Initially a "historicist" form of Christian Zionism was predominant but by the middle of the nineteenth century this version of premillenialism gave way to a "futurist" form known as dispensational premillenialism. This new view became hugely influential in British and American Protestantism by the early twentieth century, initially largely through the writings and personal influence of John Nelson Darby, the founder of the Plymouth (or Christian) Brethren and popularized for many through the marginal notes of the Scofield Reference Bible and the writing of William Blackstone whose book *Jesus is Coming* (1878) was the most popular work of its day in promoting premillenialism. In 1891 Blackstone issued a famous petition known as the "Blackstone Memorial" addressed to President Benjamin Harrison and arguing that America should promote a Jewish return to Palestine. The memorial continued to influence subsequent American presidents.[18] However, it is by no means the case that

---

17. The momentum behind Christian Zionism in the nineteenth century came from Britain. The most widely read author on the subject at mid-century—even in America—was Edward Bickersteth. Darby's activities in America came later. All of this is developed at length in my *Origins of Christian Zionism*.

18. See Moorhead, "The Father of Zionism," 787–800.

Christian Zionism today is limited to those who hold these views or that Christian Zionism is necessarily wedded to dispensational premillenialism. Many contemporary scholars continue to focus on the role of dispensational premillenialism to account for the popularity of Christian Zionism and fail to realize that this prophetic system of interpretation is increasingly out of favor with Christian Zionists across the globe.[19]

In the 1880s, Russian Jewry began to experience times of intense persecution, which led many secular Jews to seek a home for Jews where they could be free from the sort of hostility that has plagued Jews for millennia. Religious Jews were generally opposed to any talk of Zionism; the more conservative rabbis believed (and many still believe) that the restoration of the Jews to their homeland would be brought about in the future by the Messiah alone and that efforts by (largely irreligious) Jewish Zionists endangered the status of Jews in European countries where they had been settled for centuries.

But by the late nineteenth century, Christian Zionism was profoundly influencing British and American political culture in the direction of support for a "Jewish return" and was in significant ways responsible for the Balfour Declaration of 1917 that (in the closing months of the First World War) committed the British government to the establishment of a "Jewish homeland" in Palestine—an area of the Middle East that was about to be conquered by the British. The Ottoman Empire had controlled the area nearly continuously for almost 400 years but forfeited it at this point, the price of siding with Germany in World War I. American government support for the Balfour Declaration was also strongly indebted to American Christian Zionism, in particular to the ongoing lobbying efforts of William Blackstone. The League of Nations' "Palestine Mandate" of 1922 wrote the British government pledge made in the Balfour Declaration into the framework of its trusteeship of Palestine: the Christian Zionist dream was now more than a prophetic hope—it had some standing in international politics. Undoubtedly the Holocaust during World War II created a great deal of sympathy for the notion of a Jewish state where Jews might be safe in what had been their ancient homeland. All of this set the backdrop for the United Nations' vote in November 1947 to establish the State of Israel alongside an Arab state.

---

19. Much more work needs to be done on non-Protestant Christian Zionism. In the twentieth century Christian Zionism made inroads among Roman Catholics, as seen in the work of Marcel-Jacques Dubois, a French Dominican philosopher at the Hebrew University of Jerusalem, and in some sections of the Catholic charismatic movement. On Dubois see Wohlman, "Quand un chrétian." I am indebted to Dr. Curtis Hutt for this reference.

The significance of Christian Zionist influence in the twentieth century is much debated. Carl Ehle has summarized his take on its political impact in this period under three points: "1) individually Christians have directly aided Jewish Zionists in achieving political objectives, 2) to an important degree, Christian Zionists have acted as catalysts to secure Jewish acceptance of the Zionist movement, and 3) Christian Zionists have served to promote a receptive environment among non-Jews for Zionist propaganda."[20]

The Pentecostalization of Christian Zionism

The early years of the twentieth century saw the rise of Pentecostalism, and in the second half of the same century, the charismatic movement swept across both Protestantism and sections of Roman Catholicism. Recently scholars have been grouping Pentecostals and charismatic Christians under the heading of "Renewalists." These Renewalists have proven to be the most important carriers of Christian Zionism in the twenty-first century.[21] As a consequence, in the late twentieth century, the theological support base for Christian Zionism shifted dramatically. It is generally acknowledged that Pentecostalism derived much of its DNA from the holiness movement within Protestantism, which is associated with the teachings of John Wesley. Wesley was no Calvinist and strongly emphasized human ability and responsibility. The early Pentecostals were a long way from traditional Calvinism, but they did believe strongly in a sovereign God who intervened in history. Many of the early Pentecostals adopted the prophetic schema of dispensational premillenialism and with it, Christian Zionist commitments.

Early Pentecostalism clearly saw itself as a restorationist movement that was recovering aspects of New Testament Christianity that had been lost to the church—particularly, of course, the gift of "speaking in tongues" and physical healing. Yet early Pentecostalism was theologically eclectic and threw up a number of other teachings that were regarded as unacceptable by fellow Protestants and by many Pentecostals as well, including the "Jesus Only" doctrine, a Pentecostal version of Unitarianism.[22] Several of its early key leaders also advocated British Israelite teachings, which claimed that the British people (and by extension, white America) constituted the ten

20. Ehle, *Prolegomena*, 343.

21. See Williams, "The Pentecostalization," 159–94.

22. The American "Assemblies of God" was founded in 1914 to bring together those who wanted to distance themselves from "Jesus Only" teaching and affirmed a strong Trinitarianism.

lost tribes of Israel; white supremacist teachings of Anglo-Saxon superiority combined with apocalyptic speculation to reinforce the notion that its advocates were uniquely connected with the Jews, in fact, were Jews! Mainstream Renewalism today has largely abandoned the British Israelite teachings; nevertheless, within Renewalism there is currently a significant movement to nurture and symbolize connections between Jews and Christians. Many Pentecostals (and more recently the broader category of Renewalists) have adopted Israel-themed ritual displays: the wearing of Jewish garb, the blowing of the shofar in worship, and celebrations of Jewish festivals, especially the Feast of Tabernacles in Jerusalem, etc. For those who practice their faith in this way, this "Hebrew Roots" movement strongly reinforces symbolic connections with "God's chosen people." The conversion of significant numbers of American Jews in the 1970s and 1980s—with many joining the charismatic movement—led to the emergence of "Messianic Judaism." Jewish converts began to exercise leadership in American evangelicalism, forming their own "messianic congregations." A fascination with all things Jewish came to characterize Renewalists by the end of the twentieth century. Leading figures like David DuPlessis and Derek Prince sought to configure Pentecostal/charismatic history around God's dealings with the state of Israel in the twentieth century and promoted strong support for the Israel. These all have worked to place Israel, and symbolically Jerusalem, at the center of the Renewalist imagination.[23]

In the second decade of the twenty-first century Christian Zionism is alive and well in areas of the world where it was unheard of in the nineteenth century—particularly in parts of Latin and South America, sub-Saharan Africa, and amongst Chinese and Korean evangelicals/charismatics in Asia and southeast Asia. In the twentieth century, the Christian church shifted its central locus dramatically and moved from being predominantly white and Western, to become predominantly non-white and non-Western. In large measure this occurred because of the explosion of Renewalist forms of Christianity in the non-Western world.

Recent Developments

The global Renewalist movement today has asserted itself with its own brand of Christian Zionist theologies, and largely rejects dispensational premillennialism and embraces new forms of "historicist" premillennialism, the latter a reading of prophecy largely thought of as having died out in the nineteenth century. Matthew C. Westbrook, the leading scholar of Renewalist Zionism,

23. See Williams, "The Pentecostalization," 179.

has observed that "the ethos of classic dispensationalism, dominated as it was by a largely passive approach to prophecy fulfillment, which generally held that it was enough to merely watch what was happening in the world in order to understand what *God* was doing, has been jettisoned in favor of a more hands-on approach to prophecy fulfillment."[24] He points out that Renewalist Zionism tends to tie the fates of Christians and Jews more closely together than previous forms of Christian Zionism, and, together with their emphasis on supernatural triumphalism, provides the distinctive content of their Zionism versus earlier versions. Renewalist Zionism affirms both the spiritual and physical "restoration" of the Jewish people in history from a Christian perspective and is, in this way, much like the seventeenth-century Protestant Christian Zionists. Renewalist Zionism has been actively distancing itself from dispensational premillenialism in the United States, and dispensationalism has been rarely embraced by Renewalists outside of the United States.[25]

A key Renewalist Zionist network is known as the New Apostolic Reformation, which is a loose coalition that is interdenominational and generally post-denominational. Its leaders are the heads of their own networks of churches in various parts of the world, and recognize each other's leadership by acknowledging one another as modern "apostles." Some see this as the end-time restoration of the gift of "apostleship" to the church.[26] Many of them see Jerusalem as the international center of global Christianity, and are ardent supporters of the state of Israel whose founding in 1948 they see as a fulfillment of biblical prophecy. The Renewalist Zionists are broader than the New Apostolic Reformation group, and include groups such as the International Christian Embassy, Jerusalem, the largest international Christian Zionist organization in existence today.[27]

Another key promoter of Christian Zionism is John Hagee, an American pastor with a Pentecostal background and founder of Christians United for Israel. Hagee, though no longer affiliated with the Assemblies of God (a large Pentecostal denomination), believes that Jews should not be evangelized by Christians and by the common definitions of what it means to be an

---

24. Westbrook, "Broadcasting Jesus' Return," 71.

25. I am particularly indebted to Dr. Matthew C. Westbrook for his insights on these matters and to his doctoral thesis, "The International Christian Embassy," May 2014.

26. Much of the theology of this is indebted to the teachings of a group known as "The New Order of the Latter Rain." See Williams, "Pentecostalization of Christian Zionism," 179–80.

27. See chapter 13 by Susan Michael, USA Director of the International Christian Embassy in Jerusalem.

evangelical, makes it difficult for one to acknowledge him as one.[28] Hagee's prophetic understanding differs markedly from the Renewalist Zionists; he retains a darkly pessimistic futurist dispensational premillenialism adapted to his Pentecostal background.

Looking at Christian Zionism over five centuries, it is clear that it has no fixed theological home and is dependent on no one, fixed schema related to prophetic understandings of Scripture. As has been seen, the first proponents of this view in the sixteenth century were Calvinists and this tradition was the main basis for such views among Protestants down through the end of the nineteenth century. The Calvinist emphasis on the sovereignty of God and the focus on God's choice or "election" of the Jews seems to be a crucial factor in explaining Christian Zionism's appeal to Calvinists. The appeal to Pentecostals and charismatics is related to identity formation—by rooting their movement in Jewish history and symbolically identifying with the Jews as a people and Israel as a state, they find their roots going back centuries, and not just to the early 1900s.

The history of Christian Zionism is one of both novelty in that it only arose in the sixteenth century and has morphed in a number of ways over time, and of instability in that it has no fixed theological address. As Aron Engberg has observed it is now a global religious movement and must be understood dynamically as a movement, in the sense that it is "on the move."[29] But it is both dynamic and unstable and that instability concerns some Jews who look to instances of Christians professing their love for them, but then like Luther, turning on the Jews when they have not responded as expected. Or with the case of William Blackstone, the American Christian Zionist who advocated for the American government to support the Balfour Declaration, but who later soured on his relations with the Jews.[30] And the memory of British Israelite ideology's racist appeal to some early Pentecostals causes nervousness. If such thinking produces such mixed results, can Jews trust this unstable movement not to turn in an anti-Semitic direction again?

Christian Zionism thus has a very convoluted history. Over the past five centuries it has been associated with very different theological frameworks and prophetic views. It is a movement in the sense that it is "on the move" and continues to morph in the multiple locations around the world where it is being embraced. Given evangelicals' commitment to the principle of *sola Scriptura* it is likely that the next generation of evangelicals

---

28. Westbrook, "Renewalist Zionism," 45.

29. Engberg, "A Fool for Christ," 30.

30. See Gershon, *The Holy Land*.

will subject its theology to intense scrutiny to see whether they, like many of their spiritual forebears, consider it to be something that grows out of a fully-orbed biblical theology, or whether it has arisen in particular historical settings and through particular readings of Scripture, and no longer carries the persuasive power that it once did. Its validity is sure to be an ongoing debate among Christians.[31]

Bibliography

Ariel, Yaakov. "Judaism and Christianity Unite!: The Unique Culture of Messianic Judaism." In *Introduction to New and Alternative Religions in America-Jewish and Christian Traditions*, edited by Eugene V. Gallagher and W. Michael Ashcraft, 191–221. Westport, CT: Greenwood, 2006.

Ariel, Yaakov. *Philosemites or Antisemites?: Evangelical Christian Attitudes toward Jews, Judaism and the State of Israel*. Analysis of Current Trends in Antisemitism Series 20. Jerusalem: Vidal Sassoon Center, 2002.

Ariel, Yaakov. *An Unusual Relationship: Evangelical Christians and Jews*. New York: New York University Press, 2013.

Blaising, Craig A., and Darrell L. Bock. *Progressive Dispensationalism*. Wheaton, IL: BridgePoint, 1993.

Blaising, Craig A., Kenneth L. Gentry, Robert B. Strimple, and Darrell L. Bock. *Three Views on the Millennium and Beyond*. Grand Rapids: Zondervan, 1999.

Capito, Wolfgang. *In Hoseam Prophetam*. Strasbourg: Joannem Hervagium, 1528.

Cohn-Sherbok, Dan. *The Politics of Apocalypse: The History and Influence of Christian Zionism*. Oxford: Oneworld, 2006.

Clark, Christopher M. *The Politics of Conversion: Missionary Protestantism and the Jews in Prussia, 1728–1941*. Oxford: Clarendon, 1995.

Clark, Victoria. *Allies for Armageddon: The Rise of Christian Zionism*. New Haven, CT: Yale University Press, 2007.

Ehle, Carl Frederick. *Prolegomena to Christian Zionism in America: The Views of Mather and William E. Blackstone Concerning the Doctrine of the Restoration of Israel*. PhD diss., Graduate School of Arts and Science, Institute of Hebrew Studies, New York University, 1977.

Endelman, Todd M. "Introduction." In *Jewish Apostasy in the Modern World*, edited by Todd Endelman, 1–19. New York: Holmes & Meier, 1987.

Engberg, Aron. "'A Fool for Christ': Sense-Making and Negotiation of Identity in the Life Story of a Christian Soldier." In *Comprehending Christian Zionism: Perspectives in Comparison*, edited by Göran Gunner, 33–59. Minneapolis: Fortress, 2014.

Greenberg, Gershon. *The Holy Land in American Religious Thought: 1620-1948: The Symbiosis of American Religious Approaches to Scripture's Sacred Territory*. Lanham, MD: University Press of America, 1995.

---

31. Bruce K. Waltke, who formerly taught at Dallas Theological Seminary before coming on faculty at Regent College, has challenged the theological basis of Christian Zionism, a view that he was once eager to defend. His lecture on "Land in the New Testament" is available through Regent Audio (www.regentaudio.com).

Haynes, Stephen R. *Reluctant Witnesses: Jews and the Christian Imagination*. 1st American ed. Louisville: Westminster John Knox, 1995.

Hill, Christopher. "Till the Conversion of the Jews." In *Millenarianism and Messianism in English Literature and Thought, 1650-1800*, edited by Richard H. Popkin, 12–36. Leiden: E. J. Brill, 1988.

Hobbes, Gerald. "Will the Jews Return to Palestine? A 16th Century Reformation Debate." Paper presented at the Vancouver School of Theology Theological Forum, December 5, 2005.

Karp, Jonathan, and Adam Sutcliffe. *Philosemitism in history*. New York: Cambridge University Press, 2011.

Lewis, Donald M. *The Origins of Christian Zionism: Lord Shaftesbury and Evangelical Support for a Jewish Homeland*. Cambridge: Cambridge University Press, 2010.

Merkley, Paul Charles. *Christian Attitudes toward the State of Israel*. Montreal: McGill-Queen's, 2001.

———. *The Politics of Christian Zionism, 1891–1948*. London: F. Cass, 1998.

Moorhead, Jonathan. "The Father of Zionism: William E. Blackstone." *Journal of the Evangelical Theological Society*, 53.4 (December 2010) 787–800.

———. "*Jesus is Coming*": The Life and work of William E. Blackstone (1841–1935)." PhD thesis, Dallas Theological Seminary, 2008.

Popkin, Richard H. *Millenarianism and Messianism in English Literature and Thought, 1650–1800: Clark Library lectures, 1981–1982*. Publications from the Clark Library professorship, UCLA. New York: E.J. Brill, 1988.

———. *The Third force in Seventeenth-century Thought*. Brill's Studies in Intellectual History. New York: E.J. Brill, 1992.

———. "Introduction to the Millenarianism and Messianism Series." In *Millenarianism and Messianism in Early Modern European Culture: Continental Millenarians: Protestants, Catholics, Heretics*, edited by John Christian Laursen and Richard H. Popkin, 1–11. Boston: Kluwer Academic, 2001.

Popkin, Richard H., and G.M. Weiner. *Jewish Christians and Christian Jews: From the Renaissance to the Enlightenment*. The Netherlands: Kluwer Academic, 1994.

Rausch, David A. "Hebrew Christian Renaissance and Early Conflict with Messianic Judaism." *Fides et Historia* 15.2 (1983) 67–79.

Smith, Robert O. *More Desired than Our Own Salvation: The Roots of Christian Zionism*. New York: Oxford University Press, 2013.

———. "The Quest to Comprehend Christian Zionism." In *Comprehending Christian Zionism: Perspectives in Comparison*, edited by Göran Gunner, 325–35. Minneapolis: Fortress, 2014.

Toon, Peter, and B. S. Capp. *Puritans, the Millennium and the Ruture of Israel: Puritan Eschatology, 1600 to 1660: A Collection of Essays*. Cambridge: James Clarke, 1970.

Westbrook, Matthew C. "Broadcasting Jesus' Return: Televangelism and the Appropriation of Israel through Israeli-Granted Broadcasting Rights." In *Comprehending Christian Zionism: Perspectives in Comparison*, edited by Göran Gunner, 61–83. Minneapolis: Fortress, 2014.

———. "The International Christian Embassy, Jerusalem and Renewalist Zionism: Emerging Jewish-Christian Ethnonationalism." PhD diss., Drew University, 2014.

Williams, Joseph. "The Pentecostalization of Christian Zionism." *Church History* 84.1 (March 2015) 159–94.

Wohlman, Avital. "Quand un chrétian aime Israël." Paris: Les Éditions du Cerf, 2008.

12

Christian Just Peacemaking and Israel-Palestine: A Quick and Dirty Historical Account of What We are Calling Israel-Palestine[1]

Dr. David P. Gushee

I CONSIDER THE ISRAEL-PALESTINE situation the knottiest geopolitical and diplomatic problem in the world. It is a problem in which Christians are implicated and must seek to make a constructive difference today.

Israel is one of scores of new countries born in the world since 1945. At the birth of the United Nations there were fifty-one member states; in 2016 there are 193. Some of the countries that existed in 1945 don't exist now; most that exist now did not exist then. Each new nation has its own story. Most of the new nations founded since 1945, though by no means all of them, resulted from decolonialization, as the Western colonial powers gradually loosed their grip on—or had their grip forced loose from—their former colonies in the Global South. Certainly from the perspective of many Arabs, the birth of Israel marks a last gasp of European colonialization. But of course such a claim is also easily contested, as are most claims one could make about Israel-Palestine.

The history of the land we today call Israel is an ancient one with many layers. A large part of the relevant history is certainly colonial. The region that today encompasses Israel was controlled by the Turkish Ottoman

1. A longer version of this essay appeared in my 2014 volume entitled *In the Fray* (Eugene, OR: Cascade, 2014).

Empire for 400 years, from 1517 to 1917. It came under British control in 1920. If the region had followed more common global trends, the eventual receding of the British Empire and the collapse of colonialism's legitimacy after World War II would have left the land between the Jordan and the Mediterranean to its local inhabitants, the majority of whom were Arab.

In a sense, that *is* what happened. The issue in this case was that the local inhabitants were not one people. While a relatively small number of Jews had for centuries lived in what eventually became the modern state of Israel, and while Israel had been the Jews' ancient homeland, Jewish numbers increased dramatically due to waves of immigration inspired by the Zionist movement beginning in the late nineteenth century. Zionism was born in part out of the ancient Jewish attachment to *Eretz Israel*, in part as an expression of nineteenth-century European nationalism, and in part as a response to the evident and terrible anti-Semitism of European Christian civilization (so-called). The British put their stamp of approval on the Zionist project with the Balfour Declaration of 1917.

Yet this declaration was by no means welcomed by the area's Arab populations, and for most of the time of the British "Mandate of Palestine" the British actually did little to advance a new Jewish state. Eventually they favored a single binational Arab and Jewish state, an idea that surfaces sometimes today either as a dream or a nightmare of a one-state solution. Eventually, the growing Jewish nationalist movement ended up in open military conflict with the British, while also having to cope with violence from the local Arab population. The Arabs resented the British and a local Palestinian nationalism and a broader pan-Arab, anti-Zionist, and anti-British nationalism gradually emerged. The late 1930s was marked by Jews and Arabs struggling with each other and both struggling with the British.

Then of course came World War II and the horrible evil of the genocidal Nazi (and collaborator) assault on the Jews that we know as the Holocaust, which claimed six million Jewish lives as partial fulfillment of an exterminationist plan. Meanwhile, the Middle East seethed. After World War II, an exhausted Britain was ready to get out. The British handed the Israel-Palestine problem to the new United Nations. On November 29, 1947 the UN General Assembly passed Resolution 181, which offered a partition plan involving an Arab state, a Jewish state, and an internationally controlled Jerusalem. This plan was accepted by the Zionists but not by the Arabs. Palestinian fighters attacked Jewish communities the very next day, though it is not as if this was the first such attack or the first intercommunal violence. The Zionists counterattacked beginning in April 1948. With British power ebbing, and the infant UN attempting to find some kind of resolution, the forces on the ground were already in an Arab-Jewish civil war. On May 14, 1948, the day the British Mandate ended, Jews declared an independent state of Israel.

After the declaration of independence the next round of the fighting commenced. Local and regional Arab enemies attempted but were not able to strangle the newborn state in its cradle. Many died in the fighting, which lasted until early 1949. Massive population movements occurred as Jews flooded into the new Jewish state and Arabs left and were forced out. Still, when the dust settled in 1949 the Jews had fought their way successfully to an internationally recognized state (though with unsettled borders). The State of Israel was not recognized by Palestinians or surrounding Arab states. Wartime victories meant Israel controlled territory that was 30 percent bigger than what had been designated for the Jews in the 1947 UN partition plan. Palestinians had no state of their own, as the new "Hashemite Kingdom of Jordan" annexed the region west of the Jordan, while Egypt retained occupation of what became known as the Gaza Strip. Israel's near neighbors signed armistice deals rather than peace agreements. They had not come to terms with the existence of the new Jewish state.

The rest of the story is somewhat more familiar. In 1967 Israel's enemies were preparing to attack once again. This time, in a war lasting only six days, Israel prevailed decisively, conquering the Golan Heights in the north, the Sinai Peninsula near Egypt, the Gaza Strip, and most significantly the Jordanian-controlled area west of the Jordan, including East Jerusalem. This profoundly changed the balance of power in the region, and has done so to this day. As is customary in international law, occupied territories remained under military rule pending a negotiated settlement. UN Security Council Resolution 242 in November 1967 called for the establishment of a lasting peace based on Israeli withdrawal from all territories occupied in the June war, in return for an end to the state of belligerence, respect for the sovereignty of all states in the region, and the right of all to live in peace within secure, recognized boundaries. This resolution has been the basis for all subsequent peace negotiations.

Treaties in 1979 with Egypt and in 1994 with Jordan gave hope that the Arab states could one day come to terms with the permanence of Israel in the region, or even make a real peace. The Oslo Accords (negotiated in 1993, finalized in Washington in 1995) seemed to signal that Israel and the Palestinian national movement could come to terms. The 1995 Israeli-Palestinian Interim Agreement, which is as close as the parties and the world have come to an internationally recognized negotiated settlement of the conflict, allowed the Palestinian Liberation Organization (PLO) leadership to relocate to the occupied territories, granted autonomy to the Palestinians but not yet a state (though providing the framework for negotiating final issues related to a state), and committed the Palestinians to abstain from terror and change their charter, which had called for the elimination of the State of Israel. A final deal was to be negotiated by May 1999.

That deal has never been consummated, and courageous Israeli Prime Minister Yitzhak Rabin paid with his life when he was killed in 1995 by an Israeli religious extremist who opposed the Oslo Accords. Meanwhile, the very same Yasser Arafat who signed the Oslo deal planned the second intifada of 2000–2002, further deepening the immense difficulty Israelis have in believing that the Palestinians will ever fully accept their existence. Today we still live in the seemingly endless time between the times—between the establishment of an interim Palestinian Authority and an interim Israeli-Palestinian Agreement, on the one hand, and the formation of a State of Palestine and a final peace agreement, on the other.

Because Israel was established so soon after the devastation of European Jewry during the Holocaust, it was hard for onlookers not to view the birth of the Jewish state as a kind of miracle of rebirth/resurrection, though an unambiguous religious narrative of that type has never prevailed in Israel.

Of course, a miracle of rebirth was not exactly how either local or regional Arab populations viewed the birth of modern Israel. The Arabs lost territory, ever more with each successive military conflict and subsequent effort to craft a peace treaty; they lost face; many lost their homes; and of course in war many lost their lives, as was true on the Jewish side. With defeat after defeat, with the gradual economic and military strengthening of Israel over against the chronic weakness of the Palestinians, and the relative weakness of the Arab world, some also lost contact with reality. Revanchists dreamed and sometimes still dream of pushing the Jews out of Palestine altogether, no matter how absurd is/was that hope; and Palestinian leadership was often provided by romanticized terrorists who were mainly good at the routine use of attacks on civilians to express anger and inflict misery on Israelis. Every round of attacks struck directly at the Jewish state's considerable post-Holocaust trauma and insecurity.

Any review of the spate of nation-birthing and nation-dying since 1945 inspires a healthy respect for the contingent nature of nation-states. They come and go, usually in a flow of blood. Each story is unique but each is all too human.

This may suggest that attaching any ultimate significance, including theological significance, or ascribing any existential purity or innocence, to any particular nation-state with any particular territory and any particular political regime is foolish. This is true whether we speak of the US, the USSR (remember them?), or Israel. These are very human creations with very bloody births and deaths. These are stories of blood and iron.

I challenge Christians, especially evangelicals, to try to learn how to think about the history and politics and conflicts of Israel-Palestine and the region without always jumping to overlay some kind of theological interpretation on it. Ethnic groups fight each other. Nations are born in bloody, conflicted ways. Territorial disputes abound. A just peace that honors the sacred worth of each person and allows everyone to go about their daily lives in security amidst such constant bloody conflicts should always be our goal as Christians.

We need to examine the conflicts and challenges of Israel-Palestine the way we would examine the conflicts and challenges of any other region of the world, and to apply the same moral standards and peacemaking practices there as we would anywhere else. Here any particularized public theology of holy land, or holy Israel, or even primal Palestinian Christian community, needs to give way to a more universal Christian public ethic of justice, peace, and just peacemaking.

A certain kind of Christian Zionism hurts the situation in this particular region because its mystical theology of the Holy Land and of the meaning of contemporary history hinders the capacity of large numbers of American Christians to apply standard Christian public ethics to the Israeli-Palestinian conflict. Mythologizing the modern state of Israel by overlaying a certain reading of the Old Testament land texts, or of biblical apocalyptic texts, has made it more difficult for millions of evangelical Christians to understand our ethical obligations right here, right now, in the real world of real bloody history.

We need to stop treating Middle East conflicts as if they were existentially or theologically much different from conflicts over other contested land, such as the Kashmir region or Kosovo. The Israel-Palestine problem is historical, geopolitical, diplomatic, and ethical, and the overall principles of cooperative conflict resolution and other tenets of just peacemaking are where we ought to focus our attention.

The Problem of Military Occupation, Settlements, and Extremist (Religious) Zionism

If we summarize the history of the land we are discussing as consisting of the burgeoning and then new Israel outmaneuvering and outfighting Palestinians and regional Arab groups and states; over time changing the facts on the ground in her favor; gradually acquiring more and more power relative to the Palestinians in the normal way of the world; gradually claiming irreversible and internationally recognized control over more and more of the territory between the Jordan and the Mediterranean—has anything really changed in recent years? Does the Israel-Palestine problem have a new dimension worthy of our attention?

I am persuaded by a number of books by American and Israeli Jews—such as Peter Beinart and Gershom Gorenberg—that Israel as a whole has grown accustomed to a permanent military occupation of another people, which is altering her character as a people and risking the abandonment of her founding commitment to partition the land with the Palestinians. The Oslo Accords promise such a partition and the negotiations to accomplish it. Deals to make such a partition happen have come very close to being accomplished more than once since 1995, most recently in 2008 or perhaps during the 2013 Kerry Initiative. But leaders openly calling for an abandonment of any kind of two-state peace deal have moved from the margins to the mainstream in Israeli politics in the past decade.

The expansion of Jewish communities in the area of an envisioned Palestinian state has created facts on the ground that risk making a viable Palestinian state impossible. Primary responsibility for permitting and in fact subsidizing these settlements, which in some cases are in fact mid-size cities and include over 300,000 inhabitants (over 500,000 if one counts East Jerusalem), belongs to the government of Israel, both through omission and commission. Gorenberg shows that Israel stumbled rather than rushed headlong into the policies she has undertaken, but by now these policies have developed a deeply loyal constituency and a momentum of their own that is very difficult to break. (Many settlers would almost certainly fight their own Israeli Army if a peace deal required them to move. Many soldiers would not follow orders to evacuate settlers, polls show.)

Meanwhile, these settlements need to be protected. Because Palestinian territory is under military occupation, which consists for Palestinians of a life of permits, checkpoints, walls, prisons, property and natural resource seizures, settler abuses, and often fierce IDF repression of even nonviolent protests, the face of Israel for much of the world is an unsavory combination of occupation troops and militant settlers. Both Beinart and Gorenberg decry the emergence of a militant ultra-orthodox Judaism that is especially strong among the settlers and sometimes the military in the Occupied Territories, but is also becoming a major factor in Israel proper. Gorenberg suggests that in keeping and then settling occupied territories, Israel has invited the religious and political radicalization of a significant portion of her own population, and that this cannot be contained to that part to be found on the Palestinian side of the wall. This part of the population is not especially interested in protecting the principles of Israeli democracy, and its understanding of religion is not in keeping with the humane justice orientation of the best Jewish religious traditions.

When a religion under the name Judaism becomes a force for denying the human worth, needs, and rights of those outside the group, it is not true Judaism, or at least not the truest Judaism. Christians are under no obligation to defer to that kind of religious sensibility, but instead must protest it. And to the extent that there is a version of Christianity that also becomes a force for denying the human worth, needs, and rights of Palestinians in the occupied territories, it is not the truest Christianity and we must protest it. (Just as we must protest any mutant strain of Christianity anywhere else. Or a similarly problematic Islam.) This kind of religion becomes a justifying ideology for the rule of force rather than the rule of law or the standards of justice and peace, and it must be resisted in Christ's name.

Certainly Arab and then Palestinian leaders bear a significant share of responsibility for not seizing peace deals when they had the opportunity (beginning at least in 1947). Their own inability to accept sharing the land in the times before the situation mutated to what it is today is most unfortunate. But the situation that now exists on the ground is that Israel is in essence creating a two-headed Jewish state, one a quite sophisticated first-world state in internationally recognized territory with an Israeli Arab population that has considerable legal protections if not totally equal treatment, and one a rather brutal occupying power in territory with a Palestinian population that is under military rule. The trend lines are exacerbating extremist Palestinian nationalism and weakening the legitimacy of the more reasonable Palestinian Authority leaders now aging and soon to leave the scene. I am not saying that endless military occupation *creates* Palestinian voices that do not recognize the legitimacy of Israel; I am saying that such an occupation raises the profile and popularity of such voices over against the more moderate voices prepared to make peace with Israel.

It is still UN and US policy to press for a negotiated two-state solution, with an autonomous and viable Palestinian state next to a secure, recognized Israel. But the level of complexity involved in trying to arrange land swaps in order to accommodate apparently immovable Israeli settlements, while still giving a future Palestine enough land, and enough contiguity, to be a viable state, makes the 1947 partition look like child's play by comparison.

The basic Christian ethics of just peacemaking emphasizes respect for international institutions and rule-of-law structures. It calls for negotiated win-win conflict resolution approaches. It emphasizes shared responsibility for serious conflicts and for resolving them. Its brand of religiosity is interested in transforming initiatives that turn enemies into friends and spirals of conflict into cycles of peacemaking.

It is hard for me to see how Christians could not support adherence to the essential structure of UN resolutions encouraging a two-state solution, together with the Oslo Accords, together with the stated preference of the US for a negotiated two-state solution, together with respectful discussion of and with responsible participants on all sides. To the extent that there are Christians who look at the situation with a theological framework that repudiates any Palestinian claim on any land between the Jordan and the Mediterranean, or who do not respect the authority of the legal and treaty structures that have emerged to help bring some order to this situation, or who mythologize the Jewish side and demonize the Palestinian side (or vice-versa), they are not contributing constructively to Christian public ethics with relation to Israel-Palestine.

What's US Evangelical Christianity Got to Do With It?

American evangelicals bring some distinctive characteristics into the global discussion and potential resolution of the Israel-Palestine problem. Some of these characteristics are constructive; some are a double-edged sword; and some are destructive.

Evangelicals in the United States are among the last population in the world whose moral imaginations are so suffused with the stories of Scripture that the land we are talking about still remains "Holy Land" to them (us).

US evangelicals have also been remarkably better than most European Christians were in developing a positive theology of and relationship to the Jewish people. Historic Christian anti-Semitism is more often among us a contemporary Christian philosemitism. This is indeed a welcome development, except for where it precludes a philo-Palestinianism; e.g., where it trains some Christians in a one-sided love.

US evangelicals, like many other Americans, take the Holocaust seriously. It looms large in their understanding of World War II and of the twentieth century, and it helps shape a desire to assure that the Jewish people never stand alone in the world again when confronted by an enemy. I share deeply in that concern, as a Holocaust scholar and one who has served the US Holocaust Memorial Museum in an official capacity.

A significant minority of US evangelicals (and fundamentalists) has embraced a theological framework in which the birth of the modern state of Israel is an important part of the timetable of events preceding the imminent return of Jesus Christ. And the "Israel" they have in mind is not the negotiated Israel of UN resolutions and treaties but the Davidic/Solomonic Israel in the maps in the back of their Bibles.

Many US evangelicals undertake Holy Land tours that are structured in such a way as to appeal to their religious sensibilities while carefully steering clear of the problems associated with the occupied territories.

Meanwhile, US evangelicals are such an important part of the US population that our very strong instinctual and theological support for the modern state of Israel has a profound impact on US foreign policy.

More recently, of course, more and more US evangelicals have come into relationship with Palestinians, including Palestinian Christians. These have come to understand the claims of Palestinians on (parts of) the land. They have come to care about the suffering of Palestinians under occupation. They have taken dual narrative tours that have taken them through the separation barrier and checkpoints and into the Occupied Territories. They are likely to take seriously the significance of modern history and the legal-ethical-treaty framework promising/demanding a two-state solution. And they are sometimes so changed by their visits to the region that this type of evangelical polarizes toward an anti-Israel/pro-Palestinian posture.

I believe the proper posture for evangelicals is to be pro-Israel, pro-Palestine, and pro-(just) peace. We do best not when we take sides but when we function as a third side, a just-peace side. We are best postured when we are friends who come up alongside squabbling brothers and help them make peace, not when we come up on squabbling brothers and take sides.

Evangelicals who care about Israel and Palestine need to engage individuals, groups, and cultures on both sides, which is not easy, because the entire conflict somehow seems structured to keep you on one side or the other. We need to partner with constructive just peacemakers wherever we find them, and lift their voices up for special attention and emulation. We need to speak up constantly for win/win solutions. We need to help our government take a balanced and constructive role.

What is good Christian public theology in relation to Israel-Palestine? Good historical realism. Good modern respect for the rule of law. Good love of the God who makes each life sacred. Good love of each sacred individual life and each sacred people. Good, skillful, just peacemaking—so that soon there will be a just peace in the land between the Jordan and the Mediterranean.

Part IV

Political Paradigms and Perspectives

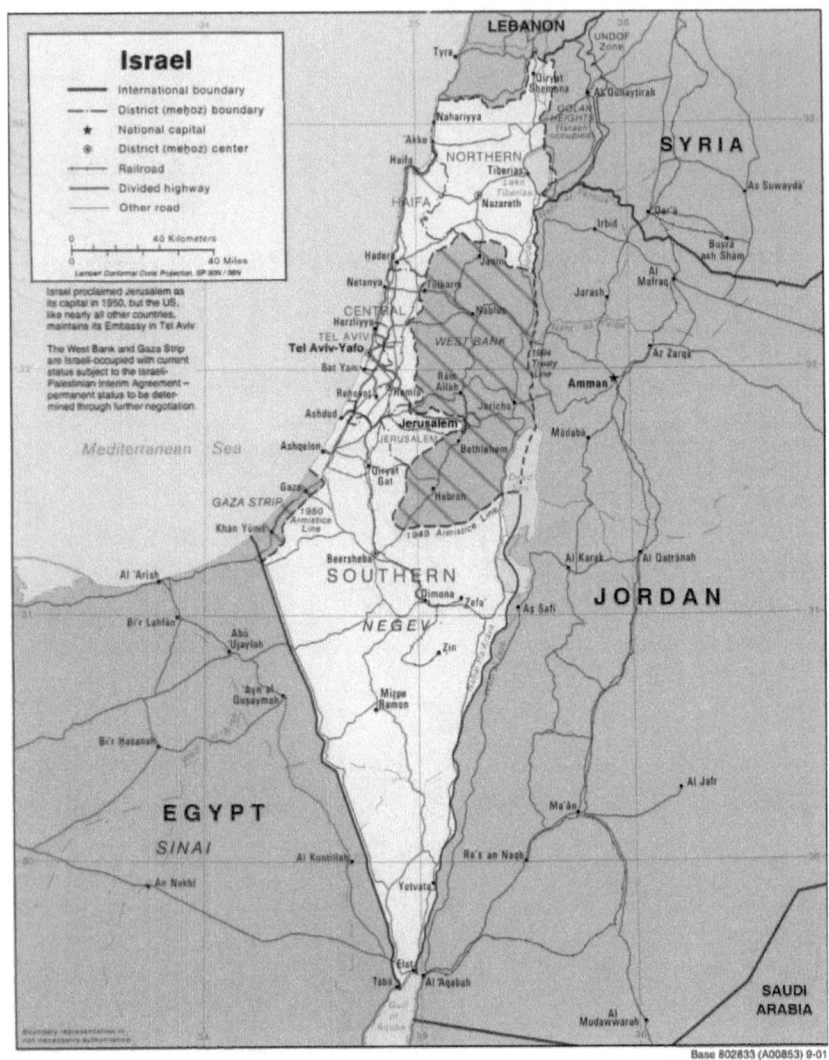

2001 CIA Map of Israel, West Bank, and Gaza[2]

2. United States Central Intelligence Agency.

13

Across the Israel Divide

Susan Michael

ISRAEL IS ONE OF the most complex issues today. It divides countries, governments, and academic institutions, along with theological communities. The issues at play are historical, theological, and political. They are also personal and, often, emotional for those directly affected. Therefore, a thoughtful Christian perspective must be one based on concern and care for all the peoples involved, and most importantly, on an honest assessment of the facts.

A striking biblical analogy highlighting the sensitivity of this issue is the reference to the Jewish people as the apple of God's eye, a very vulnerable part of the body (Deut 32:10; Zech 2:8). When handling this subject we are touching upon something that is not just sensitive to Jews, Christians, and Muslims, but to God himself.

It is made abundantly clear in Scripture that God will bless or judge people based on how they treat his people Israel (Gen 12:3, Isa 60:12, Zech 2:8–9, Joel 3:1–3). Jesus seems to confirm this in Matthew 25:31–46, where He explains that upon his return he will divide the nations for blessing or judgment based on their treatment of "His brethren."[1]

---

1. This Scripture is often said to be about helping needy Christians, or all needy people, but we cannot ignore its original meaning. The Hebrew Scriptures formed the context for all of Jesus' teachings, and he was being consistent with many passages of Scripture when he spoke here of judgment of the nations over their treatment of the Jewish people. He went further to say that he took their treatment very personally, "as you did it to the least of these my brethren, you did it to me." Jesus was Jewish and an attack on his people was an attack on him.

Another metaphor used in Scripture is likening Israel to a pregnant woman (Rev 12:1–6) because of her role in birthing the "male Child who would rule all nations." This unusual image helps to explain the special treatment and care she requires. It does not mean that she is loved more than any other of God's children, but that she has a unique role, given only to her, to birth God's plan to redeem fallen humankind. That role means that she will be vulnerable and in need of assistance.

The God of Israel takes the treatment of his people very seriously. Therefore, we should proceed in this discussion with great caution and care.

God's Banner to the Nations

The divisiveness of the Israel issue should be our first indication that something far greater is at stake here. This tiny state of eight million people, the size of New Jersey, is at the center of the world's attention. Isaiah 11:11–12 says that in "that day" when the Lord gathers His people back to the land "a second time," that he will raise a banner to the nations.[2] Indeed, the attention of all nations has been turned to Israel today.

After some 2,000 years of exile, the Jewish people have returned to their land a second time.[3] This is a historic phenomenon with no parallel. It is nothing less than a miracle that this small people group survived two exiles, maintained themselves as a nation, and have now re-established Jewish sovereignty in their ancient homeland. Isaiah says that in this second regathering God is raising a banner, or message, to the world. I believe the message of this banner is twofold based on which side of the divide one stands.

The first message is exciting and jubilant: God is faithful to keep his covenants. He never forgot his ancient people; he remembers the covenant that he made with Abraham and his descendants, and is fulfilling his promises to them. The appointed time to favor Zion has come (Ps 102:13), and whereas he may have dealt with them in judgment, despite their imperfections and failures it is now a new season, a season of favor and restoration. We Christians can rejoice: we serve a merciful and covenant-keeping God!

The second message is a warning of impending judgment to those on the other side of the divide. The flip side of the faithfulness of God to his Word is that he also promises a day of reckoning. As mentioned earlier, Scripture is very clear that God will judge the nations based on their

---

2. See also Isaiah 22:22.

3. The first exile was completed at the hands of the Babylonian Empire, the first return under the Persians, and the second exile was in 70 AD at the hands of the Romans.

treatment of Israel (Zeph 3:19–20). Israel is the fault line, and which side of that line one stands is critical.

Understanding the Challenge Israel Presents to the World

Some theologians disregard the biblical principle of judgment because it does not fit into their concept of a "God of love." However, if he really loves his children, he will protect them and deal with those who seek their destruction. There are consequences for opposing this loving God, his choice of people, and his plan.

God has lovingly given us free will, and we have the freedom to choose on which side of this divide we wish to stand. While he knows us better than we know ourselves, he allows us to encounter certain decision points whereby our decisions determine where we stand. One of those tests is Israel. God uses Israel to test the hearts of the nations, thereby exposing either their goodness, which leads to blessing, or their hatred and evil intent, which leads to judgment. In other words, Israel exposes what is in the heart of people.

George Gilder, a venture-capitalist businessman, proposes in his book, *The Israel Test,* that Israel presents a moral and ethical challenge to the world and therefore has become the ultimate fault line. At the root of the Israel Test for the world today is the knowledge that Israel is contributing more to humanity through its scientific, technological, and economic achievements than nearly any other country in the world.

According to Gilder, Israel presents the following test to the world: what is your attitude towards people who surpass you in creating wealth or in other accomplishments? Do you aspire to their excellence, or do you seethe at it? Do you admire and celebrate exceptional achievement, or do you impugn it and seek to tear it down? God is using Israel to test the hearts of the nations. Their future will be determined by how they respond.

Understanding the Challenge Israel Presents to the Church

The same test is being presented to the church. In Romans 11, the Apostle Paul addresses the attitude of the Roman church towards the Jewish people. He warns believers to make sure that their attitude is humble and honors the Jewish people. He even cautions them about possible judgment by God if their attitude is not right: "Do not be haughty, but fear. For if God did not spare the natural branches, He may not spare you either" (Rom 11:20–21, NKJV).

This is the test that Israel presents to the church: are we arrogant towards the Jews? Do we seek to replace them in advancing God's will? Or do we rejoice in the faithfulness of God to them and that he is fulfilling the promises he made to their fathers? Do we despise their return to their homeland because it does not fit into our Replacement Theology? Or do we break into praise of God's mighty ways as did the Apostle Paul when he completed his teaching about God's enduring plans for Israel in Romans 9–11?

A church that honors its Hebraic roots, as wild branches that are grafted into the natural olive tree (Rom 11:17), receives great strength and nourishment. Separating ourselves from the very root that supports our Christian faith brings spiritual decline and even death. Christianity has no meaning when separated from its Jewish context. This may explain the decline in certain denominations that belittle the biblical and Hebraic foundation of our faith.

The Heart of the Divide: Replacement Theology

The heart of the divide in the Christian world towards Israel is therefore Supersessionism or Replacement Theology. It may masquerade as a concern for the Palestinian people, or purport to be about political issues, but often the real issue lies in one's view of the Jewish people's calling and destiny.

Supersessionism is a centuries-old teaching that the Jewish people have been cursed and rejected by God because of their rejection of Jesus' messianic credentials. As a result, they have been replaced by the church; the church is therefore the new Israel of God. While God's curses may be upon the Jews, his blessings all reside on the church!

This theology provided fertile ground for centuries of anti-Semitic teachings in the church and sowed the seeds for the persecution of the Jewish people throughout Europe. Many scholars agree that the Holocaust could have never happened had it not been for the centuries of Christian anti-Semitism that was rooted in this theology.

Replacement Theology, in all of its variations, seems to imply that God's Plan A failed, so he went to Plan B with a new people, the Christian church. However, Ephesians 1:4–5 says that Plan A existed before the foundations of the world were laid, and always included the death of Christ Jesus, because that is how we are adopted as sons (vs. 5). Could it be, then, that God's covenant with the Jewish people is indeed an everlasting covenant that was not abolished nor reconstructed to apply to some other people? In fact, speaking of Israel, Paul in Romans 11 affirms that God's call over them as a nation is irrevocable (Rom 11:29). Plan A did not fail and was not annulled.

Genesis 17:8 confirms that Israel's covenant is an everlasting covenant, therefore, the land of Canaan is their everlasting possession. The land is a necessary requirement for the formation of the nation that God sought to create out of Abraham's descendants, and later for the great acts of God in the redemption of the world: the birth and death of Jesus, and the future establishment of the Messianic reign on earth.

While it was an everlasting covenant, and everlasting possession, their right to live on the land was also clearly made conditional. Deuteronomy 28:63 says that if they did not obey the Lord their God they would be removed from the land. This principle explains the two exiles the Jewish people have suffered, but even exile came with the promise of return (Deut 30:1–3). The people of Israel are not exempt from judgment, but are promised it, because of God's corrective love at work in his covenant with them.

The Abrahamic covenant also makes clear that the people of Israel will bless all the families of the earth by bringing to a fallen world the redemptive gifts through which humanity can be saved. The Apostle Paul listed those redemptive gifts in Romans 3:2 and Romans 9:4–5: the Word of God, the covenants, the law, the service of God, the promises, and Christ Jesus. Israel's work is not yet complete, and God has brought them back to the land for what may now be the final chapter of history, which is a glorious one, when the knowledge of the Lord will fill the earth and nations will learn war no more (Isa 2, 11).

Israel's Calling is for the Blessing of the World

With acknowledgement that there is a special calling placed on the Jewish people comes a belief that our conduct towards them should be based on appreciation, blessing, and honor. However, this does not mean that God loves them above all the other peoples of the world. John 3:16 declares God's love for the world: "For God so loved the world that He gave His only begotten Son, that whosoever believes in Him should not perish, but have everlasting life."

God's love for the world is why he brought into existence the nation of Israel through whom he would bring about his great plan of redemption. Their role in his plan would afford them a place of preservation and promised blessing. Unfortunately, their calling would also place them directly in the line of fire, and consequently, there would be much suffering throughout the centuries. The story of the Jewish people is filled with exiles, persecutions, pogroms, expulsions, and attempts at annihilation. There is no explanation for this history other than the biblical role bequeathed to them by God himself.

Psalm 83:1–4 explains that they are in the line of fire in a war against God Himself. "O God . . . those who hate you . . . have said 'Come, and let us cut them off from being a nation, that the name of Israel may be remembered no more'" (NKJV). God knew that the people of Israel would pay a price and their history would be full of suffering. This could explain why he promised blessings on any who would bless and help them.

Christian Zionism

While there are political, moral, and practical reasons why Christians support Israel, the biblical foundation of Christian Zionism is the belief that God bequeathed the land of Canaan to the Jewish people as an everlasting possession for the purposes of world redemption.[4] Israel's detractors in the Christian world portray Christian Zionism as heresy, claiming that it politicizes the Scriptures. However, as soon as the Bible was translated into vernacular languages some 500 years ago, which allowed Christians to read the Scriptures for themselves, preachers began to teach that the Jews would one day return to their ancient homeland. They prayed for and supported this return to the land as an act of justice for a people who had suffered persecution for centuries.

Some of the greatest and most respected evangelicals in history were what we would call Christian Zionists today: John and Charles Wesley, Charles Haddon Spurgeon, Bishop Ryle of Liverpool, Professor Jacob Janeway of the Scottish National Church, and many others.[5] The only difference between them and today's Christian Zionists is that they supported a future event, while today's Christian Zionists have witnessed the return of the Jews to their homeland and actively support a current event.

---

4. For a full treatment of the theology of Christian Zionism see the ICEJ's Biblical Zionism booklet series and "Christian Zionism in Balance," both by Rev. Hedding. Found at www.icejusa.org, or visit www.israelanswers.com.

5. For a history of Christian Zionism and quotes from some fifty Christian leaders over the last 500 years who supported the re-establishment of Israel based on their reading of Scripture, see "A History of Christian Zionism."

Who are Really God's People in the Middle East?

One of the more vocal Christian theologians leading a campaign against Christian Zionism is Dr. Gary Burge, Professor of New Testament at Wheaton College. His book, *Who are God's People in the Middle East?*, laid out a form of Replacement Theology, which claimed that the church had replaced the Jewish people as the people of God. He concluded that the Palestinian Christians are the real people of God in the Israeli-Arab conflict, arguing that Christians should support them, instead of the Jewish people.

We should indeed love and support our Christian brothers and sisters in the Palestinian territories. Yet, this does not require that we discard Israel and invalidate or discredit God's covenant with her. Instead, it requires an honest assessment of the situation facing Palestinian Christians and who is really to blame for it. Burge and others who share his view prefer to simply blame Israel, especially when it validates their Replacement Theology.

Anyone concerned for the Christians of the Middle East, including Palestinian Christians, should be applauding Israel, the one country in the region where the Christian community is thriving and growing. Israel is the only safe haven in a region where the future of Christianity is questionable, including in the Palestinian territories where the numbers are dwindling rapidly.[6] This decline is indicative of a much larger problem addressed in the next section.

Our Christian compassion should not stop with Middle East Christians. It should include love and concern for all the peoples of the Middle East. Jesus died for the whole world, including Arab and Muslim peoples, whom he loves just as much as anyone else. In fact, the many accounts of Jesus appearing to Muslims today in dreams and visions illustrate just how much God loves them and is revealing himself to those who have a heart to receive him.

The International Christian Embassy Jerusalem has a specific calling to connect the global church to Israel, demonstrating Christian love for the people of Israel. However, we make sure that a corresponding percentage of our humanitarian aid in Israel goes to its Arab minorities, both Muslims and Christians. We regularly take up the cause of the persecuted church in the Middle East in our publications, provide donations to support their care, and encourage our members to pray for them, along with the wider Muslim world, during our monthly Isaiah 62 global prayer initiative.

---

6. See Brown, "Priest to UN."

An Honest Assessment: Israel's "Unjust" Treatment of the Palestinians

A true Christian perspective must not only be based on love, but also grounded in truth. This is challenging because of a prevalent Palestinian narrative that has little regard for historical fact.[7] While the constraints of space in this article do not allow us to discuss all of the political issues associated with the Arab-Israeli conflict, it's important to examine the issues of justice and claims of oppression of the Palestinian people.[8]

How does Israel treat the 1.8 million Arabs within its country? They enjoy citizenship, voting rights, freedom of speech, worship, and the press. Women enjoy the same freedoms as men. Arabs have their own political parties, serve in the Knesset, serve on the Supreme Court, and have even been crowned "Miss Israel." It's clear that Israeli Arabs have found more justice in Israel than in any other Middle Eastern country.

Israel's detractors therefore ignore this fact and focus on the supposed injustices facing the Palestinians in Gaza and the West Bank instead. So let's look at the Palestinians. A recent Palestinian poll found that more than 40 percent of Arabs in East Jerusalem would prefer to live under Israeli sovereignty than in a future Palestinian State. They would move to a different neighborhood to stay under Israeli jurisdiction if a Palestinian State was formed. If Israel is so repressive and unjust, why would these Palestinians prefer to live under Israeli rather than Palestinian rule?

A brief review of some other statistics also shed light on the issue. When Israel first captured the West Bank and Gaza Strip in 1967 the conditions were quite dire. After twenty years of Jordanian rule, life expectancy was low; malnutrition, infectious diseases, and child mortality were rife; levels of educational attainment very low; and fewer than 60 percent of all male adults were employed.

During the 1970s, under Israeli rule, the West Bank and Gaza constituted the fourth fastest-growing economy in the world. Mortality rates fell by more than two-thirds; life expectancy rose from forty-eight years in 1967 to seventy-two in 2000, compared with an average of sixty-eight years for all

---

7. Palestinian leaders perpetrate such lies as: the Holocaust never happened, the first and second temples never existed in Jerusalem, Al-Aksa Mosque is in danger of collapse due to Israel, and that Jesus was a Palestinian. Such blatant lies are found throughout their speeches as well as school textbooks and government supported media.

8. Treatment of issues such as settlements, Jerusalem, borders, etc., can be found at www.israelanswers.com.

countries in the Middle East; and childhood diseases like polio, whooping cough, tetanus, and measles were eradicated.

By 1986, more than 100,000 Palestinians worked in Israel, and many more worked in the 2,000 industrial plants that had been built in the territories; 92.8 percent of the population had electricity around the clock as compared to 20.5 percent in 1967; 85 percent had running water as compared to 16 percent in 1967; 83.5 percent had electric or gas ranges for cooking as compared to 4 percent in 1967. Most dramatic was the progress in higher education. In 1967, not a single university existed in the territories. By the early 1990s, there were seven institutions of higher education boasting 16,500 students. Illiteracy rates dropped to 14 percent of adults compared to 61 percent in Egypt and 44 percent in Syria.

Is this the unjust and repressive Israel that the Palestinians decry?

Israel developed the West Bank and Gaza, but never annexed them. In the late 1970s, Anwar Sadat invited the Palestinians to be a part of the Camp David Accords to negotiate their own arrangements, but they refused. Israel made peace with Egypt and Jordan. It sought to broker peace with the Palestinians through a plan that was presented to the Madrid Peace Conference in 1991, which laid the groundwork for the Oslo Peace Process.

Israel sought a two-state solution with the Palestinians even though they can claim legal ownership of the West Bank according to the San Remo Conference and the League of Nations vote in 1922. The UN validated these previous conferences in the 1947 Partition Plan but proposed that the West Bank be for an Arab state. However, the Arabs rejected the plan. Thus, the West Bank is not "occupied territory" but at most "disputed territory" under international law, and Israel has repeatedly been willing to concede this area for a Palestinian State in exchange for a durable peace.

Many ask why this peace process is now stagnant. Let's review the last decade. Israel withdrew from Lebanon, Gaza, and most of the West Bank, and in return found the Hezbollah terrorist organization on its northern border, armed with more than 100,000 missiles; the Hamas terrorist organization on its southern border, which has fired more than 5,000 missiles at Israeli civilians; and the Palestinian Authority on its eastern border, which continues to foster incitement in schools and media, glorifying suicide bombers and knife-wielding youth.

Like all governments, Israel's primary responsibility is to protect its citizens from these threats, which is why it built the security fence and has checkpoints in the West Bank. The New Testament explicitly allows governments to use "the sword" to carry out this responsibility (Rom 13:1–7; 1 Pet 2:13–14). It is interesting to note that Israeli security is also credited with maintaining the Palestinian Authority government by keeping Hamas out of the West Bank.[9]

In 1999, Israel turned over control of the major areas populated by Palestinians to the Palestinian Authority (PA) in accordance with the Oslo Peace Accords, so that 99 percent of Palestinians are ruled by their own government. Israel does maintain border control and checkpoints within the West Bank, and we recognize that these security measures produce difficulties for the Palestinian people, who do not have the freedom of movement necessary to develop businesses, find jobs, and, in some cases, access hospitals in a timely manner.

However, the real cause for this suffering is not Israel's security measures, but the culture of terrorism, and the corruption of the Palestinian leadership, many of whom benefit from the continuing conflict. As a result, these leaders refuse to sit down at the negotiating table with Israel to secure a better future for their people.

The Palestinian people have suffered grave injustices, but primarily at the hands of their own leaders. While there are Palestinians who lost their lives and homes in the 1948 War of Independence, the continuing oppression of the Palestinian people by their own Arab leaders is a travesty.

If Palestinian leaders had partnered with Israel, they would have established an independent state that could be the most prosperous, free, and advanced Arab country in the region. However, under the Palestinian Authority, there is no freedom of speech or freedom of the press, children are taught to hate and murder Jews beginning in kindergarten, the unemployment rate remains exceedingly high, and impoverished refugees still live in camps. Year after year, billions of dollars in international aid earmarked for the Palestinian people are siphoned off by corrupt leaders.[10]

This is the injustice inflicted upon the Palestinian people that Israel's detractors will not acknowledge. Ascribing all blame to Israel and ignoring blatant injustices perpetrated by the Arab leaders, is not only dishonest—it is indicative of underlying anti-Semitic sentiment.

---

9. Hamas, a designated terrorist organization, would like to rule the West Bank just as they have ruled the Gaza Strip since 2006.

10 For statistics and photographs contrasting the Palestinian elite's opulence with the abject poverty of refugees they refuse to absorb, see Kaplan, "Luxury Alongside." For similar treatment of the Gaza Strip, see Booth, "Gaza Strip's middle class."

Guarding Against the New Antisemitism: Anti-Zionism

For centuries, anti-Semitism was based on Christian religious theories. Under the Nazis, it was based on racial theories. Neither of these belief systems is politically correct in today's discourse. However, a new form of anti-Semitism has become acceptable: the demonization of the Jewish State.

The truth is, one cannot demonize Israel without demonizing the Israeli people, who are an integral part of the Jewish community at large. This is made clear when a Jewish person is attacked in the streets of France because Israel has taken military action in Gaza.

The crescendo of this hate speech against Israel is building in the Muslim world, on university campuses, and amongst the social elites of the West. It is trying to infiltrate the Christian world.[11] We need to do whatever we can to make sure that this modern form of anti-Semitism does not seep into our seminaries and churches. A true Christian perspective on the Holy Land—built on a genuine love for all the peoples caught in this conflict and based on an honest assessment of the facts—will do just that.

Bibliography

"A History of Christian Zionism." *Israel Answers*. Accessed June 20, 2016. www.israelanswers.com/christian_zionism/a_history_of_christian_zionism.

Booth, William. "Gaza Strip's middle class enjoys spin classes, fine dining, private beaches." *Washington Post*, August 20, 2015. https://www.washingtonpost.com/world/middle_east/gaza-middle-class-discovers-spin-classes-fine-dining-private-beaches/2015/08/23/7e23843c-45d5-11e5-9f53-d1e3ddfd0cda_story.html.

Brown, Loretta. "Priest to UN: Israel is 'Only Safe Place' for Christians in Middle East." *CNS News*. November 3, 2014. http://www.cnsnews.com/news/article/lauretta-brown/priest-un-israel-only-safe-place-christians-middle-east.

Hedding, Malcolm. *The Basis of Christian Support for Zionism*. International Christian Embassy Jerusalem. Accessed June 20, 2016. http://us.icej.org/store/basis-christian-support-israel-booklet.

Hedding, Malcolm. *Christian Zionism in the Balance*. International Christian Embassy Jerusalem. Accessed June 20, 2016. www.icejusa.org/christian-zionism-balance.

Israel Answers. Accessed June 20, 2016. www.israelanswers.com.

Kaplan, Yael, Ryan Hartney, and Andrew Felsenthal. "Luxury Alongside Poverty in the Palestinian Authority." *Jerusalem Center for Public Affairs*, November 5, 2015. http://jcpa.org/article/luxury-alongside-poverty-in-the-palestinian-authority/.

---

11. Rev. Steven Sizer, Anglican vicar and one of the foremost Christian critics of Israel and Christian Zionism, was banned by the Anglican Church in 2015 from speaking, writing, or teaching on the Middle East due to his dissemination of anti-Semitic and racist materials.

14

Palestine and Apartheid[1]

Archbishop Desmond Tutu

I THANK GOD FOR my Hebrew antecedents. I thank God that I too am a descendent of Abraham. I give thanks to God for the gift of the Holy Scriptures made up substantially of the Hebrew Scriptures forming what we conventionally refer to as our Old Testament. Even our New Testament, which would be distinctively Christian, is incomprehensible without taking its Jewish setting seriously. For instance, Jesus is the Greek for Joshua, who led God's people into the promised land, and Christ is the Anointed One—in Hebrew, the Messiah, whose coming was predicted in the Jewish Scriptures and who was longed for so poignantly by the Jews.

I tell you nothing you do not already know. I refer to it only to assert that spiritually I am of Hebrew descent. That legacy has been of crucial importance to me in our struggle against apartheid.

Our Anti-Apartheid Struggle

At the height of the struggle—when apartheid's repression was at its most vicious and it seemed indeed as if the apartheid rulers were firmly ensconced in power, when they had all but knocked the stuffing out of their opponents and they were strutting the stage as invincible cocks of the walk—we turned to the inspiration of our Hebrew tradition and antecedents.

---

1. Much of the content of this chapter comes from: Archbishop Desmond Tutu, "Palestine and Apartheid," keynote address, Friends of Sabeel Conference, Copley Square Episcopal Church, Boston, October 27, 2007.

We were able to revive and sustain our people's hope for their vindication and the ultimate triumph of good over evil, of freedom over injustice and oppression by our references to our biblical traditions. It was often quite exhilarating. I remember once when there had been a massacre in one of our townships, which had been instigated by a sinister Third Force linked to the apartheid security apparatus, our bishops suspended a session of Episcopal Synod to be there as Ezekiel had been with the stunned exiles, to be there in a ministry of presence, and we held a service in one of our ghetto township churches. The people were stunned, devastated by the naked violence of the massacre. I preached and used Exodus 3:1–9, God's words which Yahweh asked Moses to announce to the children of Israel. I said, "Our God is not deaf—our God has heard our cries; our God is not stupid—our God knows our suffering; our God is not blind—God has seen and sees our pain and anguish and . . . yes, our God will come down and set us free." Yes, our God will come down to open the prison doors and lead our leaders from prison, lead them back from exile. For we had learned from our Jewish tradition that God, our God, is notoriously biased, forever taking the side of the weak, the oppressed, the downtrodden against the kings and powerful oppressors. Our God had been met first, not in the sanctuary, but in the mundane world of politics, taking the side of the rabble of slaves against the mighty Pharaoh. God is not neutral, God sided with Uriah the Hittite against his favorite, King David, after his adultery with Bathsheba and murder of Uriah. "Thou art the man." Anywhere else the king could have gotten away with both actions, but not in Israel. It really seemed as if the Jewish Scriptures were written specifically for us. The story of Naboth's vineyard and King Ahab and Jezebel being confronted on Yahweh's behalf by Elijah seemed to have been written especially with our situation in mind, where blacks (not exclusively, but overwhelmingly) were shipped in their millions like so many pawns in population removal schemes and dumped in poverty-stricken Bantustan homelands, hardly able to eke out a living, cut off from the more affluent so-called white South Africa.

The widow, the orphan, and the alien, who in most traditional societies would be the weakest of the weak, seemed to be particular favorites with God, who appeared to have a soft spot for them. And so worship of God's people, however elaborate and ritually correct, would be dismissed as an abomination, unless it made the worshiper have the sensitivity to care for God's favorites (Isa 1:11–16). Even something so obviously religious as a fast was rejected out of hand by this God who could declaim that the kind of fast he wanted was that which fed the hungry, set free the captives—all thoroughly secular activities but which confirmed Yahweh's bias in favor of and concern for those who were hard done by, who were at the end of their tethers, who were so low they could crawl under a snake. We could multiply references to the prophets Amos, Hosea, Jeremiah, Ezekiel, Micah, et al. It reverberates throughout the prophetic writings, this concern for the poor, the hungry, the downtrodden, the widow, the orphan, the alien.

But it was not just in the prophetic oracles. It was so also in the Pentateuch, the Torah, the Scriptures *par excellence* for God's chosen. Extraordinarily in what was perhaps the book most concerned for cultic ritual matters, Leviticus, where holiness referred most frequently to ritual cultic purity, the worshiper, or the Israelite, is bidden to be holy as Yahweh is holy, and just when we imagined that this would be concerned with ritual holiness, we are brought up short that this is a holiness that plays itself out in a concern for the hungry and the poor. "Be holy because I, the Lord your God, am holy," and so you must not glean your fields clean at harvest, leave something for the poor and hungry too (Lev 19:2, 9–10, ESV). Fantastic—God's special people must be holy but this is a holiness that expresses itself in mundane acts of caring, of kindness, and compassion, of humanitarian concern. In Deuteronomy the motive for doing acts of kindness to God's favorites, the widow, the orphan, and the alien is not emulating God's holiness, it is the memory of their former status as slaves in Egypt. That memory, it is implied, would prevent them from inflicting on others the kind of anguish they had experienced. They would never do to others, it is assumed, what had been done to them.

I think they are words to be written in letters of gold as pertinent to the situation we are in.

> Deuteronomy 24:17–22:
> "You shall not pervert the justice due to the sojourner or to the fatherless, or take a widow's garment in pledge; but you shall remember that you were a slave in Egypt and the Lord your God redeemed you from there; therefore I command you to do this.
>
> When you reap your harvest from your field, and have forgotten a sheaf in the field you shall not go back to get it; it shall be for the sojourner, the fatherless, and the widow; that the Lord your god may bless you in all the work of your hands.
>
> When you beat your olive trees, you shall not go over the boughs again; it shall be for the sojourner, the fatherless, and the widow.
>
> When you gather the grapes of your vineyard, you shall not glean it afterward; it shall be for the sojourner, the fatherless, and the widow.
>
> You shall remember that you were a slave in the land of Egypt; therefore I command you to do this." (ESV)

That is how the people of God were expected to behave. If you were set to rule over these people as king these were your marching orders, your manifesto. In the book of Psalms, they continue:

> "Give the king your justice, O God, and your righteousness to the royal son!
>
> May he judge your people with righteousness, and your poor with justice!
>
> May he defend the cause of the poor of the people, give deliverance to the children of the needy, and crush the oppressor!
>
> For he delivers the needy when he calls, the poor and him who has no helper.
>
> He has pity on the weak and the needy, and saves the lives of the needy.
>
> From oppression and violence he redeems their life; and precious is their blood in his sight." (Ps 72:1-2, 4, 12-14, ESV)

The three sections of the Hebrew Scriptures—the Torah, the Prophets, and the Writings—are unanimous in their depiction of the nature of the God revealed in these books.

It was exhilarating preaching to the oppressed and the downtrodden. The well to do, the powerful, often complained that we were mixing religion with politics and we would declare that we were doing no more than in fact preaching the gospel. We would be accused of being political and I retorted, "I don't know which Bible you are reading." "I must say I have never heard the poor complain," and "Bishop Tutu, now you're being political!" If anything they could possibly have said, "You are not political enough."

And God vindicated us. Apartheid's rulers bit the dust as all oppressors have done always, for this is a moral universe, right and wrong in matter. It cannot happen that evil, injustice, and oppression can have the last word. No. Ultimately, goodness, justice, freedom—these will prevail.

What is this to the point?

I could have spent a great deal of time rehearsing what we all know. How I experienced a *déjà vu* when I saw a security checkpoint that Palestinians had to negotiate most of their lives, that I was reminded so painfully of the same checkpoints in apartheid South Africa, when arrogant white policemen treated almost all blacks like dirt. Or, when someone pointed to a house in Jerusalem and said, "That used to be our home, but now it has been taken over by the Israelis," it made me recall so painfully similar statements in Cape Town by coloreds who had been thrown out of their homes and relocated in ghetto townships some distance from town. I could have bemoaned the illegal wall that has encroached on Palestinian land, separated families, divided property, and made what used to be a short walk to school turn into an expensive nightmare voyage running the gauntlet of checkpoints, etc. I could have said there were things that even apartheid South Africa had not done, for example: collective punishment.

I have not gone that route. No, I have chosen a different approach. My address is really a *cri de Coeur*, a cry of anguish from the heart, an impassioned plea to my spiritual relatives, the offspring of Abraham like me—please hear the call, the noble call of your Scriptures, of our Scriptures, to be with the God of the exodus who took the side of a bunch of slaves against the powerful Pharaoh. Be on the side of the God who intervened through his prophet Elijah on behalf of Naboth, hear the plea of your Scriptures, and stand with the God who intervened through his prophet Nathan on behalf of Uriah against King David. Be on the side of the God who revealed a soft spot in his heart for the widow, the orphan, and the alien; be on the side of the God whose "Spirit sends us out to preach good news to the poor." Don't be found fighting against the God, your God, our God who hears the cry of the oppressed, who sees their anguish and who will always come down to deliver them. Be not opposed to the God whose Spirit, when it anoints you, makes you concerned for the poor. This is your calling. If you disobey that calling, if you do not heed it, then as sure as anything one day you will come a cropper. You will probably not succumb to an outside military assault. With the unquestioning support of the USA you are probably impregnable. But you who are called are they who are asked to deal with the oppressed, the weak, and the despised compassionately, caringly, remembering what happened to you in Egypt and much more recently in Germany. Remember and act appropriately. If you reject your calling you may survive for a long time, but you find it is all corrosive inside and one day you will implode.

A recent report by a clinical psychologist, Nufan Yisahi Katrim, at the Hebrew University, speaks of how Israeli soldiers were gratuitously cruel and carried out acts of brutality to Palestinians in the Gaza Strip. When you uphold an unjust dispensation it corrodes your humanity. In South Africa, a former Cabinet Minister showed this. When told of the death of Steve Biko in detention, he said it left him cold.

Thanks be to God for the many, many Jews who know what their divine calling is and who want the Israeli Government to live it out. We believe in a two-state solution—of two sovereign, viable states each with contiguous borders guaranteed as secure by the international community. We condemn acts of terrorism by whomever they are committed. The suicide bomber has to be condemned for targeting innocent civilians. But equally must the Israelis be condemned for their acts of indiscriminate reprisal. We say please learn at least one positive lesson from apartheid South Africa. Under Mr. F. W. de Klerk, who must be commended for his outstanding courage, they decided to negotiate, not with those they liked but with their sworn enemy and they found the security that had eluded them for so long and that had cost so much suffering and blood. It came not from the barrel of a gun. No, it came when the legitimate aspirations and human rights of all were recognized and respected. That was thirteen years ago and the peace is still holding. Many had predicted that South Africa would be overwhelmed by a catastrophic racial bloodbath. It did not happen. It did not happen because they negotiated in good faith with their enemies.

Somebody has said if something happened once then clearly it is something possible. It happened in South Africa, why not in the Middle East?

The world needs the Jews who are faithful to their vocation that has meant so much for the world's morality, of its sense of what is right and wrong, what is good and bad, what is just and unjust, what is oppressive, and what sets people free. Jews are indispensable for a good, compassionate, just, and caring world.

And so are Palestinians.

15

Remarks at the Gaza Donors Conference[1]

The Honorable John Kerry,
Secretary of State (2013–2017)
Cairo, Egypt October 12, 2014

THANK YOU VERY MUCH, Foreign Minister Shoukry. Thank you, Secretary-General Ban Ki-moon; Vice Prime Minister Mustafa; our co-host, Foreign Minister Brende; and our colleague, Cathy Ashton, the EU High Representative. I want to particularly thank President Sisi and Foreign Minister Shoukry for their leadership and for their partnership in their efforts for the Palestinian Authority and to help bring all of us here today for their work with Israel on the cease-fire. And we respect and thank them also for their partnership with the United States, not just in working towards a durable cease-fire, but also in helping to pull together, and helping to pull together this massive reconstruction effort.

But President Sisi's efforts, I think it's fair to say, have really helped to reaffirm the pivotal role that Egypt has played in this region for so long. The same can also be said of Foreign Minister Brende and Norway, whose historic connection and commitment to these issues go back more than two decades to the Oslo Accords, and I'm personally always impressed by the deep engagement of Norway in efforts to make peace, not just here but

---

1. John Kerry, "Remarks at the Gaza Donors Conference," speech, Cairo, October 12, 2014), US State Department, http://www.state.gov/secretary/remarks/2014/10/232896.htm. Public domain.

elsewhere in the world. And of course, President Abbas, thank you for your perseverance and your partnership.

This has been a difficult few months on a difficult issue in a difficult neighborhood, and no one feels that more than the people of Gaza. This summer, as we've heard in some of the statistics that Secretary-General shared with us, more than half a million Gazans had to flee their homes and seek safety. Twenty thousand homes were destroyed or severely damaged, and more than a hundred thousand people remain displaced. And winter is fast approaching.

I have been to Gaza at a time like this, and I will never forget traveling to Izbet Abed Rabo in Gaza in 2009 and watching children playing in the rubble, seeing little Palestinian girls playing where just months earlier, homes and buildings had stood. The humanitarian challenge then was enormous, and shockingly, amazingly—and every speaker has mentioned we are back yet again—the humanitarian challenge is no less enormous in 2014. So the people of Gaza do need our help desperately—not tomorrow, not next week, but they need it now. And that's why we are all gathered here.

I am proud, personally, that the people of the United States have been working to do their part. We provided $118 million in immediate humanitarian assistance at the time of the crisis, at its height, and the $84 million that we also provided to UNRWA for operations.

Today, I'm pleased to announce an additional immediate $212 million in assistance to the Palestinian people, and obviously we will have to see how things develop in the days ahead. But this immediate money will mean immediate relief and reconstruction, and this money will help meet the Palestinian Authority's budget needs. This money will, we hope, help promote security and stability, and economic development, and it will provide for immediate distribution of food, medicine, and shelter materials for hundreds of thousands for the coming winter. And it is money that is going to help reconstruct Gaza's damaged water and sanitation system, so that Palestinians in Gaza will have access to water that they can drink and homes that they can actually start rebuilding.

Taken together, the United States has provided more than $400 million in assistance to the Palestinians over this last year, $330 million just since this summer's conflict began. But I will say to all of you, and I think everybody knows it: We come here with a sense of awesome responsibility and even resignation about the challenge that we face because we all know that so much more needs to be done, even though there have been encouraging steps.

I'm particularly grateful to UN Secretary-General Ban Ki-moon and Special Coordinator Robert Serry for helping to broker an important agreement between Israel and the Palestinian Authority for an end-use monitoring mechanism. And we appreciate Israel's cooperation in continuing to provide humanitarian access to Gaza through its crossing, which is essential if all of this is going to work.

We welcome that Israel has recently announced new measures that should allow increased trade in agricultural goods between Gaza and the West Bank, and more permits for Palestinian business leaders to enter Israel. We hope to see many more positive steps announced and implemented in the coming weeks and months. And we need to get back to the difficult work not just of reconstruction and recovery in Gaza, but of actually building Gaza's economy for the long term and developing its institutions under the Palestinian Authority.

The Palestinian Authority and President Abbas must be empowered in all that we do in order to define and determine Gaza's future. There is, simply, no other way forward, and all of us here need to help the ability of the Palestinian Authority to be able to deliver. There are many steps that we can take. We can and should see Palestinian Authority customs officials at Gaza's borders. We can and should help the PA to expand its control in Gaza, streamline Gaza's workforce, and continue to play a key role in the end-use monitoring mechanism for Gaza. And this is absolutely essential, because as long as there is a possibility that Hamas could fire rockets on Israeli civilians at any time, the people of Gaza will remain at risk of future conflict. And even as we work to reconstruct Gaza, we cannot lose sight of the importance of the long-term economic investment for the Palestinian economy that can create a vibrant private sector.

Shortly after I became Secretary of State, working with the Quartet and international local business leaders, we launched the Initiative for the Palestinian Economy. The IPE is a comprehensive plan for Palestinian economic growth in the billions of dollars. And this effort is not about donor projects or corporate social responsibility; we're talking about real investment. We had McKinsey and Company come in and make analysis of every sector of the Palestinian economy and make a determination about those areas where you could actually reduce unemployment from 21 percent to 8 percent in a period of three years. We're talking about real investment that produces real jobs and opportunities for thousands of Palestinians, and that is what is going to make the difference over the long term.

Now, we were making real progress, laying down specific projects, creating new opportunities for goods and peoples to move in and out, when tragically conflict once again replaced dialogue. But what I really want to underscore to everyone is what all of us know, but not everyone perhaps wants to confront. This is the third time in less than six years that together with the people of Gaza we have been forced to confront a reconstruction effort. This is the third time in less than six years that we've seen war break out and Gaza left in rubble. This is the third time in less than six years that we've had to rely on a cease-fire, a temporary measure, to halt the violence.

Now, I don't think there's any person here who wants to come yet again to rebuild Gaza only to think that two years from now or less we're going to be back at the same table talking about rebuilding Gaza again because the fundamental issues have not been dealt with. A cease-fire is not peace, and we've got to find a way to get back to the table and help people make tough choices, real choices. Choices that everybody in this room and outside of it understands have been on the table for too long. Choices about more than just a cease-fire. Because even the most durable of cease-fires is not a substitute for peace. Even the most durable of cease-fires is not a substitute of security for Israel and a state and dignity for the Palestinians.

As everyone here knows, last year the United States joined Israel and the Palestinian Authority in renewed peace negotiations towards a final status settlement. The truth that has not been talked about very much, and there are still legitimate reasons for maintaining that respect for the process, but the truth is that real and significant process was made on substantive issues. Longtime gaps were narrowed and creative ideas were actively being deployed to solve remaining differences.

So I say clearly and with deep conviction here today: The United States remains fully, totally committed to returning to the negotiations not for the sake of it, but because the goal of this conference and the future of this region demand it. There is nothing sustainable about the status quo. In the end, the underlying causes of discontent and suspicion and anger that exist in Israel, the West Bank, and Gaza can only be eliminated by resolving the conflict itself. There is no way to fully satisfy the parties' various demands, no way to bring the full measure of recovery to Gaza, without a long-term prospect for peace that builds confidence about the future. And everything else will be a Band-Aid fix, not a long-term resolution. Everything else will still regrettably fail to address the underlying discontent and suspicion in both Israel and Gaza and the West Bank. Everything else will be the prisoner of impatience that has brought us to this unacceptable and unsustainable status quo.

Make no mistake: What was compelling about a two-state solution a year ago is even more compelling today. Now, I know that in Israel as well as in Gaza and the West Bank, most people would quickly tell you today that as much as they want peace, they think it is a distant dream, something that's just not possible now. The problem is, having said that, no one then offers an alternative that makes sense. I say it is unacceptable to want peace but then buy into an attitude that makes it inevitable that you cannot have peace. It is unacceptable to simply shrug one's shoulders, say peace isn't possible now, and then by doing nothing to make it possible, actually add to the greater likelihood of a downward spiral.

So I say to you clearly and with great conviction: the United States will continue to work with our partners to find a way forward. We are convinced that the needs to both parties on even the most critical issues can be met, and that with common sense, goodwill, and courage we can not only address the long-term needs of Gaza, but we can actually achieve a lasting peace between Israel, the Palestinians, and all their neighbors. We have been clear from day one about the difficulty of the challenge ahead, and we knew there would be tough times. But in the end, we all want the same things: security for the Israelis; freedom, dignity, and a state for the Palestinians; peace and prosperity for both peoples.

So this is a time for leadership. It's a time for leaders to lead. And at a time when extremism, which offers no constructive vision for the future, is capitalizing on the vacuum, it is imperative for all of us to fill that vacuum with a prospect of peace. That's what the people of our countries expect from us, and that's what we must offer them—no less. So out of this conference must come not just money, but a renewed commitment from everybody to work for a peace that meets the aspirations of all—for Israelis, for Palestinians, and for all the peoples of this region. And I promise you the full commitment of President Obama, myself, and the United States of America to try to achieve that. Thank you.

16

Protestifying: A Pentecostal Reflection on Interfaith Learning and Political Action

Dr. Paul Nathan Alexander

A "TESTIMONY" IS BOTH offering a witness's account in a courtroom and going to church and telling about something good that's happened. When I was a kid, on Sunday nights at church we had "testimony services" where people would share things that God had done in their lives. We'd say "amen" and "thank you, Jesus" and rejoice with those who rejoiced. People also had "prayer requests" where they asked others to pray for things that they needed. These prayer requests weren't just "complaints," they identified real struggles and problems in the real world that people in that little church in southeast Kansas thought were worth sharing with friends and with God. In a way, those prayer requests were protests. They were protesting the flu that their five-year-old daughter had, or the difficult employee that they had to work with, or the lack of work and lack of income to take care of the family. Oftentimes, one week's protests became the next week's testimonies as children recovered and work was found. Sometimes one week's prayer request was reiterated the next week as well.

Protestimony is a word I made up that signifies a story that is both good news and bad news. It's a prayer request, complaining, and testifying all rolled into one. It's a witness's story about trouble with an eye toward better things happening. I'm going to try both to testify and protest at the same time and in so doing I might speak such a garbled word that it sounds like I'm speaking in tongues. But if I do, I trust that the Spirit will help somebody offer an interpretation so that something good can come from this protestimony by a Pentecostal country boy from Kansas.

2010

In March 2010 I participated in the "Christ at the Checkpoint: Theology in the Service of Justice and Peace" conference hosted by Palestinian Christians in Bethlehem, and three months later in June 2010 I participated in the "National Jewish-Evangelical Conversation" in Washington, DC.

At the "Christ at the Checkpoint" conference I presented an address entitled, "What Pentecostals and Charismatics Can *Do* for Peace with Justice for Israelis and Palestinians." I also met and learned from many Palestinian evangelicals and Pentecostals living on both sides of the "Green Line"—in the West Bank (Bethlehem, Ramallah, Jerusalem) and in the State of Israel (Nazareth, Jerusalem). I met a Palestinian Christian family who had lost the land that had been in their family for generations to the building of a Jewish city—called a "settlement." It didn't seem fair or just for the State of Israel to confiscate land from these Palestinian families and then build homes for Jewish families on it. It was illegal under international law, but nobody could, or would, stop Israel from doing it—and the homes were being built by the thousands. I walked in a nonviolent demonstration with Israelis, Jews, Palestinians, Muslims, Christians, and others in order to show opposition to the destruction of a Palestinian Christian's land near Bethlehem. I was videoing from within the protest when Israeli soldiers fired sound grenades into the crowd to disperse us. It worked! I ran. But we came back together a few seconds later, and I was so full of adrenaline I shouted "Salaam Shalom!" repeatedly. Then we had some engaging conversations with the soldiers and talked about what was happening (which I videoed and it's online if you want to see it). After an hour or so of the soldiers blocking our nonviolent walk down the street, we dispersed, and then the soldiers took off their helmets and laid down their guns and pulled out their water bottles, and I walked back down the same street with a couple of Palestinian friends and we walked past the soldiers and went to where we were going to begin with—the Palestinian Christian's home. I met him and he showed me what the State of Israel was planning to do to his home and land and how much he'd already lost (several acres). His granddaughter was swinging in a swingset that was soon to no longer exist. My Palestinian friend, who is committed to nonviolent resistance, said, "I will never give up. I will never stop [working] against you, against your occupation, and your army, if you work in our land. I promise you, where[ever] you go, you will see my face." I felt sad, and frustrated.

While I was there I also helped write the Bethlehem Evangelical Affirmation, which seemed to be remarkably safe and set a low bar.

> We recognize that this is the time to resolve the Israeli-Palestinian conflict. Therefore, we are convinced that the Holy Spirit is leading us at such a time as this to unite as Christians throughout the world in order to pray and work for a just peace in Israel and Palestine. To this end, we commit to reconnect with the local Palestinian church and to listen and learn from all those who follow Jesus in the Holy Land and to share their stories with our own faith communities. We further commit to work together to advocate changes in public policy and so achieve a just and lasting resolution of the conflict. Our vision and our hope is that Israelis and Palestinians will live in justice and peace in the land of the Holy One.[1]

Notice that the affirmation included both learning and sharing stories as well as advocating policy changes. It seemed to us that it was okay to try to influence policy makers (not only in Israel, Palestine, and the USA, but throughout the world) toward justice and peace for everyone in the land. Sometimes laws need to change and Christians can use their voices to speak up for changes that they think are just.

Three months later, I was in Washington, DC, along with fifteen or so other evangelical/Pentecostal leaders meeting with about fifteen or so American Jewish leaders. I mentioned the "Christ at the Checkpoint" conference and learned from a few rabbis that the name of the conference was very offensive to some Jews. I also learned that some Jewish leaders thought I shouldn't be associating with several of the Palestinian Christians at the conference (as well as others who were there). I wanted to learn how to advocate for both Israelis and Palestinians, so I asked questions and listened carefully. I was glad to learn about the "Three Ds" that are used to test what people say about the State of Israel—Delegitimization, Demonization, and Double Standards. I knew I hadn't delegitimized Israel, demonized Israel, or applied double standards. However, I realized that just as some people use those methods against Israel, some use the same three methods against Palestinians and delegitimize their national aspirations, demonize Palestinians, and apply double standards. It also helped me see clearly that not only do I not want to demonize anyone, I also don't want to romanticize either Jews or Palestinians. I'm just a person and prefer neither to be demonized nor

---

1 Kuttab, "Where Do We Go," 181–82.

romanticized—both are false images of me—and both demonizing and romanticizing are ways of not relating to people as the people they are. I realized that "humanizing" everyone as much as possible, and me too, would be better for all of us (except that sometimes being romanticized can help your cause). The conveners of the "Jewish-Evangelical Conversation" invited me to give a presentation at the next year's meeting in 2011.

2011

In June 2011, the participants of the "National Jewish-Evangelical Conversation" met again in Washington, DC. The topics we discussed included "Zionism and Varieties of Jewish Identification," "Current Trends in American Evangelicalism and Christian Zionism," and the one that I helped lead, "Middle East Christians: What are the Circumstances of Christians in Israel, the West Bank, and throughout the ever changing Middle East?" We also devoted a session to exploring "How evangelicals and Jews, out of their specific traditions, study and arrive at religious, moral, and ethical positions concerning new and emerging issues in society."

I began by sharing about my Pentecostal tradition that emerged in Los Angeles in the early 1900s to a significant degree because of the leadership of William Seymour, a son of former slaves from Louisiana. Their multi-ethnic and gender inclusive church worshiped in a barn. In order to illustrate dangerous theology and ethics I showed pictures of a light-skinned, European looking Jesus with a rifle and a light-skinned, European looking Jesus with an M-16 and a Colt 45 knocking on the door "of our hearts"and commented that even though I followed a violent God for many years (and many Christians still do), I found a different way of seeking justice and making peace. Then I showed a picture of the darker-skinned "Forensic Jesus" that the British Broadcasting Company (BBC) developed based on archaeological excavations of first-century human remains in the area where Jesus lived.

I then showed pictures of Palestinian and Israeli Christian families who live and minister and work in Israel and the West Bank, and I highlighted the "Christ at the Checkpoint: Hope in the Midst of Conflict" mission statement for the then-forthcoming 2012 conference in Bethlehem.

> The aim of *Christ at the Checkpoint* is to provide an opportunity for Evangelical Christians who take the Bible seriously to prayerfully seek a better awareness of issues of peace, justice, and reconciliation. The conference will: 1) Empower and encourage the Palestinian church. 2) Expose the realities of the injustices in the Palestinian territories and create awareness of the

obstacles to reconciliation and peace. 3) Create a platform for serious engagement with Christian Zionism and an open forum for ongoing dialogue between all positions within the Evangelical theological spectrum. 4) Motivate participants to become advocates for the reconciliation work of the church in Palestine/Israel and its ramifications for the Middle East and the world.

I am a very ignorant person and I make a lot of mistakes. I then showed a picture of John Hagee with a word bubble above his head that read, "Christians United for Israelis and Palestinians! Peace, justice, and security for all!" John Hagee is a Pentecostal preacher who founded the Christian Zionist organization Christians United for Israel (CUFI) and I thought it would be good to tweak it to include both Israelis and Palestinians—CUFIP. I concluded with a slide that read, "Now what? What the world needs, and what Palestinian Evangelicals are hoping for, is Christians United for Israel and Palestine. Better yet, Christians and Jews United for Israel and Palestine. I am encouraged to be pro-Israel and pro-Palestine at the same time, how is this possible?"

I later asked several rabbis how one both engages in interfaith dialogue and learning while also advocating for specific policy changes in the USA, Israel, and Palestine, and one rabbi responded, "You can't." He is only one Jewish leader, and other Jewish leaders disagree with him, but he shared the genuine perspective that talking with some people precludes working with others (or vice versa).

I felt sad about this. I have Palestinian friends and Israeli friends, Muslim friends and Jewish friends. I appreciate learning from all of them. Which is why I was pleased to be invited to participate in the Christian Leadership Initiative sponsored by the American Jewish Committee and the Shalom Hartman Institute in 2012 and 2013.

2012 and 2013

In March 2012 I attended the second "Christ at the Checkpoint" conference in Bethlehem. At the conclusion of the conference the organizers distributed the "Christ at the Checkpoint Manifesto" that they had written.

- The kingdom of God has come. Evangelicals must reclaim the prophetic role in bringing peace, justice, and reconciliation in Palestine and Israel.
- Reconciliation recognizes God's image in one another.

- Racial ethnicity alone does not guarantee the benefits of the Abrahamic Covenant.
- The church in the land of the Holy One has borne witness to Christ since the days of Pentecost. It must be empowered to continue to be light and salt in the region, if there is to be hope in the midst of conflict.
- Any exclusive claim to land of the Bible in the name of God is not in line with the teaching of Scripture.
- All forms of violence must be refuted unequivocally.
- Palestinian Christians must not lose the capacity to self-criticism if they wish to remain prophetic.
- There are real injustices taking place in the Palestinian territories and the suffering of the Palestinian people can no longer be ignored. Any solution must respect the equity and rights of Israel and Palestinian communities.
- For Palestinian Christians, the occupation is the core issue of the conflict.
- Any challenge of the injustices taking place in the Holy Land must be done in Christian love. Criticism of Israel and the occupation cannot be confused with anti-Semitism and the delegitimization of the State of Israel.
- Respectful dialogue between Palestinian and Messianic believers must continue. Though we may disagree on secondary matters of theology, the gospel of Jesus and his ethical teaching take precedence.
- Christians must understand the global context for the rise of extremist Islam. We challenge stereotyping of all faith forms that betray God's commandment to love our neighbors and enemies.

In July 2012 and July 2013, I, along with fourteen other professors from the USA, participated in the Christian Leadership Initiative in Jerusalem, hosted by the Shalom Hartman Institute and the American Jewish Committee. For two weeks each summer I thoroughly enjoyed studying "the central ideas of Judaism in the areas of ethics, faith, and politics, canonical Jewish texts, the challenges of modernity and the State of Israel, diverse ideologies and religious practices of contemporary world Jewry, intellectual foundations of religious pluralism and interreligious studies, and practical methods for Christian engagement with Jews."[2] I learned so much through *havruta* study and engaging conversations. One strong area of empathy that I have

2. "Christian Leadership Initiative."

with Israeli Jews in particular but the Jewish people as a whole (recognizing that some Jews don't desire my empathy for this) is with their efforts to build a state in the same ways that so many other nations and peoples have tried to build states—on land owned or lived on by others that is taken and held with violence and law. But this deserves no special critique because that's just the way states are built—either through conquest or revolution. So Israelis are in a particularly difficult position as they try to justify their existence to other people who benefit from predecessors having done the same thing. I specifically think of Euro-Americans, i.e., "white" people, in the USA who continue to benefit from the fact that their ancestors took the land from Native Americans through violence and law. The State of Israel, like all others, came into being with bloodshed, shifts in who controlled land and resources, and the use of law. The State of Israel, and every state that exists, continues to exist and flourish (to greater or lesser degrees) with the threat or actuality of killing and the use of political power. This is the way states exist, and Jews again have one, and it's a hell of a mess for them to figure out how to make it a good one—although they're doing much better than some other states in the region and in the world. If Palestinians ever get one, or the Kurds, it'll be a hell of a mess figuring those out too—just like any pluralistic society that allows open argument, debate, and shifts of power and control.

Another wonderful highlight, of many, was singing and fellowshipping with young "charismatic" Jews in Tel Aviv who were practicing Judaism in ways that resonated deeply with me. From the guitars to the relaxed structure to the youthful intensity and desire for renewal, I "got it" and was so thankful for the experience.

In December 2013 I helped convene an ecumenical conference in Philadelphia entitled "Impact: Holy Land." The speakers consisted of Messianic Jews, Israeli Christians, Palestinian Christians, and American Christians. People of all faiths were welcome, but all of the speakers were "followers of Jesus." We described the event like this:

> The lands of Israel, Judea, Samaria, Galilee, the West Bank, Palestinian territories, Gaza, State of Israel, State of Palestine, the land of holy origins, and the Holy Land are contested areas with contested names. Different followers of Jesus (as well as many others of no faith tradition and other faith traditions) have different perspectives on the histories and potential futures for the peoples living in these lands. Many are seeking to have a positive "impact" on the area—for Israelis, or Palestinians, or both.
>
> We think that North Americans need to listen well to the diverse stories and perspectives of Palestinian Christians,

Christian Zionists, Messianic Jews, and other followers of Jesus. All of these perspectives reflect serious engagement with both scriptural texts and political realities in lands that carry deep meaning for many of us.

We seek not to solve the Israeli-Palestinian situation at this conference, but we do seek to convene a conversation where diverse brothers and sisters in Christ—Palestinian, Israeli, North American—can share honestly and lovingly in a space where their perspectives are respected, even as we know we will not agree on everything.

We invite you to participate with an open mind and an open heart in this important conversation. We welcome Jews, Muslims, and anyone interested to participate in the conference.

The goals for our time together are modest. After our few days together, we hope that you will:

- build relationships with other people committed to loving one another and being active peacemakers.
- get to know Christians from Palestine, Israel, and other parts of the world.
- see that folks can disagree on something very important, while still learning together and loving one another.
- be able to model peacemaking.
- increase support and love and relationship with Israelis and Palestinians in a way that values both.
- engage in deep church-building and discipleship.

Everyone has a reason not to come—what's yours?[3]

2014

In 2014 I was on sabbatical and did not attend either the "Christ at the Checkpoint" conference in March or the "National Jewish-Evangelical Conversation in June." Perhaps I was tired. However, I did drink some tea with a few American Jewish leaders who shared with me a very helpful document: "Elevating the Discussion to Advance Peace: Distinguishing Between Criticism of and Bias against Israel," most of which is reproduced below.

> To enhance understanding and inter-group civility, it is necessary to distinguish between criticism of and bias against Israel. Stifling debate or dissent is NOT our intent. The Israeli-Palestinian conflict is deeply complicated. A fair hearing must

3. "Why Impact Holy Land."

be given to the claims and aspirations of both sides. We seek a richer discussion, one that is not sidetracked by base and baseless assertions. Fortunately, the universe of criticism about the policies and actions either of Israel or the Palestinians is very broad. There are a handful of limited situations in which that criticism moves into troubling territory. Criticism of Israel is not necessarily anti-Semitic any more than criticism of Palestinians is necessarily anti-Muslim or anti-Arab. Context—as well as clarity of intent—is important. For instance, a critical comment about an Israeli or Palestinian policy or practice made by someone who recognizes the right of each people to self-governance resonates differently than a similar comment made by someone who rejects that right. Among the issues that are legitimate topics for discussion are: land for peace, the status of Jewish settlements over the 1949 Armistice Line, future borders of a Palestinian State, Jerusalem, and treatment of Palestinians.

These are appropriate topics of debate, both within the Jewish community and general society. Israel, as a Western democracy, is often held to a different standard than other countries in the region. When fair-minded people offer such critiques they should be respected and heard. When debate is free of the concerns detailed below, others will listen with respect.

We are concerned when critique of Israel is characterized by:

1. Denying the very legitimacy of the State of Israel and the right of the Jewish people as a nation to sovereignty in any portion of its ancient homeland.

2. Criticizing the efforts of the State of Israel to defend itself without considering the right to self-defense or the causes that lead to the need for self-defense.

3. Assigning to Israel responsibility for all Palestinian violence and incitement, or justifying all Palestinian violence and incitement.

4. Failing to acknowledge when Israel takes risks for peace and takes positive steps in the treatment of Palestinians and to end the conflict.

5. Criticizing Israel for its wrongs while not criticizing others involved in the conflict for their wrongs or identifying Israel as the root of all the problems in the Middle East, because moral integrity is linked to moral consistency.

6. Employing certain anti-Jewish motifs, such as those that assert Jewish control or conspiracy to control finance, media, or government.

7. Using outdated Christian theological understandings of Judaism and the Jewish People, which most Churches have repudiated since the Holocaust, in discourse about the Israeli-Palestinian conflict. These include: A) Those supersessionist and replacement theologies that cast Jewish religious beliefs and practices as primitive, legalistic, tribal, and parochial in the face of Christian universalism, in application to the Israel-Palestinian conflict; B) Assignment of biblical responsibilities and judgments to the modern state of Israel that are not assigned to any other country; C) That theological view that holds that the Jewish people lost all right to the land because of their rejection of Christianity; D) The use of biblical texts that assign to Israel only prophecies of punishment and doom and not those of restoration to the land; E) The use of the *adversos Iudaeos* tradition which employs classic medieval Christian anti-Jewish stereotypes and extends the classic Christian teaching of contempt from Judaism and the Jewish people to Zionism and the State of Israel. These theologies betray deep-rooted theological bias, not just against Israel, but also against Judaism and the Jewish people. Careful attention must be given to use of the language of the cross or deicide imagery in describing the actions of the modern Jewish state.

These criteria and ideas express a broad consensus amongst American Jewish leadership. When consistent with these criteria, those who raise critiques of Israel's policies will find conversation partners in the American Jewish community.[4]

I heard a joke in Jerusalem. After one trip to Israel and Palestine people think they can write a book. After two trips to Israel and Palestine people think they can write an article. After three trips to Israel and Palestine people aren't sure what to say any more. The more I listen and learn the more I see the complexity, but I'm not convinced that this means I must be silent. I think the State of Israel is trying to be a religiously pluralistic democracy and there are many Jews working for justice and peace despite the fact that others are not—the range of Jewish religious and political perspectives from the "lefts" to the "rights" is tremendously broad. Palestinians are continuing to lose their land and hope for a Palestinian state is diminishing, and many

---

4. Felson, "Elevating the Discussion."

Palestinians are working nonviolently for civil and human rights even while other Palestinians are not.

I wrote an article during the Hamas-Israel war in Summer 2014, entitled "Let Hope Die." Perhaps it is the protest part of my protestimony. So I'm sharing it as my most recent fumbling attempt at engaging in interfaith learning and political action after my body has shared space, and my eyes have shared contact, and my ears have listened, and my mind and soul have struggled with Jews and Palestinians in cafes, meeting rooms, synagogues, churches, and dusty roads.

Let Hope Die[5]

"Keep Hope Alive" is a rallying cry for disenfranchised and marginalized people, and it's been around for a long time—especially among Palestinians regarding their hope for a Palestinian state. But hope is also dangerous, for "Hope deferred makes the heart sick" (Prov 13:12).

In *The Dark Side of Hope: A Psychological Investigation and Cultural Commentary*, Karen Kress argues that when adults "hope for the impossible, genuinely useful steps toward getting much of what they want may be ignored." Social psychologists have also found that hope increases one's ability to tolerate pain.

> In an interesting experiment, Carla Berg, Rick Snyder, and Nancy Hamilton (2008) used guided imagery in what they called a hope induction. For about 15 minutes, research participants were asked to think of an important goal and to imagine how they might achieve it. A comparison condition asked participants to read a home organization book for fifteen minutes. All participants were then asked to immerse their non-dominant hand in a bucket of ice water for as long as they could (up to five minutes). This is a standard measure of pain tolerance, and it is painful but not harmful. Participants receiving the brief hope induction kept their hand immersed for about 150 seconds, whereas those in the comparison condition kept their hand immersed for about ninety seconds. Hope did not affect reports on how painful the experience was, but it did increase the ability to tolerate it.[6]

The Israeli-Palestinian situation is not a bucket of ice water. But the correlations are that hope can be a way of keeping people in situations of suffering

---

5. Alexander, "Let Hope Die."
6 Kerry, "Can Hope Be Bad?," and Peterson, "Good Hope."

for longer periods of time and that if they hope for the impossible they can continue to be taken advantage of and not do practical things to make their situation better. Hoping for something you don't have the power to change or that is unrealistic can be destructive.

- Hamas isn't fighting for a Palestinian state next to Israel. They're fighting futilely against Israel, and there is no way they can ever win. They're outgunned, outflanked, out-resourced, and engaged in a foolish, deadly, self-destructive, anti-Semitic battle that they will perpetually lose. Every time. If they think their little garage-welded rockets can actually do anything against the Israel Defense Forces they're deluded—even if they get better weapons. Yes, they tragically kill civilians and soldiers, but it's a losing battle, and Israel will continue to overpower them. This can (and probably will) continue for decades and decades and decades, unless Hamas changes its charter and accepts Israel and uses means of negotiation other than violence. That would be wisdom. But I'm not hopeful.

- Israel is fighting violently to exist and flourish. And it always will. To expect otherwise is naive. When Israel is attacked, it will bomb the life out of whoever does it—pretty much like any other nation or state with the military and political ability to do so. Israel will fight overpoweringly hard—and win. I don't think anyone should be hopeful that this will change, because it won't. Don't waste your time with that.

- If you think Jesus is going to come back and solve this in your lifetime, let that hope die, too, friend. It ain't gonna happen (if you don't believe me, check back ten years from now and see where that hope got you, and then ten years after that, and then ten years after that . . .). And neither Israel nor Hamas is going to follow Jesus' teachings to "love your enemies." The relevance of Jesus to this situation is not as a flying-through-the-sky Savior who will make it all okay, nor as a teacher of moral wisdom to organizations not interested in his inability to defend one's self or cause with violence. The relevance of Jesus could, however, be for people who give a damn about his teachings and think Christianity can sometimes be a good thing (as well as acknowledging that it can be a destructive thing, too), and then if those people actually live them out in at least authentic (even if clumsy) attempts at doing something slightly helpful.

So don't put your hope in Hamas to be wise, and don't put your hope in Israel not to fight disproportionably hard, and don't put your hope in Jesus to magically fix this. Don't. Or, if you insist on one or more of the previous three hopes, let's start there and move on. Perhaps something like this:

- Dear Hamas, accept the existence of the State of Israel and stop fighting. You just look ridiculous.
- Dear Israel, don't kill so many civilians with all your super powers. We know, you're a badass, but you look ridiculous, too.
- Dear Jesus, please come back and fix the world. It sucks.

There, now that we've either let hope die or implored the people with power to do different things, now what?

- Reconsider the situation from a centuries-long economic perspective. If you buy a good investment—like a rental property—it can appreciate over time, becoming more valuable, and it can also produce a decent income along the way. That's what nation building is. It's land and resources, wealth and control—a long-term investment. The Holy Land is perhaps some of the most valuable real estate in the world because it's sacred to at least three religions totaling several billion people. Israel and the West Bank and Gaza aren't for short-term flippers who buy a house, rehab it, and then sell it for a profit—or for stock day traders. It's a buy and hold (but nobody's selling, so it's more of a take and hold).
- Regardless of what you think about political solutions for all the people living in the region (one state, two state, three state, four; if you've got a clue please tell me more), I think it's good to know that there are Jews and Muslims who get along and work together and that there are Israelis and Palestinians who get along and work together. So perhaps the place to focus our energy is on building up and strengthening relationships and joint projects among the diversities that will be ever present.
- Which brings us back to Jesus (since he's not coming back to us). "Blessed are the peacemakers, for they are the children of God." But blessings can also be curses, so "Cursed are the peacemakers, for they are the children of God" also has a nice ring to it. And regardless of whether it's a blessing or a curse (or both), it's important. Because real people are really suffering, and hatred, racism, bitterness, revenge, and death are intensely real. So go meet some Israelis and tell them you love both them and Palestinians (and want the best for both), and go meet some Palestinians and tell them you love both them and Israelis (and want the best for both). Really. And then just listen (and ask a few questions). Let hope die, but not love.

But telling Israelis and Palestinians that you love them both is not enough (oh, that it were). But if you do love them, or think you can (and even if you can't, love is hard sometimes and not necessary to do good work), go ahead and support and work with organizations that help bring Israelis and Palestinians (and others) together for difficult conversations, pained truth-telling, and humble learning; for collaboration and creativity in the arts, humanities, and sciences; for inter-religious dialogue and education; and for political action for civil and human rights that improves the lives of the citizens of Israel and Palestine—regardless of the status of a final status.

An interminable conflict has winners and losers—some benefit from the status quo (those with more power and resources). And the resolution of a conflict has winners and losers—some lose when the status quo changes (those who get less power and fewer resources). So both Israelis and Palestinians have a lot to lose in a "solution," and neither of them is going anywhere.

So this war still rages, with Israelis and Palestinians huddled in bomb shelters and innocent civilians dying and people with weapons both killing and being killed. And yet it shall end. And there will probably be another one. And if you let go of hope, you can get to work building a better society that's still going to be there when the sun rises the day after your funeral.

Bibliography

Alexander, Paul. "Let Hope Die." *Evangelicals for Social Action*. July 24, 2014. http://www.evangelicalsforsocialaction.org/holistic-ministry/let-hope-die/

"Christian Leadership Initiative." Hartmann Institute. Accessed June 18, 2016. http://hartman.org.il/Programs_View.asp?Program_Id=15&Cat_Id=291&Cat_Type=Programs.

Felson, Ethan, Yehiel Poupko, and David Sandmel. "Elevating the Discussion to Advance Peace: Distinguishing Between Criticism of and Bias against Israel." 2014. Accessed June 18, 2016. Http://engage.jewishpublicaffairs.org/blog/comments.jsp?blog_entry_KEY=7127&t=.

Kerry, Susan K. "Can Hope Be Bad?" *Psychology Today*. March 22, 2013. http://www.psychologytoday.com/blog/creating-in-flow/201303/can-hope-be-bad.

Kuttab, Johnathan, "Where Do We Go From Here?" In *Christ at the Checkpoint: Theology in the Service of Justice and Peace*, edited by Paul Alexander, 179–82. Eugene, OR: Pickwick, 2012.

Peterson, Christopher. "Good Hope and Bad Hope." *Psychology Today*, July 24, 2010. http://www.psychologytoday.com/blog/the-good-life/201007/good-hope-and-bad-hope.

"Why Impact Holy Land." *Evangelicals for Social Action*. Accessed June 18, 2016. http://impactholyland.org/why-impact-holy-land/.

Part V

An End to Violence and Vision for Peace

©Mae Elise Cannon
"Turn from evil and do good; seek peace and pursue it."
Psalm 34:14 (NIV)

17

Millennial Voices for Peace[1]

Statement of Principles

MILLENNIAL CHRISTIANS ACROSS AMERICA are uniting in an emerging movement seeking peace and justice in the Holy Land. As inhabitants of an increasingly interconnected world, as followers of Christ who believe that faith should inform action, as United States citizens invested in the endeavors of our country, and as friends and family members of those actively experiencing the conflict in the Holy Land, we hold a personal connection to this land and to its people.

We share in the heritage of faith and tradition that was born out of the Holy Land, and we desire to see redemption and flourishing in the land. We hope to be ambassadors of peace and reconciliation and advocates for both the Palestinian and Israeli people (2 Cor 5:18–20).

We are inspired by those of different faiths who seek to understand the experience of the other under a mutual respect and shared commitment to peace. We are inspired by all who live in fear and oppression yet choose to love their enemies and pray for those who dispossess, terrorize, or oppress them (Matt 5:44).

We believe all children—be they Israeli or Palestinian—have the right to live in safety, free from violence, fear, and want. We believe it is God's will that all the children of this land live in peace and without fear (Matt 19:14).

We believe that frustration without action or compassion will never lead to positive change. Thus, we are dedicated to working towards

1. Available on the Millennial Voices for Peace (MVP) web page at http://www.millennialvoicesforpeace.com/statement-of-principles/.

constructive outcomes for those who experience the destructive power of conflict. We are committed to being quick to hear, slow to speak, and slow to anger (Jas 1:19).

We call for the end to all violence, vengeance (retribution), fear, and hatred of Palestinians toward Israelis and Israelis toward Palestinians. We are committed to reconciliation and nonviolent bilateral change, believing that this is the only way to achieve a long-term solution and a lasting peace that affirms the God-given dignity of all people. We reject the notion that advocacy is practiced within a narrative in which we must choose between polarized sides. We challenge all arguments that place narratives unavoidably and inalterably in opposition to each other. We instead seek to tread a different path, in which the historic and present pain and suffering of all peoples are heard, felt, and validated, and in which a future solution represents the legitimate, holistic needs of both Palestinians and Israelis.

Violent acts of terror do not advance the cause for peace and justice, but undermine those who pursue it. We believe that sustainable peace cannot be fully realized in the presence of terrorism, nor under the realities of military occupation. Long-term solutions do not include an indefinite occupation, as it is a significant contributor to poverty in the Palestinian territories and source of fear and oppression for all people in the Holy Land. We stand alongside the Israeli and Palestinian men, women, and children leading the way on this difficult journey toward peace and justice.

It is time to venture beyond solidarity and into peaceful activism. As Millennial Voice for Peace, we, as a group and as individuals, are committed to a movement that mobilizes our US national resources (churches, communities, government) to act as a catalyst for establishing peace and justice in the Holy Land.

18

Barriers to Peace

Dr. Bob Roberts

It's so easy to blame the conflict in the Holy Land on the Israelis or the Palestinians. Have you ever thought as an evangelical how you might be playing a role without even realizing it? In the past, I fit into that category. Let me start with some of my story . . . .

I grew up in the Deep South of East Texas, up and down Highway 69. My dad pastored small Baptist churches from northeast Texas in Lindale to Port Acres in southeast Texas where the Sabine River ran into the Gulf of Mexico and a few places in between. There was one sense in which prejudice, if not racism, reigned supreme. It trumped love, grace, mercy, and acceptance. Jesus died for the sins of the world, but we didn't accept the whole world that was closest to us, with good reason, or so we were led to believe. It was great to pay for missionaries to go to parts of the world where people were black or brown, among other colors—but here, they had their place. There was no sadness in my tribe when Martin Luther King, Jr. was assassinated—sad, but understandable for troublemakers like him. There was more concern over the fact that there might be riots or unrest than the fact that a man had been murdered. I grew up near centers of the Ku Klux Klan. This was my first exposure to terrorism, though at the time I never would have thought of it like that. Yes, they were extremist, but circumstances forced them there—or so we thought.

I stumbled into the world in a rather unexpected way, working with community leaders in society instead of preachers and missionaries, and it changed how I saw everything as a committed Baptist. I studied missions and was deeply committed to the goal that the whole world might be won to Jesus, the Baptist way. I knew little of Jesus and his way apart from my Texas upbringing. I counted on my tribe to interpret the ways of Jesus for me. I knew even less of the international community, but it didn't matter as long as I could see them saved and in a Baptist church. I was one of the committed few who studied the message of Jesus being taken to all of the corners of the earth: we call it missiology. Looking back, I had only a tribal view of Jesus and virtually no understanding of the world, let alone the people and cultures around me that were non-Anglo. Why did I need to understand a "lost" world? It didn't matter, the world was damned. I had a very minuscule understanding of God's image present in all creation.

Here's what I've learned: the seed of discrimination against a single person or group opens the door to discrimination among all groups and people—it doesn't stay with a single group.

There was prejudice against blacks and Jews for sure. I understood some of the prejudices against the black community, but I never really got the "Jew" part. I remember that was challenged—we even had a man who had been a Jew who found Jesus and became an evangelist came to preach at our church. You can't hate or be prejudiced towards Jews and be a dispensational premillennialist. That's reserved for Arabs and Muslims. The church was packed to hear this Jewish believer talk about Jesus. In the fourth grade I sat by a little boy in school that was Jewish and did the best I could every day to convert him. Poor kid, he got no relief from me!

After all, the Jews were the chosen people of God. The Old Testament, which I was raised on, told the story of the Jewish people and how we all now share in the promises of God that had primarily and initially been directed toward a single race or nationality. In addition, Jesus was Jewish—that should count for something. If that wasn't enough, Jesus was coming back! But, for him to return, the Jews first had to be restored to the Holy Land. And the temple had to be rebuilt for Jesus to come, right?

I don't believe a physical temple has to be rebuilt anymore, much to the chagrin of dispensational premillennialists. I do believe in the second coming of Jesus, but not a snatch and patch kind of hermeneutic that doesn't see Jesus as the fulfillment of all things and things to come. For me I was taught, and still believe Jesus was more than a prophet, and though the Messiah, even greater than the messianic role for the Jews—but he was God. That Messianic rule would come from the Jewish God-Man Jesus, but he was the Messiah for the whole world, not just one tribe. The kingdom of God will not revert to the past but move forward in the future. The kingdom of God that began with Jesus is a kingdom that lives inside of all people who follow him, not a nation or a race. The kingdom Jesus introduced isn't repeat but fulfillment and moving forward. The temple has been rebuilt inside of me when Jesus came within and now, as 1 Corinthians 3:16 says, we "are God's temple."

Historically, there has been a kind of rationalism and denial that caused good Baptists from accepting the sin or prejudices of racism. I remember an old Baptist deacon telling me racism was wrong. He made the commitment that he no longer required black people coming to his home to enter from the back door—they were as welcomed as anyone else. He viewed anything less than complete hospitality as a sin. I also remember being in my early twenties and on staff at a megachurch. One Sunday, I had brought a lot of children to church with me. One of them happened to be black. A man let me know I had no business bringing that black boy to our church, even though this man was wearing his "Jesus First" pin. My response? I told him, "Sir, I really don't know that much about you, but one thing I know for sure, is that Jesus isn't first in your life. You should take that pin off." I was told I needed to be more understanding.

I remember another Sunday afternoon after I had become a pastor. I was lying on the couch after having preached several times, exhausted and taking a nap. The TV had been left on PBS. I slowly woke up to the series *Eye on the Prize* that dealt with the civil rights struggle. I watched the old footage from Alabama and saw the fire hoses turned on people as German shepherds were set loose on protesters in Birmingham. I remember thinking, what was wrong with those white people that had so much hate? I was thinking, why would those white people do something like that? I then wondered: how could it be that white people acted that way 100 years after the Civil War? Then it hit me, and I was devastated to realize, they were my tribe! I felt the full weight of that on my shoulders that afternoon. I was causing someone else pain.

What does this have to do with Israel/Palestine? Everything! The core sin isn't racism or prejudice—it's the willingness to categorize a group of people as less than and others as more than. The same thing I experienced with my tribe growing up around African Americans was the same exact root that grew another shoot directed against the Palestinians in favor of God's Chosen, the Jews.

For me, something unexpected happened that helped me move further down the road. The church I had started decided to focus on Vietnam, even though it was a "closed" country. We wanted our members to volunteer there. This meant no one could go do "religious" work—only humanitarian work. We were forced to work with the government leaders and others—people in the society whom the church didn't normally work with. As a result of our engagement, I became friends with people I would never expect. I didn't agree with them, but I heard their narratives and began to understand them. The Vietnamese people, mostly atheists, were a community we had feared. But there was something about these people. Although I didn't agree, I began to understand their story. We have had over 100 exchange students come to the US to live with church members—two with my wife and I. To have an atheist, Buddhist, communist, and animist live in your home takes things to a whole different level! Had I not read books about the Vietnamese people and communists as human beings—I would have never believed there was anything good about any Vietnamese people. As our work continued, I became friends with many people—too many to discredit an entire nation and group of people. If I was wrong about Vietnamese people and didn't have the full picture, what about others from other parts of the world?

After 9/11 our church was asked by a friend of mine to do the same kind of front door, people-to-people kind of engagement in Afghanistan that we had in Vietnam. This was my first experience with Muslims. Afghanistan was a hard place to do community engagement, which demanded starting with relationship building. Much fear abounded. But once again, without going into the story, I don't just become friends with Muslims but with imams, leaders within the Muslim community. The picture that had been painted by my tribe, and by the media, were not the people I experienced. The Afghani people were beautiful, intelligent, artistic, and very unique. Yes, they had some nut cases—just like my tribe. They had reservations with me, and with evangelicals in particular, that I didn't understand. Their reservations had something to do with Palestine and Israel, but I didn't understand it.

Earlier in the year, I had preached a series on loving others. I used scenes from the movie *Schindler's List* as illustrations in my sermon. One scene in particular, at the end of the movie, Schindler was looking at his watch, car, and other things. He thought to himself, if only he'd sold those things, then more people would have lived. I loved that movie. But that scene would come back to haunt me.

Our work in Vietnam and Afghanistan opened doors for me to do work in other nations on delicate issues. As a result, I was invited to go with a group to visit Israel/Palestine on more of a diplomatic trip. I couldn't wait to see the sacred place I'd studied for years and preached about so many times. But, I didn't want the first time I saw the Holy Land to be about diplomats and meetings running from one place to the next. So for Christmas that year, my wife and I decided to go to the Holy Land together first as tourists. We envisioned no meetings, no special visits. Only my wife and I slowly experiencing the land of Jesus. We decided to stay in Bethlehem. I had heard you could stay at an Intercontinental Hotel there for only $80 a night only a few miles away from Jerusalem. We booked it.

We landed in Tel Aviv and were picked up by a Palestinian pastor someone wanted me to meet. He took us straight to a church service in a kibbutz of all places where he preached, as a Palestinian Christian to Jewish Christians! It was at a place where many Russian Jews had become followers of Jesus. I was amazed at meeting them, hearing their stories, and seeing them follow Jesus with such passion. I only knew of one or two Palestinian pastors. They were evangelical. I wondered how they dealt with the whole Jewish issue. This was certainly one way! After the service we were taken to Bethlehem. I was stunned by what I saw. Pulling into a special checkpoint I saw a concrete wall—much more than a fence—thirty-plus feet into the air with machine gun turrets strategically placed on top of the wall. What was I getting myself into? What was this place? Going through the checkpoint was no easy thing. Evangelical pastors in the United States are among Israel's strongest supporters, yet this Palestinian pastor was having a challenge getting across the separation barrier between Israel and the West Bank. Everything I heard, saw, and experienced caused me to question things I had learned and thought I knew about the place and its people. I was feeling what I had felt towards the Palestinians was a lot like what I went through when some of the blinders on the race issue came off my eyes, and some of the blinders towards the Vietnamese had come off my eyes.

The next day Nikki and I went to the Church of the Nativity and walked around the streets of Bethlehem—a mostly Muslim city—we were treated like royalty. I met many evangelical pastors and followers of Jesus. Back in the United States, all I had heard was that Palestinians rejected the right of the Israelis to exist. But, when I was in Bethlehem, none of the Palestinians I met expressed that view. I talked to them on the streets. They wanted peace. A two-state solution was just fine for them. I heard the stories of how land that had been in the Palestinian community for generations was taken from them illegally. I heard from evangelical pastors who believe God called them to fulfill the Great Commission just like I felt. I couldn't help but think how much more effective Arab-to-Arab sharing of the good news of Jesus was than American-to-Arab sharing.

As a result of these experiences, and many more since then, I realized I contributed barriers to peace. Here's how I had been a part of creating barriers:

First, I swallowed speculative theology innocently which led to a detrimental response to the Palestinians and the Israeli wars. Basically, we evangelicals had marginalized the Palestinians. Palestinian Christians are our brothers and sisters in Christ, but we had cut their missional legs out from under them. I saw why no Arab could take any evangelical seriously because of the ways evangelical Americans have ignored the Palestinian community. Today Palestinians live under harsh realities, which include special travel permits and walls to hold them in or keep them out. Seeing these things broke my heart.

Second, I still support the Jews. Because of my love for the Jewish community, I, and other evangelicals, must be willing to critique and challenge when things are unjust. It is wrong and hurtful to both sides as well as detrimental to the spread of the gospel. Who wants to hear a "gospel" that's driven by war and justification of bombing innocent women and children? I support the Jews, but not their unjust actions. Neither do I support terrorist actions by the Palestinians. Israel is the official and legal occupier of another people living in the West Bank and Gaza. To treat these Palestinians with disrespect or to use unnecessary, overwhelming, and disproportionate force is wrong. Israel is better than this. The Hebrew Scriptures and story teaches a better way. This isn't to say Palestinians are right in some of their responses. Many people have told me, "As a Texan you would never allow bombs from Mexico to be lobbed at Texas." Fair enough. But I will tell you as a Texan, neither would we allow ourselves to be enslaved for sixty years and never do anything about it and just be silent. Ever heard of the Alamo? As a Texan, when it's war, it's to the death. I love the Jews, but to exalt them above the Palestinians as better or superior isn't a Jesus solution.

Third, I lost the big picture of Jesus in my narrow eschatology. My false eschatology "justified" my prejudice. Jesus brought down the walls between Jew and Greek, male and female, slave and free. In the end, we have shown prejudice, if not racism, by our universal support of one side. Jews were chosen as God's first, not his last. They are chosen, but the rest of us are not second-class followers of God. We can keep doing things as we are, but it will lead to nothing good. You can't keep pushing people down, treating them with disrespect, ignoring basic human rights, and simply expect things to go away. As a Christian, regardless of what people do, God will see. In the end, sin is exposed and people always pay a penalty. Jesus died for all humanity—not just the Jews.

Fourth, because I was so determined in my own view of right and wrong toward the Holy Land, I never once listened to the story of Palestine and the people who were living there before the majority of Jews came in the early 1900s. I began to meet people—good people—who told stories of when the Jews came during the 1948 war and how many Arabs had to flee their homes. Their homes and land was taken away from them. They became refugees and had nowhere to go. Where is the justice in this? Hearing these stories forced me to begin to read about the history of how and when the Jews came and the Zionist movement that started in the nineteenth century. Why did the Palestinians lose their homes? All of these questions forced me to do a lot of reading and learning that I previously had not done. I had painted a people with a broad brush in a monolithic sort of way. It is also wrong to view all Jews as not caring for Palestinian land rights and their freedom. I've met many Jews from the Knesset (the national legislature of Israel) to business people to everyday men and women who strongly support Palestinian aspirations.

Fifth, I allowed myself to uncritically listen to my tribe and be affected by the crowd instead of thinking on my own and taking a fresh look at things. It seems I've had to learn this again and again in my life. First my perspective was changed toward the Vietnamese, then it was the Muslims, then how I relate to African Americans, and now it was the Palestinians. Today there is more news than ever before, but it is also niched in such a way as to reinforce many already existing views. MSNBC caters to the liberal. FOX caters to the ultra-conservative. News is a market that is for profit, that doesn't make for a free press. You have to listen to many different views and sources of news for a clear understanding.

Sixth, and finally, I allowed my faith and my national flag to be wrapped together. That is very dangerous. The kingdom of God is bigger than any national flag, the United States included. The reality is God's kingdom and Man's kingdom are in direct conflict more often than not. I do not look at the world as an American; I look at it as a "Kingdom Ambassador" that represents the Prince of Peace. His kingdom will not be established with guns and war, but with love and understanding and respect for every human being. That's good for us, and it's incredible for the gospel of peace.

We don't realize how our prejudice impacts how we look at others and how we feel about them, especially when we feel things en masse. I didn't. I didn't shape foreign policy, I didn't occupy the Palestinians, I didn't persecute the Jews—I didn't do any of the bad stuff you see on the news. No, I just contributed to an atmosphere that was toxic and allowed all those bad things to happen—without realizing it.

So the next time you hear the news, or someone makes a derogatory statement about someone or a people or group, ask yourself—is that right? Do they know them? Do you know them? Are your actions or your attitudes contributing to a culture of hate or a culture of love and peace?

19

Middle East Crisis and Peace Building

Dr. David A. Anderson

There is an old African proverb that says:

> From afar, I thought you were a monster. When you got closer, I thought you were just an animal. When you got closer I noticed that you were a human, but when we were face to face, I realized you were my brother.[1]

Distance demonizes. From a distance one might perceive others as monsters; or maybe just animals or, at a minimum, merely human. From a distance "those people" are not like me. They are different. But when people look one another in the eye, face to face, we realize an important truth. Namely, we are brothers and sisters.

Someone once put it like this: "It is hard to hate up close!" I have often stated privately and publicly that comprehension begins with conversation. Such a foundational principle to bridge building has never been more necessary to embrace.

The deep divides that separate cultures, communities, and countries jeopardizes our common desires for peace, prosperity, and respect. Yet conversation and dialogue afford us opportunities to close gaps of misunderstanding and mischaracterization.

Recently, I was invited to speak about world peace from the perspective of Jesus, my religion's founder. What's interesting is that the invitation came from an unlikely source: the Ahmadiyya Muslim Community. The

---

1. Anderson, *Graceism*, 159.

headquarters for their religious group in America was hosting peace talks and reported that one of the reasons they invited me was because, in their words, "He is so kind to Muslims." The person who called to extend the invitation made it sound as if it was such a rare thing for a Christian preacher like me to be kind to Muslims. Since I host a daily radio show in the nation's capital I receive a lot of calls about faith in general, and Islam in particular. Clearly there are Muslims who listen and, from time to time, even call in.

Kindness doesn't mean that I don't have my own convictions as a follower of Jesus that differ from the founder of the Islamic religion. Conversely, kindness means respecting other worldviews and not ratcheting up rhetoric that inflames negativity, stereotyping, and at worst, hate.

A Lonely Man of Faith

Having been to the Middle East many times for multiple purposes, I can say that the hotbed of division is deep and wide. When I went through a Palestinian checkpoint into Bethlehem to interview Palestinian Christians, it was a humbling and penetrating experience for me spiritually. As I sat in the back of a jewelry shop and spoke with a man about his faith, he was as devout, if not more so, than I was. Yet ethnically he was Palestinian. As a Christian he felt lonely. Why? Many around the world don't know that Palestinian Christians exist. The Palestinians are mostly Muslim and because he was a member of the Christian minority, he often felt overlooked by the global community. In the eyes of Israelis, little differentiates Muslim and Christian Palestinian men other than the religious designation on their ID cards. Our fellowship was warm until I asked him questions about suicide bombings and the Jewish community on the other side of the checkpoint. His voice elevated four octaves, his passion rose significantly, and the rapid speed with which he spoke increased significantly as he explained the levels of oppression he and "his people," the Palestinians, feel at the hands of the Jews.

When I speak with Jewish people about the prejudice and the terrorist attacks, they too are saddened and befuddled by the sense of hostility and insecurity they feel, living on pins and needles wondering when the next attack will come.

How do we as spiritual leaders build bridges in such circumstances? How do we build trust?

Building Trust Between The Israelis And Palestinians

We must understand that from an Abrahamic perspective, trust can begin by acknowledging that our respective faiths are rooted in common ground.

In reality, the Christians and Muslims have more in common religiously speaking than Christians and Jews in several regards. First, many Jewish friends reject Jesus and may even be offended by his name. Yet Muslims honor and respect Jesus as a spiritual leader. Second, many Muslims pray and practice their faith in reverence to God while many Jewish friends are secular and scant in their reverence to God. Their greater conviction is to their cultural heritage and physical survival than from a deeper sense of conviction from a scriptural or spiritual standpoint. Finally, the holy book of all three faiths point back to Abraham, yet so many religious scholars and leaders hesitate to invite others of different faith traditions into relationship to solve problems or build bridges.

First, we must understand the Hebrew admonition from the Jewish Scriptures in Proverbs 3:5–6, which says, "Trust in the Lord with all your heart and lean not on your own understanding; in all your ways submit to him, and he will make your paths straight" (NIV).

Trusting in God, and not just ourselves, is our common need for dependence that indeed a "higher hand" is guiding us. As we willingly surrender to such divine leadership our steps will be ordered and our crooked paths will be made straight.

Second, we must hear from Islam's Holy Scriptures, which say:

> And what reason have we that we should not rely on Allah? And He has indeed guided us in our ways; and certainly we would bear with patience your persecution of us; and on Allah should the reliant rely (Qur'an, Surat Ibrahim, 12:12, Shakir).

Third, we must heed the words of Jesus, who says:

> Do not let your hearts be troubled. You believe in God; believe also in Me. . . . Peace I leave with you; My peace I give you. I do not give to you as the world gives. Do not let your hearts be troubled and do not be afraid" (John 14:1, 27, NIV).

We can see a relationship between troubled hearts and trust. Jesus encourages us not to allow our troubled hearts and fear to drive us, but to allow his peace to settle our troubled hearts and to quell our fears.

One of the books I wrote is called *I Forgrace You*. Forgraceness goes beyond forgiveness. Forgraceness not only forgives past hurts, but it is the concept of extending grace to those who have hurt you. *I Forgrace You* is about doing good to those who have hurt you. When trust is broken, forgiveness is essential, but forgraceness is wholly redemptive and healing.

We trust in the God of Abraham. We must hear from our Holy Scriptures, and we must walk in a bestowed peace from on high with one another. It is the job of spiritual leaders and leading scholars to speak to nations, governments, and congregations alike that those from other cultures and religions are friends, are not monsters. They are not animals. They are even more than just humans. They are our brothers and sisters . . . Selah!

As I search the Christian Scriptures, there is an interesting pattern of peace that we see from Paul's writings as we look at what Jesus did. A pattern of peace emerges in Ephesians 2:16–21. In this Scripture passage we can find a model of bridge building that can be helpful whether in the Middle East or elsewhere. Look at the five ways to effect peace:

Five Ways to Effect Peace

Patterned after Jesus, Ephesians 2:16–22

1. Point People to God as Our Help

He "reconcile[d] both [Jews and Gentiles] to God" (Eph 2:16a, NIV).

Remember that integrating God into the Middle East debate is actually what elevates the debate toward a workable plan. It lifts the hardest issues to a divine place where help can be found beyond the control of humans only. An open dependence on God increases the level of respect for humanity amongst those who are divided and calls them to a higher plane.

2. Put to Death Hostility

"He put to death their hostility" (Eph 2:16b, NIV).

Decreasing conflict by decreasing hostile words, phrases, and attitudes will encourage civility and call upon our highest selves as we communicate with one another forthrightly and with honesty. By not allowing conflict to escalate to rage through hostile words, threats, and hate speech we will help to prevent outrageous animosity.

3. Preach Peace to All Humanity

He "reached peace to you who were far away and peace to those who were near" (Eph 2:17, NIV).

Peace to all can and should be preached by all religions and by all people, regardless of their faith. Living in peace is not only the desire of the world's citizens but it is the job of its leaders to cast such a vision and seek to attain it.

4. Provide Access to Heights Of Power

"For through him we both have access to the Father by one Spirit" (Eph 2:18, NIV).

Everyone wants to be heard and wants to feel like they have a voice. Equal access to power and promise is critical to peace throughout the world. It was even true in Jesus' day. Paul, the Scripture writer of Colossians, wanted all people to know that they had open access to God through Jesus Christ and that there was equality among those who were followers of Jesus. Here are a few Scriptures below:

- "Here there is no Gentile or Jew, circumcised or uncircumcised, barbarian, Scythian, slave or free, but Christ is all, and is in all" (Col 3:11, NIV).
- "There is neither Jew nor Gentile, neither slave nor free, nor is there male and female, for you are all one in Christ Jesus" (Gal 3:28, NIV).

When considering peace, equality and equity must be considered and seriously explored in order for uprisings to be limited. Access at every level of leadership should be available for all citizens even if such levels may only achieved by a few.

5. Participate Together to Build Something Honorable

"In Him the whole building is joined together . . ." (Eph 2:21, NIV).

Working together on a unified project toward a common goal will assist in the strategic alliances for a better future. When the self-interest of a person, a community, or a nation can be seen within a plan then there is a compelling reason for distinct groups to work together for the common good. In so doing, everyone is honored because everyone is contributing to something honorable.

Conclusion

Peace is possible. Comprehension begins with conversation. Bridge builders must be willing to host such conversations in a positive, spiritual, and honest way. Striking religion out of the dialogue is a mistake that has cost way too much. My premise is that the three Abrahamic faiths have the ability to seek common ground by elevating the conversation to higher ground.

Bibliography

Anderson, David A. *Graceism: The Art of Inclusion.* Downer's Grove, IL: InterVarsity, 2009.

———. *I Forgrace You: Doing Good to Those Who Have Hurt You.* Downer's Grove, IL: InterVarsity, 2011.

20

Hope in the Midst of a Mess

Dr. Darrell L. Bock

It does not take a rocket scientist to know the Middle East is a mess and has been for quite some time. The conflict there, for most people, is a fairly recent twentieth-century phenomenon. However its roots go back centuries, as far back as Isaac and Ishmael millennia ago, according to the book of Genesis. Just looking at the mix of faiths, Jewish, Christian, and Muslim, reveals Jerusalem as a holy city in an area of the earth that has been contested for a long time.

The Old Testament in Genesis 12:1–8, 13:14–17, and 17:8 says the land was given to Israel as a people by God. This gift of a place to reside has been a source of controversy. In Genesis 17:8, promise of land is said to be an "eternal" or "enduring possession." Such claims and the history tied to it make Israel the first of the three monotheistic faiths to have a claim on the land.

This sacred trust and deed explains why Jews are, as a people and a nation, wedded to the land and sense a deep right to be there. I speak of a people and a land, because the promise to the people of a land led to the formation of a nation, as well as a national identity beyond their religious commitments. That nation existed long ago in the past as the Hebrew Scripture chronicles and has been reformed in the recent past of the twentieth century. In today's world, where many operate on strictly secular values, such religious and covenantal claims mean little. But to people of faith, such claims mean everything.

Christians also value the land. It is here where Jesus, the Christ, ministered and made his call to Israel to see him as the fulfillment of other promises God had made to the nation bound to God by covenant, a blessing promised to the nation yet also said to open up blessing for the world (Genesis 12:1–3). His crucifixion in Jerusalem and the nature of his ministry throughout Israel has made it a sacred land for Christians, though in ways that do not evoke the need for a Christian nation-state nationhood from this locale, despite the Crusades when Christians tried to regain the land lost to Islam.

One needs only to see a picture of Jerusalem today to know that for Islam, Jerusalem is also a sacred site. The golden dome of the Dome of the Rock is placed, ironically enough, on the site Jewish tradition says Abraham was to sacrifice Isaac. It also is the locale of the Holy of Holies of the Jewish temple. For Muslims, it is the site where Mohammed was taken up into heaven, celebrated as the *Isra and Mi'raj* (see the seventeenth chapter of the Qur'an).

It is a tangled web in a place many people of different faiths regard as not just the Holy Land, but *their* Holy Land. All of this makes for claims of entitlement to this real estate. In the mix, is a belief of some that people of the other faiths represent an unclean presence in the land, making seeing "the other" as a legitimate neighbor hard. In a place seen as sacred space, the presence of others who do not believe is seen as a stain on land that is seen as special. This view exists for some Muslims and Jews about others in the land. Add to this centuries of conflict, and it is no wonder the Middle East crises cannot be solved in a few weeks or through a few years of negotiations.

It is such a tangle I experience when I travel to Israel. I have been on both sides of the now famous Wall or Separation Barrier, which separates Israel from the West Bank. As a Christian, I have Jewish and Palestinian friends in the land. They live on opposite sides of the Wall, a wall whose erection was claimed to be, by those who built it, for mutual protection because of concerns about security and human life in the face of multiple random attacks. Whether those actions be called acts of terrorism or acts of liberation from occupation does not matter, the effect and danger to human life was the same and was real. Seeing the dispute only from one angle can also contribute to the cycle of violence and retribution.

I listen to the stories of people on both sides of the divide. I lectured over ten years ago at Ben Gurion University and was hosted by my Israeli friends at a dinner. In a conversation I still recall, I was told of what it was like to dodge rockets regularly fired from Gaza. That decades-old reality still continues today as rockets are regularly fired in from the outside. Life was and is gauged by the ability to respond instantly to the sound of a siren signaling a threat. I have met with Palestinians who have told me their stories of what it is like to live in a caged environment, in some cases handled very roughly simply for being who they are. What is it like to be seen and viewed with suspicion automatically because of the environment where one lives? I hear similar stories of injustice from each side, only the people in the white and black hats change. If fixing injustice is our standard for solving the Middle East problem, then no one escapes a need to think through what damage has been done and the complexity of the causes. The Middle East is trapped in a cycle of blame with plenty of cause to go around and with all possessing specific, retained memories of injustice that are hard to let go of or dismiss.

One of the key themes of the Christian faith is the pursuit of forgiveness, the golden rule, and reconciliation, lived out in a context where love for one's neighbor means having respect for them because every human is made in God's image. Forgiveness is sought through Jesus from God for spiritual debts one knows he or she cannot repay on his or her own. Reconciliation meant and means that Jew and Gentile can now worship the same God and respect each other through a personal embrace of the forgiveness Jesus provides. God has given those who seek this forgiveness a worth that allows them to share the same God, the same Savior, and participate in the same faith community. No text says this as clearly as Ephesians 2:11–22. Such respect means there is an ability among those of different ethnic background to share space well. Is there something to learn from this spiritual example of what becoming a Christian should mean?

It seems we have two options in the Middle East. Either 1) we continue down a path where each people and faith does what is right in its own eyes in defending only its interests or 2) those in the land work to figure out how to agree on sharing space and resources together in peace.

One cannot get to option two without recognizing other dimensions to a solution. One problem is that it will take all three faiths plus all secular citizens to agree to this shared space, or else the violence will continue. If multiple faiths or primary people groups are willing to negotiate honestly, while any remaining group stays committed to violent extraction of the other, there will be no peace. This is something no one outside the land can negotiate for those who live in it. Those in the Middle East, those of all faiths or of no faith in Israel and her neighbors in the region, will have to determine if and how they can live together in peace.

I have defended elsewhere my own belief that Israel has a right to be in her land because of the scriptural promise that gave her the land in an everlasting covenant with God,[1] but that position does not represent a *carte blanche* for everything the modern State of Israel does. The Hebrew Scripture is full of exhortations to Israel about how those from outside her land should be treated with equity in it. Examples are Exodus 22:21 and 23:9. Israel's experience as foreigners in Egypt was to dictate how they treated those in their land with justice, mercy, and compassion. On the other side, those who act with violence to get what they want can expect violence in return, both out of protection and as a means to attempt to prevent of future acts. When I have had frank conversations with my Palestinian and Arab brothers in Christ about their situation I have said that one cannot ignore genuine security concerns Israel possesses since she is charged with protecting her citizens from genuine threats. I have also contended before Jews in Israel that concern for injustice to Palestinians is also something that must be addressed.

I cannot pretend as an outsider to the situation in the Middle East to be able to solve a dilemma that is centuries in the making or break a cycle that runs so deep. All one can suggest from the outside is a general way forward. The Christian values of forgiveness, the golden rule, reconciliation,

---

1. Bock, "The Restoration," 295–312. Some biblical texts promising Israel the enduring right to the land were cited above. Some argue that the land is Jesus Christ's, so now the land belongs to his people, but this ignores two key points. (1) Jesus held up hope for Israel as a functioning nation himself as the noted chapter above argues. (2) The promises God is said to have made in covenant to Israel were made for and to her, including the promise of land as an enduring possession. If these are divine promises, their content does not change for Israel regardless of what additional blessing comes to other people as a result of the full redemption Jesus will bring one day. Whatever peace Jesus is said to bring in the future to all the earth would include this Israelite dimension within it, since Jesus also foresees a future embrace of him and promise for her. See Luke 13:34–35; Acts 1:6–7, where Jesus simply says the restoration of the kingdom to Israel is the Father's business without denying it will take place. Peter in Acts 3:18–22 argues that what comes in the return of Jesus is detailed in the Hebrew Scripture, texts that see a role for national Israel in the future peace.

and love for one's neighbor do provide a way towards a solution. Still many knotty problems remain that require local solutions. None of this will come easily as the pain and sense of injustice runs deep on all sides and has existed for a long time. Moving beyond keeping score will be required for things to change. One thing is for sure: either those in the Middle East figure out a way to respect their mutual presence or the violence and cycle of the centuries will continue. Any hope of a peaceful resolution requires a change of heart on all sides. Without that, only God bringing justice directly can bring a way out—and that experience will be difficult for those the Creator holds accountable.

As for those of us located outside the area of this conflict, it is important to understand the history of the situation, the promises people claim are tied to the area, and the complexity of the current problem given these conflicting perspectives. Israel has a right to be concerned about her existence and security. Palestinians have a right to a life of dignity. No one has the right to terrorize. Human life should be respected. It is a problem only those who live there can solve. They have to determine a solution to the tensions the history of the past has handed to them. They have to be able to live with the results. Those of us on the outside cannot fix it for them, but we can hope and pray that God will help those who live there to see a better way through than the mess that currently exists.

Bibliography

Bock, Darrell. "The Restoration of Israel in Luke-Acts." In *The People, the Land and the Future of Israel,* edited by Darrell Bock and Mitch Glaser, 103–14. Grand Rapids: Kregel, 2014.

21

Navigating Minefields: Explosive Wisdom for Modern Pilgrims[1]

Jerry White

WHEN I WAS TWENTY years old, I was camping in northern Israel with two friends, and suddenly the earth exploded around me. I looked down at my shredded bloody legs in confused horror, wanting to know where my right foot had gone. It was 1984. Our innocent pilgrimage had led us through an unmarked minefield from the 1967 Arab-Israeli War.

That fateful explosion taught me early in life how to dig deep into myself—mind, heart, soul—to find out who I really was, and what I wanted to accomplish in the life I still had. This reach for resilience, grace, and transformation has been an ongoing process.

One of the fundamental lessons I have learned is so darn obvious I'm embarrassed to write it: life will scar you painfully and challenge your faith. And people will both surprise and disappoint you, because you run into human beings wherever you go—mothers, fathers, sons, daughters, brothers, sisters of all stripes. Whether you're wearing a navy suit and tie, a camouflaged jacket, torn jeans or sacred tunic, you are always and everywhere dealing with saintly and sinful people. These are individuals of diverse faiths—with values, concerns, hopes, and anxieties—just like you and me. It's so simple and obvious that we can easily forget. We fall into a

---

1. Adapted from Jerry White, "Explosive Wisdom: What Landmines Teach Us about Liberation and Leadership," *KOSMOS Magazine*, Spring/Summer 2012, http://www.kosmosjournal.org/article/explosive-wisdom-what-landmines-teach-us-about-liberation-and-leadership/. Used with permission.

trap of misunderstanding, making "the other" different than ourselves. We inadvertently create adversaries, even among our friends, co-believers, and colleagues.

Fasting forward a decade, I unexpectedly came to lead a small band of resilient landmine survivors, activists, and jaded politicians in a campaign to clean up thousands of minefields in Israel, Palestine, and Jordan. The Middle East should be dubbed the "landmine heartland" of the world because it is so heavily contaminated. Israel alone has up to one million mines buried from the Red Sea in the south up through the Arava Valley to the Dead Sea, up through the Jordan Valley to the landmine-infested Golan Heights.

In 2009, Israel was invested in the idea that these minefields were somehow critical for their security, and they were not interested in giving them up. These mines had long ceased being useful for security and instead posed a threat to Israelis themselves, wounding innocent civilians, not soldiers or terrorists.

In 2004 I thought (prematurely) I might be ready to launch the Mine-Free Israel Campaign. After all, I had already "practiced" my landmine leadership on a global scale. I had worked closely with Diana, Princess of Wales, and celebrated with my colleagues the 1997 Nobel Peace Prize awarded to our International Campaign to Ban Landmines. We had negotiated an innovative treaty to ban anti-personnel mines, now signed by 160 countries. In 1998, Her Majesty Queen Noor of Jordan became the new patron of Landmine Survivors Network (an organization I co-founded in 1995 with another American survivor, Ken Rutherford). At that time, King Hussein of Jordan pledged to ban all future landmine use, to destroy stockpiles within four years, and to clear the Jordan River Valley of mines within ten years. (Sadly, the king passed away just as the Mine Ban Treaty entered into force and didn't live to see Jordan accomplish this visionary goal in 2012.) I thought these credentials, along with my personal experiences, would be sufficient to trigger Israel to take serious action. After all, I had the "knowledge" of how to get this done.

Wrong. Unfortunately, I did not yet have the wisdom or understanding.

Israel is one of the toughest countries I have worked in, beating Bosnia-Herzegovina, Ethiopia, Vietnam, and Colombia—combined. There's a saying about Israel that it's just like any other country, only more so. It wasn't enough for me to have studied Jewish history and Hebrew, nor to have shared scar tissue and limb loss locally. When it comes to barrier-busting shifts to bring about fundamental change of thought and behavior—what matters more than street cred is who you are at your core and what you are communicating in the present moment. What I conveyed during that first attempt at changing Israel's defense policy was primarily my own personal crusade to "clean up Israel." I held a handful of perfunctory meetings with mid-level officials at the Ministry of Foreign Affairs in Jerusalem and then at the Defense Ministry in Tel Aviv. I spoke forthrightly about how Israel was ten years behind most other countries when it came to the landmine issue. I recounted my personal experience in 1984 and announced with some bravado how I was now ready to help Israel address this gap, to engage in this fight for what was right (as if the country had been awaiting my return!). Upon reflection, the energy and vocabulary were all wrong. "Crusader" energy, whether medieval or modern in manifestation, never ends well.

"Lama-mi-ata?" asked one irritated Israeli Colonel: "Why-Who Are-You?" It's a saying that implies something like: who made YOU the boss of me anyway? My naïve ideas of preparing a media campaign to publicize their Holy Land as a deadly land, including a *60 Minutes* and *Vanity Fair* partnership, wasn't exactly viewed as friendly fare. "This type of activism never turns out well for Israel. We will be slammed in the international media. Forget it." As I got up to go with my well-meaning American tail between my legs, the same colonel asked another pointed question—this one cut to the quick: "Jerry, are you ready to do this in a way that is not about you? Something more low key that will take several years of quiet work and patience?" Patience? I thought there wasn't time to be patient. This was clearly a "wrong" that urgently needed to be made "right." But, the defense establishment in Israel was not inclined to work with individuals or civil society, and they certainly were under no obligation to listen to me, some naïve American tourist injured on an ill-advised camping trip two decades prior.

It took a couple more years for me to learn how to make the issue about others, their vital interests and values, rather than about me and my wishful thinking. By the time I returned to Israel in 2009 to relaunch the Mine-Free Israel Campaign, I arrived with a more humble and clear sense of what I could bring to the table.

It was not cameras, criticism, or angry activism, but a growing capacity to stand firmly in wisdom and magnify the qualities I so admire in others: Light. Wholeness. Liberation. They aren't magic words, but a mantra of sorts to remind me of the positive energy we can inhabit in any boardroom or living room. These qualities humble me because they are not possessions. They can be accessed anytime, anywhere by grace.

Before meeting the key decision-makers—from Prime Minister Benjamin Netanyahu, or Defense Minister Ehud Barak, or his Deputy Matan Vilnai, to the Opposition Leader Tzipi Livni and her Kadima party colleague, Tzachi Hanegbi, then chair of the powerful Knesset Foreign Affairs and Defense Committee—I wanted our Mine-Free Campaign to be very clean and clear. We would look each and every individual straight in the eye as a human being created equal in dignity and rights. There would be no old-school attempt to stain reputations with shame-and-blame tactics that divide the sheep from the goats, the angels from demons. "All is One," as His Holiness the Dalai Lama reminded me pointedly. We would assume there was inherent greatness and resilience in each politician, and we would remain absolutely neutral regarding personal politics or past history. After all, we were after hearts, minds, and votes. To pass minefield clearance legislation would require approval from the top security brass in Israel as well as support from a majority of politicized Knesset members across all parties, from the far right to the far left.

Before meeting Tzachi Hanegbi, I was told he'd be a cool customer, tough, calculating, fiercely pragmatic, as he sized me up. I invited him for an afternoon coffee in the lobby of a seaside Tel Aviv hotel. "What do you want?" he asked. It seemed pointedly abrupt, at least to this American, preferring to warm up a bit more relationally. Hanegbi was there on business. His demeanor, with arms crossed and no notepad, quickly reminded me that my notions of "Light, Wholeness, and Liberation" could not remain pie-in-the-sky fluff, but had to be brought down to earth: tactical and operational. I sobered up, kicking into action with a twelve-minute briefing on the landmine problem, handing Hanegbi a one-page map of the most contaminated areas. I then invited his leadership, as the influential chair of the Knesset's powerful Defense and Foreign Affairs Committee. Hanegbi didn't just accept the challenge, he rose to it. "I will do this," he pledged. His steel-blue eyes matched his departing handshake. We both knew this was easier said than done.

We discussed nothing about his past or political future. This was about where he stood here and now on the issue of liberating land and lives in Israel.

When I first queried Israeli diplomats at various UN arms control meetings in Geneva and New York about their take on landmines, there were the knee-jerk responses: "This is a security issue, and landmines are a cheap way to keep terrorists from crossing our borders." And, "We would love to live in an ideal world without mines, but our neighbors are so hostile that we can't make progress without regional peace." There was the odd deflection: "The United States hasn't signed the Landmine Ban Treaty, so why should we?" or even outright denial and offense: "We don't have a problem in Israel—*you* are our landmine problem!"

These were predictable refrains. Landmine ban activists had heard similar statements from other defense establishments, including the

Pentagon and members of NATO. Fair to say that it is not their *modus operandi* to surrender weapons they've spent decades stockpiling. This is the entrenched and rehearsed response of any bureaucracy not wanting to give up their gadgets or tools that might come in handy one day. Without understanding, many mine-ban campaigners took the issue personally and ascribed to the military an evil motive. Most of the civil society campaigners had no military experience and found it difficult to argue credibly within a security framework.

It's true that advocates advocate from where they sit, from their self-interest. De-miners wanted money for mine clearance; survivor advocacy groups wanted money for prosthetics and rehabilitation; lawyers wanted money to lobby new legal frameworks and policies. Each and every technical fix, however seductively pragmatic, risks short-circuiting the ultimate paradigm shift—the need to delegitimize anti-personnel mines once and for all, ensuring an end to the use, production, stockpiling, and transfer of these indiscriminate weapons that can't tell the difference between a child and a soldier.

To underscore the importance of human security—to make it about everyone, not just our positions—we organized landmine survivors worldwide to speak out, to share their undeniable stories of horror and pain. Survivors became the lifeblood of the mine ban movement. Their courageous testimonies highlighted the fact that the landmine campaign was never just about landmines, but it was about people and their right to personal safety and mobility.

One of the overreaching goals was to transform outdated military security frameworks into human security frameworks that would in fact increase citizen and public safety. Eradicating landmines would strengthen international norms against any and all indiscriminate weapons. This system change would also help repair devastated rural economies, increase prospects for livelihood and promote peace.

We brought this human understanding and newfound wisdom to the Campaign for a Mine-Free Israel. We recognized how important it was to engage all diplomats and militaries and not to turn them into reactionary enemies of the cause. Our language had to engage around what each of us stands for—our shared values—rather than what divides us. What was it we all could agree on? Well, surely none of us wanted our own children maimed or killed by mines, right? How might we work together to stop this madness?

If we had proceeded on a rabidly adversarial march with blood-drenched "ban mines" posters, picket signs, and strident chants—I can assure you that very little progress would have been made in the Holy Land.

Modern advocacy need not follow the zero-sum patterns of last century's Cold War, where one side wins at the other's expense. I believe everyone will win by eradicating indiscriminate mines.

Meanwhile, my passionate advocacy has not always been wise. I remember with regret writing a sizzling ten-page memo to US Senator Patrick Leahy criticizing his USAID War Victims Fund, enumerating all the things they could and should do better. For years, that memo, filled with righteous footnotes, put significant distance between me and otherwise like-minded individuals trying to deliver artificial limbs and humanitarian assistance worldwide. As a close friend advised, "Jerry, being right doesn't win you friends, or get the job done." That remark stuck deep inside, daily.

By the time I returned to Israel, where I had stepped on my mine, I was learning quickly about all the different types of minefields in the world—political, social, and human. It was humbling to realize that even little me was responsible for creating some of them.

Re-approaching Israel on this issue required me to know myself better, and to better understand my audience. Israel presented a particular challenge with a traumatized population that perceives itself under siege from all sides. Most Israelis believed landmines were critical to bolster border security and prevent terrorists from infiltrating. Most knew very little, if anything, about the extent of the contamination. Up to one million buried mines threatened the lives and livelihood of Israelis and Palestinians alike. There had been sporadic accidents, including my own and other civilians over the years—mostly non-Jews, non-Israelis, and livestock. Nothing shocking or painful enough to awaken the country's collective consciousness to action. I was looking for a tipping point, something that would make clear to this battered country that the cost of landmine pollution was too high.

Suddenly, tragically, I found it in an eleven-year-old boy, a prince, Daniel Yuval.

It was February 6, 2010 and Israel had just had its first snow of the year. Daniel and his four siblings had never actually made snowballs, let alone a snowman. They parked on the side of the road and raced into an open field. Then, BANG! There was a muffled explosion and everyone froze. Daniel had detonated a mine and his right foot was blown off. Shrapnel had sprayed his older sister's face. Within the hour, news cameras were capturing a bloodstained father bravely carrying his children out of a useless unmarked minefield, while their mother watched in desperation.

Several months earlier, a local Kibbutznik had confided, "Israel will never take action to clean up this mess until one of our very own children—a Jewish boy or girl—gets hurt or killed, God forbid." I went to visit Daniel

Yuval in the hospital, just to show him that recovery from a mine blast was not that scary, that if I could do it he could do it. By the time I'd left, Daniel had told me that he wanted to make sure this pain didn't happen to anyone else. "What can we do, Jerry, to make sure no other kids get hurt?"

Daniel became the wise-beyond-his-years Youth Ambassador for the Mine-Free Israel Campaign. Instantly, the landmine issue was reframed. Young Daniel became the iconic focal point, just as Princess Diana had electrified twelve years before the International Campaign to Ban Landmines. One wonders if Israel would have found the political will to pass legislation (one year later) to clear the country of all non-operational minefields if it were not for Daniel's innocent courage. This brave little boy was broadcast in living rooms across the country, teaching Israelis about the true nature of an insidious and indiscriminate weapon that maims children.

In Israel, families routinely drove by minefield signs and stretches of barbed wire for kilometers and had grown immune to their dangers. The information about the perils of minefields was simply unavailable, and the mythology that mines enhanced Israeli security was entrenched. Even after stepping on a landmine, I myself didn't comprehend the extent of the contamination.

We found a series of hiking maps in Israel first published in Hebrew in 2004 to alert tour guides and local hiking groups to the presence of landmines. One of the problems was that there were no maps in Arabic or English, or in Russian for that matter. Tourists, new immigrants, and laborers were the most at risk of injury or death. So we set out to research and independently publish the first open-source map showing the minefields throughout the country and the West Bank.

Our small research team examined years of media reports, public statements, and records from past casualties. Most Israelis were unaware, for instance, that hundreds of square kilometers of land are rendered unusable and dangerous due to landmine contamination. We were determined to put information out to the public, the media, and policymakers, including bulleted one-page fact sheets in multiple languages and accessible formats. Small steps made a big difference.

In 2010, we published the first comprehensive study of the problem in English, Arabic, and Hebrew: *Explosive Litter: Status Report on Minefields in Israel and the Palestinian Authority*. Importantly, the research uncovered a trail of official correspondence, including the fact that the Israel Defense Forces (IDF) had publically declared that hundreds of their minefields were no longer operational, and that the IDF did not object to their removal.

We set out to develop a network of individuals who understood the issue or lived next to minefields. We built a small diverse group of landmine survivors, news reporters, rehabilitation specialists, and public officials who were committed to change.

We stood against the insidious landmine, our sworn enemy that had stolen our limbs and lives. We were also against inaction, passivity, and cynicism. We stood for the possibility of a mine-free Israel within ten years. We stood for the liberation of fertile land for farming. We stood for families living in safety, free of fear. We stood for the healing of people and the environment.

The vision for change goes beyond knowledge and understanding. Such vision can only come from reaching deeper into our collective wisdom. Tapping into something bigger than all of us makes it possible to bring change that can benefit future generations of Israelis, Palestinians, and Jordanians. Yes, even the world.

On February 7, 2011, Daniel and his older sister, Amit, and younger brother, Yoav (who were also hurt in the Golan minefield) joined me and our campaign coordinator, Dhyan Or, in Jerusalem to meet virtually all Knesset members and head of factions. We hired the savvy Tel Aviv government relations firm, Policy, to arrange meetings with anyone inside government who would agree to see us. This ended up including the Prime Minister, the Minister of Defense, the Minister of Foreign Affairs, and the Head of the Opposition. Careful to avoid anger and castigation, we urged them to fulfill the promises they had made to young Daniel and our campaign in the previous year, and called on them to stand with us and vote in favor of the proposed mine clearance bill. That day, the bill passed its first reading by an unheard of unanimous vote across all party lines (60–0). Remarkably, Daniel was summoned to the front of the plenary room, normally reserved only for members of Knesset. The following week, the bill was returned to the Foreign Affairs and Defense Committee for hearings to resolve a number of outstanding issues.

After negotiating final language that would mandate compliance with International UN Mine Action Standards and a pilot project to be initiated within months of passage, the proposed legislation was brought back to the full Knesset for a final historic vote on March 14, 2011. As Daniel and I sat with our fellow survivors and campaigners in the honorary balcony, senior Knesset member Ronnie Bar-On (former Minister of Finance) publicly credited us for this historic moment before presenting the bill for the second and third final readings. Once again, the vote was unanimous, and we all but burst into tears of joy, light, wholeness, and liberation. Israel had unanimously agreed to clear its non-operational minefields.

Nothing like this had happened since the successful "Don't Pick the Wildflowers" campaign run by the Society for the Protection of Nature back in the 1950s. Our campaign had pushed the boundaries of military-civilian collaboration on a border security issue, just as the "Arab Spring" was signaling regional unrest.

This was a victory for everyone who cared for land and lives held hostage for decades by minefields. Liberation is never about the one obvious boulder blocking your way.

Having worked with leaders from all walks of life and from over 100 countries, I have come to appreciate the special type of wise leadership needed for the global challenges ahead. There are a growing number of people who are learning how to summon the courage to take on some of society's most rigidly embedded institutions in pursuit of life-saving, economy-enhancing change.

It will take more than technology and military expertise to clean up hundreds of thousands of minefields we have created across the planet. We must call forth a new generation of wise young liberators to chart a path forward where we can walk freely and safely in peace.

Part VI

We Belong to Each Other: Relationship Across Divides

©annegeorg. IStockPhoto.com. Photo ID: 84059219. Jan 23, 2016.
Downloaded June 26, 2016.

"If we have no peace, it is because we have forgotten that we belong to each other."

—MOTHER TERESA

22

Standing Beside the Vulnerable[1]

Shane Claiborne

I HEARD A RABBI say that the Scriptures are kind of like a diamond. You keep turning them, and they give you new light. The diamond we are going to look at is the familiar story of the Good Samaritan[2] in light of the current realities in the Holy Land. It's a story that I think a lot of us are familiar with. To me, it has everything to do with the conversation around the struggle in the Holy Land. At the "Christ at the Checkpoint Conference" that I was a part of, a friend and theologian—Stephen Sizer—explained this parable beautifully. I'm going to take some of Stephen's thoughts and add some of my own.

The story of the Good Samaritan is one of the most scandalous stories that Jesus tells. The likely heroes, the religious folks, are actually the ones who pass by. The Samaritan, the social outcast, doesn't believe all the right things. Maybe he believes some unorthodox theology. Yet, the Samaritan is the one who is moved with compassion and does something about injustice. As Sister Joan Chittister says, "God consistently challenges the chosen and he includes the excluded."[3] I love that idea, and I see it consistently in Jesus, that whenever someone thinks that they have the corner on the market of God's chosen people, Jesus challenges that. Whenever someone thinks they are outside of anything that God could be doing, Jesus brings them in to the

---

1. Based on a talk given at *Impact Holy Land*, Friends Meeting House, Philadelphia, December 2013. Used by permission from Evangelicals for Social Action.
2. Luke 10:25–37.
3. Claiborne, https://rachelheldevans.com/blog/ask-shane-claiborne-response.

story. It doesn't get any more scandalous than Jesus saying to the teachers of the law, "The tax collectors, the prostitutes, and the Samaritans are entering the kingdom ahead of you."

What I love in this parable is that we can see God working outside of the boundaries of our own ideas about where God is at work. This story is an illustration that as Christians we can't hold the Spirit hostage. The Spirit moves as the Spirit wants. We look in Scripture and God is using Samaritans, pagan kings, and brothel owners. I am reminded of a quote from Rich Mullins recounting something one of his professors said: "God spoke to Balaam through his ass and God's been speaking through asses ever since."[4] So if God should choose to use us, we shouldn't think too highly of ourselves. If upon meeting someone we think God could never use them, we should think twice. Because God spoke to Balaam through his donkey. This story of how God uses the unexpected is woven throughout Scripture and is a concept we still struggle to believe and embrace today.

I think that's one of the clear points of the story, but there is so much more in it. One of the things that occurs to me as I read the story is that the story never would have happened if people weren't walking down a road where people get beat up. Everything in our world is compelling us to move away from the streets where people get beat up, from the neighborhoods where there is high crime or there are people who don't look like us. The inertia of our culture is pulling us away from suffering. Yet, the gospel pulls us into it. We should be drawn into places where people are beat-up because our hearts are moved by compassion. As Christians, we are called to be re-oriented by Jesus so that suffering isn't something we try to get away from but something we cross into the ditch and get dirty in the midst of. That is the call of the story of the Good Samaritan. That is our call when we talk and learn about the complexities of struggle in The Holy Land.

There's a great song that Derek Webb from Nashville sings, that says, "Where we're all living so good, we moved out of Jesus' neighborhood."[5] He's pointing to the funniness of how our culture sees it as an achievement to be able to withdraw from places of suffering. Or, as I heard one preacher say one time, if we find ourselves climbing the ladder of success, we best be careful because on our way up we might pass Jesus on his way down. The whole story is about God entering into the suffering and the pain of our world.

The other thing that occurs to me about this story is that people get beat up at really inconvenient times. Injustice often happens when we're on

---

4. *Ragamuffin*.
5. Webb, "Rich Young Ruler."

our way somewhere. Half of the stories in the gospels are interruptions and surprises. Jesus is on his way and someone pulls on his shirt or says, "My daughter is sick!" Or, "We ran out of wine at our wedding, can you help a brother out?" These miraculous stories come from interruptions, and yet interruptions and inconveniences are the very things that we try to work out of our lives. We love our routines and our Daytimers and the predictability of our schedule. We have no room for interruptions. But I think injustice anywhere should interrupt our comfort and our routines. Just as it did for the Samaritan. When I went to the Middle East, that's what happened. Injustice interrupted my theology and my thinking. The injustice I saw caused me to want to do something.

As we think about this story a little more, the other thing that occurs to me is that we really don't know much about the person who got beat up in the ditch. (And, this is where I'm stealing from Stephen Sizer's talk on this parable a little bit.) The person in the ditch is robbed of his clothing; he is left naked. He's knocked out unconscious; he's robbed of his language and dialect. The two ways that you would be able to identify someone are stripped from this person. We are left with a clear answer to the question, "What do we know about the person in the ditch?" That answer is they are a human being. We don't know who they are. Where they are from. We don't know what religion they are. We don't know their sexual orientation, their national identity, or their views on any current topic. All that we know is that this is a human being, created in the image of God, who has been beat up.

That should be enough to move us into compassion. It was enough for the Samaritan. It seems so beautiful that the Samaritan who responds didn't have all his ideas in order, but he has his heart in order. The Samaritan's heart is what moved him; maybe the ideas come later. I think that theology is really important, and that what we believe about God is really important. However, at the end of the day, if our theology doesn't move us to compassion for the most beat-up, marginalized person pushed in the ditch, then what good is our theology? Throughout history, the person who is beat up is different. Any time a person is beat up and in the ditch—whether they are Israeli or Palestinian—we have to remember they are created in the image of God, and we should be moved to respond.

When I first moved into North Philly, we began to see that our neighborhood had a lot of gun violence. I say this as a person from Tennessee; we shot stuff in Tennessee. I grew up killing squirrels and eating squirrel brains. I'm not just saying that because of *Duck Dynasty*, we really did. I grew up hunting. Half of my family is in the NRA and my dad was in Vietnam. There's a song in Tennessee that goes, "Our houses are protected by the good Lord and a gun. And you might meet 'em both if you show up here not welcome, son."[6] That's my land.

But, I came up to Philly, and I couldn't make sense of the violence.

When I looked at Jesus and what Jesus said, and I looked at our neighborhood and our world, I knew that there was work to be done. I knew that as Christians we were called to move towards this pain and offer hope and healing the way the Good Samaritan did. Perhaps without all the answers, but with the right heart.

I can remember one of the times that we heard the gunshots ring out, I came outside and on our front porch I saw this kid fall, bleeding. He was nineteen years old. I held him, and I prayed for him, only to find out the next morning that he died. For me, from that moment, gun violence wasn't some political debate; it was a nineteen-year-old kid named Pepito who I knew and who was made in the image of God. He mattered to God.

That is the kind of fire that fueled my heart against injustices. It is not just about debating ideas. It is about any time a human being's dignity is stepped on, or any time a person is beat up or shot or called a name. All of those injustices should break our hearts because part of the image of God is wounded in the world.

Once, when I was at the University of Pennsylvania, there was a hate crime against one of the Jewish communities there. It broke my heart. I couldn't even speak about it without crying about it. Then when I went to Israel and Palestine, I saw what is happening in some of those communities and it broke my heart as well.

In Philadelphia, a movement called "Heeding God's Call" started, not just to address the victims of gun violence on the streets, but the epidemic of gun violence that 300 folks are dying from in our city every year. Ten thousand in our country. And every one of those lives matter to God. It is a historical conversation of peace churches. All kinds of friends and allies gathered together to wrestle with gun violence. They said, "We got to do something. Not just lift people out of the ditch." As MLK said, "We are called to be the Good Samaritan, but after you lift so many people out of the ditch you start to ask, maybe the whole road to Jericho needs to be repaved."[7] We began to hold vigils in the streets. We had one of the vigils at one of the historic gun shops in Philadelphia—Colosimo's gun shop.

6. Thompson, "Way Out Here."
7. King, "A Time to Break the Silence."

We had Good Friday vigils. When a representative group of "Heeding God's Call" said we also have to put our bodies in the way of this injustice, they did a sit in in the spirit of the civil rights movement. They were arrested inside the gun shop. They went to trial. There were schools that let their kids come to the trial. Those arrested were mostly pastors and nuns. What happened through the course of the trial is that all the defendants were found not guilty and the gun shop went on trial. People began to wrestle with the question of, "How is it that we sell semi-automatic weapons in the streets of Philly?" As one of the kids in our neighborhood said, "Why do we have so many gun shops when there aren't that many deer?" As a kid from Tennessee I said, "Great question!"

We started wrestling with and exposing that injustice. In the ensuing days, Colosimo's shop closed down. I think it is now a bicycle shop, which is a great testimony to the world. I do not say that triumphalistically, but we were praying that the violence would stop. We were getting in the streets. We were putting in our bodies, trying to say, "This has to stop." The closure of Colosimo's was a significant step in stopping some of the gun violence in Philadelphia. There is also power in the prophetic witness when it becomes public. "We must expose injustice" as Dr. King said, "and make injustice so uncomfortable that it has to be dealt with."[8] I think that's what we need to be doing with the situation in Gaza right now. I love the idea of faith-based flotillas to bring relief into Gaza, to raise questions of, "Why can't we bring basic medication? Basic living needs into this place?" These people matter to God. I would say the same thing if they were on the other side of the border. Every human being matters to God.

One of the things we started in Philly is we said maybe we need a prophetic witness. So we got inspired by these "beat-your-swords-into-ploughshares"[9] prophets in Micah and Isaiah. We partnered with some Mennonite builders and blacksmiths, and we looked around for some guns. We had an AK-47 donated. So, we took that sucker and we beat it into a shovel and a rake. Then we started getting other people around the world sending us images of things like a guitar made out of guns. We received a picture from a guy in Mozambique who was playing a saxophone made out of a semi-automatic gun. Our most powerful transformation was when we took a handgun off the streets of Philadelphia and we heated the metal up in the barrel of the gun. Red hot. Then one of the mothers who had lost her son to gun violence took the hammer and she started beating on the barrel on that gun. As she beat it, after every hit of the hammer, she said, "This. Is.

---

8. Campolo and Claiborne, *Red Letter Revolution*, 153.
9. Isa 2:4; Joel 3:10; Mic 4:3.

For. My. Son." I can't even tell you how powerful that was. We saw the barrel of that gun transformed into farm tools. There is this image of turning the tools of death into things that bring life. A farm tool was made out of the barrel of a gun that had previously been a tool of violence on our city streets.

What we need in the movement for peace and justice is imagination. I have a dream of the folks on both side of the wall—the Israeli nationals and the Palestinians; Christians and Jews and Muslims—together taking weapons, together beating them, and declaring together, "We. Will. Not. Kill. One. Another. Our God is a God of love." That dream is the dream the prophets lead us to.

Everywhere I go I see a young generation that is drawn to that kind of imagination, that finds the hatred, the divisions, and the polarities of political agendas absolutely nauseating. And, sadly, a lot of times they see religion not as the solution, but as part of the problem. All religions have had people who have distorted the best of their faith. Muslim, Jews, and Christians that have done terrible things in the name of God. God has been terribly misrepresented in the world.

And yet, what is beautiful about the conversations that happen between people who want to work for peace and justice is we are saying, "We will not let the haters high-jack the headlines." We want a movement that looks like Jesus again. We want a movement sprinkled with the fruits of the Spirit. If, in the end, our ideas don't move us to compassion for the beat-up persons—whichever side of the wall they are on—then our ideas have fallen short of the call to be the body of Christ in the world.

Bibliography

Campolo, Tony, and Shane Claiborne. *Red Letter Revolution: What if Jesus Really Meant What He Said?* Nashville: Thomas Nelson, 2012.

Claiborne, Shane. *The Irresistible Revolution, Updated and Expanded: Living as an Ordinary Radical*. Grand Rapids: Zondervan, 2016.

King, Martin Luther, Jr. "A Time to Break the Silence." Sermon, Riverside Church, New York, Apr 4, 1967.

Ragamuffin. Directed by David Schulz. 2014. Color Green Films, 2014. DVD.

Thompson, Josh. "Way Out Here." In *Way Out Here*. Columbia Nashville, 2010. CD.

Webb, Derrick. "Rich Young Ruler." In *Mockingbird*. Integrity Media, 2005. CD.

23

The Power of Unlikely Friendships

Carolyn Custis James

"THOSE ARE YOUR GUYS!" a Canadian neighbor shouted sarcastically at me above the din of jet engines as he pointed to the cloud covered skies in Oxford, England. On January 17, 1991, an American-led coalition began air attacks on Iraqi forces in a multinational response to Iraq's invasion and annexation of Kuwait—a major source of US oil. At the time, my husband, daughter, and I were living in Oxford where Frank was pursuing doctoral studies. From where we lived, we could hear the thunderous roar of US military planes overhead, departing from the nearby base for the battle in the gulf.

Our flat in university graduate housing was something of a mini-United Nations that put us in close proximity with people from all over the world. During our four years in England, I discovered Oxford offers more than one kind of education for those who come to reside within her borders. It was an enormous privilege to live in a global village with neighbors from all over the world sharing meals, talking politics, religion, and encountering a cornucopia of cultural diversity all amid the anxiety of doctoral studies. I learned a lot through friendships with those neighbors.

Operation Desert Storm, as that war came to be known, created tensions in Oxford where anti-war sentiment in general and opposition to American involvement in particular ran high. As Americans, we were blindsided by a cooling of friendships, even with Christian friends, from other countries who viewed the war as a battle for the American automobile. The isolation that resulted as a consequence had the unexpected effect of drawing Frank and me into unlikely friendships and eye-opening conversations about the war with other neighbors—an Indian Muslim and a Jewish Israeli. Both were experiencing a similar isolation, but for different reasons—Ali because he was Muslim and Gabi because his country (which at the time was under attack from Iraqi scud missiles) was so strongly allied with the United States. In both cases, our conversations inevitably turned from what was happening in the gulf to the situation in Palestine.

Our Muslim neighbor, Ali, was from a region in India where Muslims were a persecuted minority and where the oppression was so bad that it was unsafe for Muslims to travel. His wife couldn't safely visit her sister who lived only a short distance away. He explained to us how Muslims have been oppressed all over the world, leaving many with a pent-up rage, especially against the West. He and his Muslim friends were outraged by Saddam Hussein and his merciless invasion of Kuwait. In fact, they hated him for his attack on Iran resulting in a nearly decade-long war between Muslim neighbors, his brutal repression of his own people, and now his assault on Kuwait. At the same time they were profoundly offended by the double standard they observed at work in Operation Desert Storm. What was the difference between Saddam's takeover of Kuwait and Israel's annexation of Palestine? Yet Israel's seizure of Palestine drew global support, especially in the West. But, in the words of Saddam's Deputy Prime Minister, Tariq Iziz, the world "raised a stick" when an Arab country did the same thing.

Ali didn't hide the fact that he and other Muslims had conflicted feelings of their own. On the one hand, they hated Saddam because of the brutality of his regime, and his wars with fellow Muslims. Still, they could not help but admire a Muslim leader who defied the US and its allies. Startling evidence of the intensity of the fierce inner conflict Muslims felt came from Ali's fellow Muslim, who openly rejoiced that Saddam was striking a blow against the Great Satan, but in the next breath swore that, given a weapon and the opportunity, he would personally kill Saddam.

Much to our surprise, our Israeli friend corroborated Ali's perspective on Israel's takeover of Palestine. Like every young Israeli, in his pre-Oxford days Gabi served in Israel's military. He fought in Southern Lebanon as part of Israel's 1982–1985 battle against the Palestinian Liberation Organization's infiltration into the region. Conversations with Gabi were especially interesting because, much to our surprise, he was profoundly sympathetic with the Palestinians and deeply troubled over their plight. Because of his expertise on Middle Eastern politics, Gabi was often a guest commentator for British news networks during Operation Desert Storm. He was the first person I ever heard raise the question of injustice in Israel's treatment of the Palestinians. Both he and his wife believed the Israelis committed horrible injustices and that the leaders of their country used terrorists' tactics to eject the Palestinians who had called Palestine home for over a thousand years.

Conversations with those two men were both shocking and disturbing to me. They exposed realities and perspectives I hadn't considered and revealed how little I really understood about the situation in Israel and in the Gulf, but most importantly, how easy it is to grow up in a country where only one side of a story is told. Conversations with those global neighbors introduced realities I could no longer ignore.

Escapist Theology

I was raised in a Christian tradition that embraces an exalted view of Israel as God's chosen people and the center of his purposes in the world. One of the distinctive features of this tradition was that the Christian church is relegated to "a parenthesis" in God's story, living in expectation of the rapture—a concept popularized through *Left Behind* books and movies where Jesus suddenly returns to carry Christians away to heaven. As a pastor's daughter, the church was my world, and I thrived on the rich Bible teaching that gave me a biblical foundation for which I'll always be grateful. But the worldview of this tradition had a mixed effect on me.

This theological system instilled in me a profound admiration and support for Israel as God's chosen people. Indeed, being Jewish took on an aura of celebrity. A Jew enjoyed a special place in God's eyes that I as a non-Jew (or Gentile) didn't and couldn't attain. Of course it was special to be a Christian, but nothing was more desirable than being a Messianic or Christian Jew. As a young girl I even thought it would be the ultimate privilege to marry a Jewish Christian. (Alas, life is full of disappointments. I ended up with a Gentile Texan named Frank.)

Growing up with this worldview inevitably reduced the Christian church to a secondary role in God's purposes and made "being ready" for the rapture paramount (meaning make sure you're saved and don't get caught doing something you want to be explaining through all eternity). Furthermore, it narrowed the church's mission to evangelism so as many people as possible would be raptured. The theology behind this anticipation of an imminent escape colored how I viewed the world and the evening news. Hope was bound up with escaping the messy brokenness of our world, rather than engaging it with the radical power of the gospel and answering God's call to be agents of justice, mercy, and the kingdom of God on earth.

Conversations with Ali and Gabi poked holes in my tradition by raising issues of injustice that I, as a Christian, couldn't ignore.

Confronting Realities

That earlier theological tradition no longer shapes my worldview or governs my perspective on the Israeli-Palestinian crisis. My work in biblical studies, with a primary focus on how the Bible engages global gender and justice issues for women, may seem unrelated to that crisis. But I have been surprised and impacted by the connections.

My research involves delving into issues of injustice, oppression, and atrocities against women and girls worldwide—sex trafficking, systemic poverty, gendercide, child marriages, honor killings, rape as a weapon of war, domestic violence, and a plethora of other disturbing issues. Sometimes the things I've learned have been so dark and incomprehensibly evil, there aren't words to describe the nightmares women have experienced and are still enduring. But as a Christian and as God's image-bearer, I knew I couldn't turn a blind eye. I have responsibility to do what I can to understand and engage these problems.

The overwhelming scope of the suffering coupled with a profound sense of powerlessness to make it stop can easily lead to despair. These realities have driven me back to dig into the Scriptures, determined to find out if the message of the Bible for women and girls globally is robust enough to hold up under the weight of these twenty-first-century horrors, to test God's heart for his daughters, and to see if the Bible speaks hope, meaning, and purpose into the lives of every woman and girl in today's world no matter how her story is playing out. I have not been disappointed, but rather have been armed with a larger, stronger, more enduring vision for women than I ever hoped to find.

The realities of this misbegotten world have compelled me to dare to ask the hard questions and to refuse to settle for simplistic triumphalist answers that presuppose prosperity, freedom, peace, and privilege. We are only fooling ourselves to think we can count on answers for ourselves that collapse under the weight of other peoples' lives.

Some of the same core issues I encountered as I probed the plight of women in the world also surface in the Israeli-Palestinian crisis. If I have learned anything about the marginalization of women it is that the roots of the problem run deep into the human psyche. That is also true of the Israeli-Palestinian crisis, for both Jews and Palestinians bear the scars of unspeakable persecution, oppression, and atrocities. Undoubtedly, Post-Traumatic Stress Disorder (PTSD) runs at epidemic levels among both Israelis and Palestinians and impacts the ongoing crisis. Injustice comes in many forms and produces an undercurrent of rage that is not easily diffused. The long shadow of the Holocaust has burnished into the souls of the Jewish people a fierce "Never again!" resolve as they seek safe haven in the promised land, no matter the cost. The Palestinians' worst fears have been realized as the Jewish population surged and encroaching Israeli settlements displaced them from land they had long occupied. Thousands have fled in abject fear, lives have been lost and more physical, psychological, and spiritual wounds than can be counted result from the exchanges of rocket fire, bullets, rocks, and words. The Ancient Near Eastern ethic of *lex talionis* (eye-for-an-eye retaliation) fuels the desire for revenge. Little wonder peace negotiations are so difficult and cease fires so fragile.

The wisdom of Solomon may be able to sort out the dilemma caused by two women claiming to be the mother of the same baby. But two nations claiming indigenous rights to the same land is not so easily solved.

Despite the depth of the challenges I see, I still remain determined to fight for women and girls. That same tenacity must stiffen our resolve to stay in the battle for peace in Palestine.

Keeping Hope Alive

How do we keep hope alive? We must never forget that God has not given up, nor will he, on the vision he cast at creation—a vision for both men and women. And he will ultimately have his way. No matter how dire and hopeless the situation or how absent he may seem, God is in this battle too. That alone is reason for hope. Injustice, oppression, and violence have no place in the world he created and loves. His vision is of a unity—a Blessed Alliance—among his image bearers that bridges all that divides us and mirrors the Trinity's oneness in diversity. Although the fall drove a wedge between male and female and led to deadly violence between brothers, beginning with Cain and Abel, Jesus' mission was to reunite a fallen humanity with their Creator and to break down the walls that divide us from one another. The oneness he restores among his followers is intended to give hard evidence to a watching world that Jesus has come and that his kingdom is not of this world.

We must also remember that God's heart for the Arabs is just as great as his heart for the Jews. God doesn't play favorites. Not only are the Old Testament stories of Hagar and Ruth two of the most emphatic counter-cultural statements in all of Scripture of God's heart for his daughters, their stories are jaw-dropping demonstrations of God's overflowing love for the Arabs.

Both young women came from countries that in today's world are key Arab nations—Egypt and Jordan. According to today's demographics both would be classed as Arab. So it is highly irregular, to say the least, for both of them step out onto the pages of the Jewish Scriptures and command the spotlight. But they do. Furthermore, God gives them strategic roles in his story. This is unusual for females within a full-blown patriarchal culture where men own center stage. Their non-Jewish ethnicity makes their appearances in and contributions to Jewish history even more striking. Both are in desperate circumstances. Hagar is an Egyptian slave. In today's parlance, she was a trafficked girl. Ruth is an impoverished immigrant who scavenges for food. In both stories, everything turns on the fact that God is at work in the lives of both young women. The world may marginalize them, but God pursues and deploys them for his purposes for the world.

Who would believe the Angel of the LORD would track down a trafficked, abused, and frightened Egyptian slave girl running for her life into the wilderness? Not only does this meeting mark a stunning breakthrough in the desperate fugitive's life and a resounding affirmation of her value in God's eyes, Hagar becomes a prophetess who teaches God's people then and now of the intimately personal love of "the God who sees me"—a message both Abraham and Sarah desperately needed to hear. Hagar's contribution to Jewish and Christian theology is monumental.

Who would believe that an Israelite family's desperate flight to Moab to escape a famine was also a divinely orchestrated rescue operation for Ruth, the young Moabites whose father off-loaded her by giving her in marriage to a famine refugee? Who would guess that God's purposes for the world were riding on the shoulders of this young non-Jewish destitute immigrant or that her calling would require a strong alliance with a powerful Jewish man? Contrary to traditional interpretations, her alliance with Boaz is not based on romantic self-interest, but is *solely* for Naomi's sake. Everything Ruth and Boaz do is selfless, sacrificial, and intended to benefit her. We do them an enormous disservice by reducing their story to a romance. They ensure that Naomi is well fed and they rescue this childless widow's dying family by producing and giving her a son. Unbeknownst to them, their love and sacrificial actions for a grieving widow were advancing the purposes of God for the whole world, for the son they produced became the grandfather of King David and the ancestor of King Jesus. Their cross-cultural alliance models what is possible for Arabs and Israeli's in today's Palestine. And there are plenty of contemporary examples that show that this is actually happening.

Breaking Down Walls in Palestine

In 2006, Charles Gibson, ABC news anchor at the time, made the wry comment, "We don't usually look to the Middle East for uplifting stories." Then he told one. It started with the story of an attack on an Israeli border town that took the lives of two Jewish brothers—both husbands and fathers. A third surviving brother, devastated by grief, was nevertheless determined to do more than bury his brothers. He took action to donate his brothers' organs. Among the waiting candidates was an Arab man who was losing his sight and who was completely dumbfounded and humbled to receive the gift of sight from a Jewish victim of an Arab missile. A successful cornea implant restored sight to the man and broke through a barrier most people would have thought impenetrable. They met—a grieving Jewish man and an Arab—wept together, embraced, and called each other "brother," while in the distance the battle continued to rage.

When an eighteen-year-old Palestinian was arrested for throwing rocks, beaten for refusing to confess, released only to die from internal injuries, his younger brother, Aziz Abu Sarah, was outraged, bitter, and filled with a thirst for revenge.[1] When Aziz turned eighteen and enrolled in a class to learn Hebrew for a job he wanted, for the first time he encountered Jews who were not soldiers. It was life-changing. Friendships developed that convinced him to dedicate his life to dismantling the wall of anger, hatred, and ignorance that divided them. With two Jewish friends he cofounded Mejdi Tours—an innovative way to connect people and promote friendships that can make a difference. Tours are led by a Jewish and a Palestinian guide who tell stories and history from entirely different perspectives and take tourists to meet and share meals with Palestinians and Israelis. These encounters and the friendships that follow allow basic humanity to bubble to the surface, understanding to grow, hostilities and prejudices to die, and friendships to thrive.

On reflection, Oxford proved to be much more than an educational experience. It was a revelation of the complexities of this world, where black and white answers fade to gray. It was also an opportunity to experience the power of unlikely friendships. For in that global village, I had the opportunity to listen and learn from an Indian Muslim and a former Israeli soldier who were our friends. That we could have those conversations at all gives me hope.

---

1. Read more about Aziz Abu Sarah and his work with MEJDI Tours in the Foreword.

24

A Truer and Deeper Peace

Lynne Hybels

"I WISH MY HEAD were a well of water and my eyes fountains of tears, so I could weep day and night for the slain among my dear, dear people." You may recognize that from the prayer of the weeping prophet Jeremiah, recorded in Jeremiah 1:9 (The Message).

It was also the first line of an email I received from a friend in Bethlehem, a pastor's wife, during the war between Israel and Gaza in July 2014.

"Our hearts grieve continually," she added, "as we hear of whole families being killed, women becoming widows, mothers collecting the parts of their children's bodies. We pray for this killing to come to an end! Lord, have mercy on your people!"

She ended with a question: "So how, my friend, can a normal human being put his or her head peacefully on the pillow and go to sleep?"

How, indeed?

I also received notes from friends in Israel. One young Jewish woman wrote: "I fear every moment for my friends and family living in the line of rocket fire from Hamas, and I grieve every moment for the horrific loss of life in Gaza."

Another Israeli Jewish woman, a follower of Jesus and a poet, sent me lines from a poem she wrote during the fighting:

> War's cost is paid incrementally
> drop by crimson drop, tear by tear
> rent from ruptured hearts

The young, the old,
all bleed red on never satiated earth.

All bleed red on never satiated earth . . .

While the war raged between Israelis and Palestinians in Gaza, my then–two-year-old grandson fell on a hardwood floor and sustained a bone-deep gash on his perfect little forehead. I sat like any grandmother in the emergency room, snuggling her grandbaby, willing him with heart and soul to be whole and healthy again. But a part of my mind was elsewhere, thinking of a grandmother in Gaza, holding her broken baby. Nine stitches and my little guy was good as new. But there were not enough stitches in the world to fix the babies of Gaza.

Nor is there an end to the fear an Israeli grandmother experiences, living as she does on Israel's border with Gaza. Each time the municipal air horn sounds, warning of rocket fire from Gaza, she has to shuttle her grandchildren into the nearest bomb shelter. She has fifteen seconds to get her little loved ones to safety.

I frequently visit one such Israeli grandmother, who will never forget the day her now-grown daughter's childhood friend was killed by such a rocket. Despite her grief and fear, this grandmother advocates for a better life for Gazans. "We will never have a better life," she says, "until they have a better life too." Surprisingly, I visit many people on both sides of this conflict who advocate for reconciliation and peace with their supposed "enemy."

We Americans can—and do—talk of the complexity of the conflict in the Holy Land, and talk incessantly! But we must not forget there are real people behind that complexity, real people who are suffering. What do we do with that complexity? And with those suffering people?

An Israeli Christian friend wrote me once:

> In the complexity of the conflict, with continually divergent narratives of even the simplest events, I seek the place of prayer for all I see, and more so for what I do not see and cannot know. . . . I'm learning to expect the unexpected and with it the ache that uncertainty engenders.
>
> Engagement for me means raising my voice [in a community of Israeli and Palestinian women committed to reconciliation] in hope that many will hear "another voice" coming from Israel/Palestine. It also means raising my voice in prayer and supplication for the Prince of Peace to come into the lives of all the peoples of this region, Jew and Arab alike. I've learned that even when I'm inundated with feelings of powerlessness and vulnerability, I can hold tightly to the knowledge that "He has

the whole world in His hands," and that includes Israel/Palestine. *Being a positive presence, a pursuer of peace and a person of prayer in my small world has to be enough whether or not I ever see results.*

"A positive presence, a pursuer of peace, and a person of prayer in my small world." That's the kind of person I was looking for in 2009 when I began traveling regularly to the Holy Land. I had just attended a conference in Amman, Jordan taught entirely by Arab Christians from Jordan, Lebanon, Egypt, Iraq, and the West Bank. They had challenged me to understand how American engagement in the Middle East was making their lives miserable. "As Christians we used to live in relative peace with our Muslim neighbors," they explained, "but now we're being equated with 'Christian America' that appears to be militaristic, imperialistic, and insensitive to the plight of our brothers and sisters in Palestine. Suddenly we're becoming 'the enemy' in our own neighborhoods. American Christians don't understand what they're doing to us."

Expert analysts may or may not agree with their assessment, but I could not hear their claim or see their pain without committing myself to learning as much as I could about the region in general and the Arab-Israeli conflict in particular.

Two decades earlier I had traveled to Bosnia and Croatia during the Balkan war, haunted by a single question: *What does it mean to follow Jesus into a place of violent conflict?*

Later I asked that question as I traveled to the Democratic Republic of Congo, where the deadliest war since World War II was raging.

I ask the question still as I travel repeatedly to the Holy Land. That question has compelled me to seek peacemakers, and I've found them—on both sides of the conflict, in all three of the Abrahamic faiths, and among some who claim no religion at all. One peacemaker, a non-religious Israeli Jew, told me on one of my first trips, "If you're here to pick sides, go home. We don't need you. But if you're willing to figure out what it means to be a friend to both Israelis and Palestinians, then we welcome you. Either Arabs and Jews will learn to live together, or we'll die together. Help us learn to live together."

Certainly there are strong rejectionist voices: people from both sides and from all three faiths who want nothing to do with peace, who are so overwhelmed by fear and filled with hatred that they cannot even imagine peace. I listen to them. I learn from them. But I align myself with those who live out a willingness to forgive and to be forgiven; who listen to "the other" not to find the flaws in their arguments but in order to understand them;

who believe that loving our enemies is not just a suggestion Jesus made in a thoughtless moment but a call to deep Christian discipleship. Christians in the Holy Land who choose this daily discipleship inspire me; Jews and Muslims who walk the path toward peace—whether or not they acknowledge it as the way of Jesus—humble me.

As an American Christian, I am aware, of course, that engagement in the Holy Land is theologically controversial. Some Christians make a strong case that the birth of the modern State of Israel in 1948 and the ingathering of the Jews to the Holy Land is a fulfillment of Old Testament prophecies that are tied to end-time events and the second coming of Christ. Other Christians emphasize Jesus' fulfillment of Old Testament prophecies, and the spiritual nature of God's kingdom that is not connected to a physical place. Jewish followers of Jesus—Messianic Jews—tend to fall more in the first theological camp, and Palestinian Christians tend to fall in the latter.

I knew these theological differences existed, but I was still caught off guard after I gave a talk about my engagement in the Holy Land, when a Messianic Jewish theologian from Israel told me he believed I had totally violated Scripture by talking about the plight of the Palestinians. He reminded me that God had given the land to the Jews, and if the Palestinians were suffering it was because God's will related to the Holy Land was being violated. If I thought the treatment they were receiving was unjust it was because I didn't understand God's purposes in the world. It was a very awkward and disturbing conversation.

Now, fast-forward two years. I gave another similar talk, and again that same Messianic theologian approached me afterwards. I assumed we would have another awkward conversation.

Instead, he said, "Thank you for that talk. That was a great talk. In fact, I think you should give that talk to some of our Jewish congregations."

What happened during the two years separating those conversations?

What happened in me is that a wise Palestinian friend challenged me to spend as much time with Israelis as I had been spending with Palestinians.

So I began doing that. In subsequent trips I met with secular mainstream Jews and those in the Israeli peace movement. I talked with Israeli families who'd lost children to the violence of suicide bombers. I ate Shabbat meals with Orthodox families, and listened to the perspective of Messianic Jews. Perhaps most significantly, I walked slowly through the halls of Yad Vashem, the Holocaust Memorial in Jerusalem.

In my second talk in Bethlehem, I described those experiences. I also said, "I will never bring a group of people to visit Israel and Palestine again, without taking them to Yad Vashem. How can we begin to understand this place without holding the reality of Jewish history in our conscious awareness?"

So, my heart had been broken on a deeper level for the Jewish people and that came through in my talk.

What also happened during those two years was that the Jewish theologian spent time with Palestinians in the West Bank, and he actually saw the reality of their daily lives. He said to me, "I still support the State of Israel and believe the Jews have a unique role to play in God's redemptive plan. *But the kind of injustice I've seen in the West Bank, and that you have described in your talk, is unconscionable. It can't continue.*"

That story—of those two very different conversations—greatly encouraged me. I've been similarly encouraged by many people with whom I disagree on some points of theology, but for whom I have the deepest respect, and whose level of compassion and wisdom humbles me. Israeli and Palestinian followers of Jesus in the Holy Land have to struggle with a very difficult blend of theology, politics, and history—all bound together with fear and hurt and repeated disappointments. Yet I've met theologians on both sides who, because they actually live in the complex reality of the Holy Land, speak with the careful nuance that complexity requires. Together they hold to an image of Jews and Arabs, Israelis and Palestinians, living together in the land in peace.

Some see a measure of peace achievable through a political solution; others envision peace only in a distant day when Jesus' kingdom is here in fullness. But they are united in their desire and commitment to see Jews and Arabs living peacefully and equally as brothers and sisters.

Because of the peacemakers I've met "on the ground" in Israel and the West Bank, I believe it is possible to be truly pro-Israeli and pro-Palestinian at the same time.

The first step toward that is to acknowledge that Israelis and Palestinians have very different, and often conflicting, histories and narratives, each of which must be sought out and respectfully heard. When you pay attention to both narratives, it's easy to understand why the Jews would want a homeland in that little strip of land where they have biblical and historical ties. And it's easy to understand why the Palestinians feel they have an equally valid claim on the land based on centuries of residence there.

Certainly, either narrative can be mythologized and distorted and used to demonize the other. So, part of our task as people seeking peace is to listen with a discerning ear, to study well, to question what we hear, and to learn from a wide variety of people.

I had just such an opportunity several years ago in Bethlehem. I attended a meeting of Palestinian women, both Christian and Muslim. There were two speakers at the meeting. One was an Israeli Messianic Jew from Nazareth. The other was a Palestinian Christian woman from Jerusalem. Each of these two women described, in turn, the typical narrative that is commonly held by her people, and then she critiqued it.

The Jewish woman said, "You won't like what I'm going to say, but this is what most Jews believe: that Jewish violence in the war of 1948 was purely defensive; Jews were simply defending themselves against Arab aggressors. But before you get mad at me, I need to tell you that I realize that is not true. The tragic truth is that in 1948 many Arabs were aggressively forced from their land and/or brutally killed by Jewish fighters." She said, "Admitting this makes me pretty unpopular with some Israelis, but we must be open to self-criticism."

The Palestinian woman described some of the hardships of the occupation, but then she said, "We Palestinians tend to think that all our problems are caused by the occupation. But that's not true." She said, "We must accept culpability for allowing a victim mentality to dominate our actions and for making many poor choices along the way that have hurt us collectively." That was hard for some of the Palestinian women to hear, and they discussed it at length. But at the end of the meeting they asked to meet again so they could continue such discussions.

It was such a privilege to sit in on that meeting. How admirable, how wise, how courageous, for these women to be willing to listen to the narrative of the other and also to critique their own. Surely, they are laying an important foundation for peace.

When I say I'm pro-Israel, I mean that I support the existence of the State of Israel as a home for the Jewish people. I long for the day when Jews can live there without the fear of rockets from Gaza, or suicide bombers, or any other kind of violence against them. In a world in which anti-Semitism is, tragically, still alive and well, I am thankful for the State of Israel. While I may disagree with some policies of the government of Israel, that doesn't mean I'm anti-Israel or anti-Jew, anymore than my disagreement with certain policies of the US government means that I'm anti-US or anti-American.

When I say I'm pro-Palestinian, I mean that I believe Palestinians have an equally valid right to live in the land and should have the same civil rights that are afforded to Israeli Jewish citizens, whether that's in one state, two states, or however many states. I believe Palestinians—whether in the West Bank or Gaza—should be free from military occupation or blockade. They should be able to travel freely between their own communities, engage in commerce, and have easy access to the outside world.

I believe that the ongoing military occupation of the West Bank and the continuing blockade of Gaza is a violation of human rights; as such, it deeply harms the security, freedom, and dignity of both Palestinians and Israelis. The very fact that I use the word "occupation" has led some people to judge me as an enemy of the State of Israel; they have told me the only "occupation" is the one perpetrated by the Arabs who are occupying the land of Judea and Samaria that belongs to the Jews.

On the other hand, I've met many Israeli Jews who believe the occupation is wrong; that it violates their Judaic ethic; that it breeds hostility and undermines security; and that it has to end.

In an op-ed, an Israeli journalist wrote, "Why can't 'pro-Israel' mean anti-occupation, support for human rights, equality, democracy for all peoples under Israel's control? Why should we perpetuate the conflict, by supporting Israeli government policies that perpetuate the conflict?"

I've met many Israelis who, like this journalist, claim to be patriots fighting for the soul, security, integrity, and future of their country—they just don't want to do that at the expense of the Palestinians.

These people believe, as I do, that any violence against civilians, whether carried out militarily or through guerrilla tactics, is illegal under international law, damages prospects for peace, and must not be tolerated. I have never—and will never—condone the violence of Hamas. But grieving the death of innocent Palestinian civilians in Gaza does not equal support for Hamas. Likewise, grieving the deaths of Israelis and being empathetic to the sense of terror created by continual rocket fire does not equal support for all Israeli policies.

In the years since I began traveling to Israel and the West Bank, there has been a fluctuating level of hostility between Palestinians and Israelis. As I write these words, in early 2015, I watch sadly as that hostility manifests itself in open hatred, expressed both in vitriolic words and acts of violence. However, I truly do not believe that hatred and violence reflects the hearts of the majority of Palestinians. Nor do I believe it reflects the hearts of the majority of Israelis.

I may be wrong. But I began traveling to the Holy Land specifically in search of peacemakers, in search of people committed to nonviolence, forgiveness, and reconciliation. And I found them, in both Palestine and Israel. From what I can see, they're still there.

Several months ago, thirty American, Israeli, and Palestinian women met for two days in Washington, DC. We were Christians, Muslims, and Jews, religious and secular, young, and old—united by our commitment to equal human rights for all the people of the Holy Land.

Some of the Palestinian women had been criticized by their friends in the West Bank for attending a meeting with Israelis, their oppressors. Some of the Israeli women had been criticized by their friends for attending a meeting with Palestinians, their enemies. Some of the American women showed up at the meeting licking wounds sustained from journalists who wrongly judged our character and motives.

So, there was a rather high degree of emotional "rawness" in the gathering. While that rawness could have pushed us all to put up protective barriers, it actually had the opposite impact. There was an unusual level of honest communication and vulnerability, with Israeli and Palestinian women talking about the fears they have for their children and the loneliness they often feel as women committed to peace and reconciliation.

There was a particularly profound connection between a young Palestinian woman and an older Israeli woman. They were both psychologists, highly educated and articulate, but neither could quite contain their emotion as they spoke.

The young Palestinian woman described what it was like to send her teenage son through a checkpoint, knowing that he would feel frustrated and humiliated; she feared that the humiliation, repeated over and over again, would turn him into an angry young man, maybe even a violent young man. She tried to keep him away from checkpoints, but she couldn't keep him locked in one little neighborhood. So she feared for his future.

The older Israeli woman described what it was like knowing that her teenage grandson was an Israeli Defense Force (IDF) soldier, standing at a checkpoint with a gun in his hand, terrified of using the power of that weapon, and yet terrified not to. She didn't want him to become the oppressor, but he was becoming just that. She feared what that would do to him, inside.

The two women agreed: "We are both victims of this conflict, this occupation, this ongoing tragedy. We are both victims of the fear that sets our people against each other."

Then the Israeli woman spoke out of the wisdom of her years: "But look at us here," she said, "in this room. Today we talked about our fear, and instead of fear driving us apart, it has brought us together. We need to keep talking with one another, deeply and honestly. We need to use this fear to draw us together."

In that room filled with broken women, something deeply holy happened.

I'm coming to believe that the key to peacemaking is *brokenness*. Speaking personally, the haunting question I mentioned at the beginning of this chapter—*What does it mean to follow Jesus into a place of conflict?*—has led me into a journey of ongoing brokenness. Over and over again I am broken: broken every time I have to face, again, how poorly I live out Jesus' call to peacemaking; how quick I am to pick sides and go for easy answers; basically, how unlike Jesus I am.

Jean Paul Lederach wrote a book called *RECONCILE*. He suggests that the main thing Jesus brought to his role as a peacemaker was his presence. There was something in his *presence*—something in who he was and how he showed up—that made the way of peace more likely.

I think that *something* that was in Jesus is what the Holy Land—and every region of conflict—needs now. A friend from Bethlehem, who has been engaged in nonviolence and reconciliation for many years, wrote this to me at the height of the 2014 violence between Hama and Israel: "When all the dead are buried and the dust settles, a truer and deeper kind of peace needs to rise up from the rubble of the Holy Land."

I agree with him. Yes, of course, there is need for political change in the Holy Land, and I do not hesitate to advocate for such change. And certainly, there are important changes related to human rights and freedom that need to be made. But political decisions and changes in legal status, even if supported by the international community, will not be enough to bring sustainable peace to the Holy Land. Something more is needed, something deeper. While we work and advocate for practical change, we must also work and pray for something deeper: not a peace that depends on the decisions of politicians or that trips off the tongues of activists, but a peace that bubbles up from the spring of God's love as it fills us—and fills our Israeli and Palestinian friends—and then pulls us all beyond the limits of our own self-interest. We need a spiritual transformation and healing that pulls us to that place where we are free to see and love the other as God does.

To see and love the other as God does. That doesn't come naturally to us. I think it only comes through prayer and silence and deep listening for the still small voice of God. I am more committed than ever to the journey of transformation that is peacemaking. And I know there are Palestinians and Israelis more committed than ever to that journey. Together, let us pray and work and sacrifice and encourage one another as we pursue God's true and multifaceted vision of peace in the Holy Land.

25

Overrated:
The Holy Land and Discipleship

Rev. Eugene Cho

IN 2006 I FOUND myself in a village in a remote area of the jungle in Myanmar (otherwise known as Burma). United Nations officials had deemed the genocide in certain parts of Burma similar to the crisis in Darfur in the 1990s—but it had been widely forgotten in the global media.

I learned about the challenges violence impresses upon their community. The village—comprising mostly of internally displaced refugees—like many others, didn't even have a name because its residents often had to pack up quickly to flee when they heard news of an imminent attack; the village was simply designated by a number. Despite the hardships and challenges the villagers faced, I was genuinely compelled by their sense of hope and courage.

I asked, "What are your biggest challenges?"

"Schools. Teachers. Paying teachers hard," replied one of the village elders in broken English, knowing that I had visited one of their makeshift schools earlier in the day.

The school couldn't hold on to its teachers because they kept leaving to take jobs across the border in Thailand, where schools offered higher salaries. Out of curiosity, I asked this village elder about the salary of their teachers.

"About forty dollars," he responded.

Without even thinking, I replied, "Forty dollars a day?"

He laughed and then shook his head.

Embarrassed, I said, I'm sorry. Forty dollars a week?"

There was no laugh this time. He just shook his head. Oh my goodness. How could their salaries be forty dollars per month?

"Forty dollars a month?" I asked.

While I expected an affirmation the elder shook his head and I couldn't fathom the possibility of my next guess being accurate.

With hesitation and incredulity, I asked, "Forty dollars a year?"

And he finally nodded his head.

I couldn't believe it. That's what I'd spend on a cheap date night with my wife, a few books, a cell phone bill, or a tank of gas. But forty dollars prevented this village from keeping their teachers around.

After that, we couldn't sit and go back to life as usual. Convicted and moved, my wife Minhee and I decided we had to do something. We would ask people to give up what they earned for just one day's work—about 0.4 percent of their annual salary—and that money would *impact* lives in real ways. This became One Day's Wages (ODW), a grassroots movement of people, stories, and action to alleviate extreme global poverty.

However, this wasn't just about starting something. It wasn't just about doing a work of compassion and justice. There was more. Far more dangerous and uncomfortable. God was challenging us not just to "change the world"; he was inviting us to change. You see, it's easier to talk about wanting to change the world; to talk about the need to change this and change that; to start this movement and start that organization. But if I'm honest, we don't always do it, and we don't always want to think that we, ourselves, have to change in the process.

Minhee and I spent time discussing how to respond to the convictions of our hearts, we prayed for direction, vision, and clarity.

What we sensed was not pleasant. Not pleasant at all. Maybe I could craft a nice thirty-minute sermon, write a serious of blog posts, or recommend books and links for people to check out on Facebook. But isn't that what makes discipleship so uncomfortable and challenging? God often leads us on a journeys we would never go on if it were up to us. It's our ideas versus God's will. It's our agenda versus God's will. It's our plans versus God's will.

In prayer, both Minhee and I sensed an invitation from the Holy Spirit to give up an entire year's salary. Thus our journey began, but I began this quest, in part, because I sensed *I could do it*. However, Minhee and I had no idea exactly how difficult this conviction would be to live out.

The months and years that followed brought us to our knees and led me to a simple, yet piercing confession: I am more in love with the idea of changing the world *than actually changing the world*. And in wanting to change the world, I confess to neglecting a posture of humility in which I must be aware that *I, too, must change.*

Let's be honest: most of us love justice and compassion. In terms of popularity, justice has *really* taken off in recent years. So quickly, I sometimes fear the true meaning gets lost in the fray. I fear that our passion for justice might end up in a cardboard box next to our Jesus Freak T-shirts and W.W.J.D. bracelets. I fear the fullness of biblical justice will not take root, and be nothing more than a passing trend.

Justice is the act of restoring something to fullness after it has been harmed. Justice is making things right. But that definition for me is still a little incomplete. Even more fundamental than a definition of justice is the place from which our understanding of justice emanates. It is hard to restore what has been wronged if you don't have a point of reference. We need to know what this fullness looks like in its pure form. We need to know where this restoration comes from. If fullness is the goal for us as the church and as Christians, we must seek to understand the fullness of what God intended for his creation. We need to more deeply understand God the Father, Jesus the son of God, and the Holy Spirit. We need to more deeply grow in intimacy with the creator, redeemer, and sustainer. More often than not, we're fixed in the brokenness of our world because we are constantly surrounded by brokenness. But if we're not careful, we lose sight of God. We lose sight of God's purpose and intent for creation. We lose sight of God's promise to restore our brokenness and fallen world.

This is why for us, as Christians, the person of God, the deity of God, God's justice, and God's goodness are such powerful things. God's justice is his plan of redemption for a broken world. God's justice is renewing the world to what he would have intended it to be.

Justice is not just a thing that is good. Justice is not merely doing well. Justice is not something that's moral or right or fair. Justice is not, in itself, a set of ethics. Justice is not just an aggregation of the many justice-themed verses throughout the Scriptures. Justice is not trendy, glamorous, cool, or sexy. Justice isn't a movement. Justice is so much more, and the understanding of this fullness is central to the work that we do in pursuing justice.

I do believe this truth is making its way into the hearts of this generation and I truly believe this is our calling to all peoples *and* I believe there is an imperative thrust upon the church to live out the gift of justice and compassion in Israel and the occupied Palestinian territories.

This conflict, the Israeli-Palestinian conflict, has successfully divided and entrenched the church and society at large to such a degree that even fundamental beliefs about love and charity, of which there is wide agreement across Christian traditions and denominations, have been suspended if not abolished from discourse.

By and large we have chosen to suspend inquiry, compassion, and justice for one of two things: (1) biblical themed recreation or (2) a proxy war for our political and eschatological predispositions. All the while the people of this land—Muslim, Christian, and Jew—are living on a different plane. We do not see the anger, suffering, prejudice, and deep personal wounds . . . and if we do, it's severely limited and heavily qualified.

It's in this context that we should offer a confession similar to the first: We have been in love with the idea of the Holy Land more than the people that *actually* live there. We have not allowed the land and all its people to impact us, change us, make us think, and grow. If we seek to confront this reality, to do works of compassion and justice, if we seek to follow Jesus into the land of his birth, we must confront the realities of this broken Holy Land and understand that we too need to be changed along the way.

I wanted my first visit to Israel and Palestine to reflect as many perspectives and histories as possible. I'm not, and we should not, be afraid to have more information or to love more people. I met with Israeli security experts, Israeli and Palestinian activists, kids, faith leaders, lawyers. It's important to learn about the histories and daily lives of these people. Learn about anti-Semitism, which, largely perpetrated by Christians, has afflicted and even sought to destroy the Jewish people for centuries. We should learn about the Palestinian families that were displaced in 1948 and still live as refugees. The populations of these communities are relatively small by US standards, and the pain and fear is personal for everyone.

And while one can experience and empathize with diverging opinions, occasionally, you have an experience that's beyond a difference of perspective. Even when engaging an issue as complex as this, there are times when perspective doesn't justify an unconscionable injustice. I reached this conclusion in Ofer Prison watching the court proceedings for a Palestinian teenager on trial before the Israeli Military Court.

What many don't understand about the word *occupation* is that it is not just an evocative buzzword or a rallying cry for Palestinians. It's a technical term (not limited to the Israeli-Palestinian conflict) to describe the effective provisional control of a ruling power over a territory which is not under the formal sovereignty of that political entity.

I think many of us in North America have a hard time understanding the realities and implications of occupation, and there are many. But one important implication for the Israeli-Palestinian conflict is that an Israeli legal system has been imposed on people in the West Bank. While there is a

Palestinian government and Palestinian civil court system, all Palestinians in the West Bank are ultimately subject to Israeli Military Law.

When I say all Palestinians in the West Bank, I mean all Palestinians. That includes children.

The Israeli "Youth Law" states that the incarceration of minors is a last resort employed when no alternative exists. A separate legal apparatus has been created in recognition of how a child's age affects not only criminal responsibility, but also the experience of arrest, interrogation, trial, and imprisonment. It explicitly prohibits the incarceration of minors under the age of fourteen, the arrest and interrogation of minors at night, and it provides both for consultation with a lawyer and for the presence of a parent during questioning.

To put it simply, in contrast to these legal protections afforded Israeli children under Israeli civil law, Palestinians children have far fewer rights under Israeli military law; arrest and imprisonment remain to be the *primary* means of coping with offenses. By a very wide margin, Palestinian children are most often accused of and arrested for throwing stones.

UNICEF has been tracking and regularly reporting on this issue for several years. A recent report featured sworn testimonies from 208 Palestinian children gathered from September 2013 up until September 2014, reporting ill-treatment at the hands of various Israeli military and police authorities while under military detention in the West Bank. One hundred and thirty-nine of the children interviewed were aged sixteen and seventeen; sixty-nine were aged fifteen and younger. Of the 208 interviewed:

- 162 children were blindfolded at the time of their arrest
- 189 children had their hands painfully bound at the time of arrest
- 171 children experienced physical violence during arrest, interrogation, and/or detention
- 144 experienced verbal abuse and intimidation
- eighty-nine were transferred from the place of arrest to the police station on the floor of a vehicle
- seventy-nine were awoken and taken from their homes in the middle of the night
- 163 were not informed of their right to counsel and right to remain silent
- 148 were strip searched at the police station, seventy-six at the detention facilities

- twenty-eight children were held in solitary confinement
- sixty-three were forced to sign a confession in a language they do not understand

At the time of arrest, parents are rarely informed of the allegations against their child, they are rarely informed where their child is taken, and they are rarely present during the interrogation. Parents are unlikely to see their child for days, often not until the trial.

In November 2015, I sat on a bench in the back of a double wide trailer on the compound of Ofer Prison beside the parents of a teenager arrested, detained, and now on trial for throwing stones. Most of the children I saw that day had been accused of throwing stones. One of them had been accused of carrying a knife with the intention of harming an Israeli soldier.

The court proceedings were hectic. It was hot and sun poured through the windows of this trailer turned court room. Three Palestinians were being tried at the same time; only one of them was a minor. All court personnel and most of the dozen attendees were in the Israeli Defense Force uniform. The room swirled as clerks shuffled papers to and from the judge, defense lawyers shouted over one another, staff moved in and out of the cramped space. Arab and Hebrew could be heard intermittently in the loudness of the courtroom. The trial was conducted in Hebrew and on occasion, although rarely, translated into Arabic; the child and his family often didn't know what was happening (nor did I), even though we had translators. A soldier sat down next to me and offered to translate. He said the youth attempted to stab someone and had confessed his guilt. Having discussed the case with the child's lawyer, I knew the soldier's story was different than what the youth claimed.

If this young man decided to plead not guilty, he would remain in prison several more months. He would be away from his family, his friends, and would fall behind in school. There was no choice but to plead guilty. This is one of the reasons about 99 percent of cases involving children produce a guilty verdict.

On average, there are between 250 and 300 Palestinian children in Israeli military detention at any time.

I do not condone stone throwing. This is a serious offense that has harmed and even killed Israelis. And yet, this unjust system, both in its noncompliance with principles of due process and its disregard for the needs of children, is unacceptable. And the problem is not cosmetic. By its very nature, military occupation cannot facilitate community level restorative justice for children. Full stop.

This is what military occupation is.

This is how it plays out.

This is one reason among many that peace must be forged and occupation brought to an end.

I am more in love with the idea of changing the world . . . than actually changing the world. And in wanting to change the world, I confess to neglecting a posture of humility in which I must be aware that I, too, must change.

I carry a passion for peace and justice in the Holy Land, and my heart did change in that courtroom on a day I will never forget. But that change cannot be the last. No matter how unjustly they have been treated, my compassion cannot be exclusively reserved for Palestinian children. True Christian discipleship and love is too radical to end there.

I think about that day. I think about the Israeli clerks in that court room. Several young men and women in their early twenties, required by law to serve in the military. I have to imagine they didn't want to be there either. I think of other Israeli soldiers I met at checkpoints. Young. Bored. Tired. Angry. Spending their youth herding people like cattle day after day. I think about their parents. Parents who lovingly brought their children into the world. Who now pass on a conflict they too once fought and, as much as they tried, could not resolve. I think of the terror attacks on buses and cafes. I think of the Jewish people who have longed for safety and peace for so long.

I am unapologetic about acknowledging the injustices children face in the military court system and under occupation. And that reality is not threatened, undermined, or dismissed by compassion and love. It's not absolved when I ask young Israelis about their fears and aspirations. The injustice is not forgotten when I learn about and pray for Israel's security. I have no less urgency to right this wrong when I learn about and enjoy Jewish tradition.

There are many who will insist that you stop growing.

You empathize with Israel: that is enough.

You empathize with Palestine: that is enough.

It is not enough. There is always more.

The gospel we love and seek to administer is not just about salvation, but also about a commitment to the kingdom of God, a kingdom that was ushered in by the incarnation and ministry of Jesus, the Christ, in the very land of which we speak.

If we believe in this kingdom and gospel of Christ, we believe that Christ came, Christ died, Christ was raised, and Christ will return. The power of the Holy Spirit is at work all around us so that we don't have to wait aimlessly until that day. I believe a sincere discipleship demonstrates itself by being active in kingdom work, because of Christ's example, and out of gratitude for God for everything we've been given. Few places are as worthy and in need of this work, the work of Shalom, restoration, and redemption.

In seeking to do justice and kingdom work in the Holy Land, we have to be open to the reality that God will challenge us, change us, and transform us. In doing justice and in doing things that matter to God, we actually grow more in his likeness. We will begin to reflect more of the character of God. We grow more intimate with the heart of God. We will do things because they embody the kingdom of God. And it is right in the eyes of God.

May we continue to pray for peace and justice in the Holy Land and continue to be transformed into the likeness of God.

Part VII

Future Hope: Action & Engagement toward a Just Peace

©Mae Elise Cannon
Candles in the Church of the Nativity – Bethlehem

26

Praying for Peace in Jerusalem

Jim Wallis

THE ANCIENT WORDS OF Psalm 122 lyrically and beautifully call us to "pray for peace in Jerusalem." Today's headlines remind us that these prayers remain urgently needed, as Jerusalem continues to symbolize both the hopes and dreams of the Abrahamic faith traditions and the pain and division of the enduring Israeli-Palestinian conflict. This conflict has claimed countless lives, caused unimaginable trauma, and devastated families and communities for decades. Many perceive it as irresolvable, but such pessimism betrays a lack of theological imagination. Arriving at sustainable solutions involves a new commitment to the peace, security, and prosperity of all God's people.

Our prayers for peace will be meaningless if we do not understand the depth and complexity of the meaning behind that word. Peace has become a thin concept in the world today. We assume peace exists wherever violence is absent but this is an incorrect and shallow understanding. There is no constant, open warfare between South Korea and North Korea but peace can hardly be said to exist between those two nations. The constant tension between community members and law enforcement in so many US cities does not qualify as peace. Many women face discrimination and oppression in societies around the globe. While many do not actively resist, their daily acts of passive protest demonstrate the lack of peace.

Expressing centuries of Christian wisdom, Martin Luther King, Jr. once said, "true peace is not the absence of tension; it is the presence of justice."[1] Peace requires not simply the cessation of shooting, the removal of troops, or an end to the threat of imminent violence. It requires that the dignity of each person be acknowledged and respected. True peace demands fair treatment across society and equality before the law. It is not possible unless economic and political opportunity is accessible to everyone.

So, how can true peace prevail in Israel/Palestine?

Before attempting an answer to that question let me say something that is both unpopular and true: Christians—regardless of their intentions—have often been an obstacle to peace in the region.

How so?

First, many evangelical Christians have historically been uncritical and unequivocal supporters of Israel. Even when the Israeli military and government take actions warranting critique and condemnation, evangelical support in the US has often been unflinching. This support is frequently rooted in the dispensationalist belief that a Jewish state must exist in the Middle East in order for Christ to return.[2] These Christian Zionists have historically been unwilling to criticize or even question Israel's behavior and have even financially supported destructive behaviors such as settlement expansion in the West Bank. Some in this community conflate Israel and the will of God, rendering critical analysis of the state antithetical to God's will. As a result, Israel's actions are seen as advancing the second coming of Jesus, and override all other considerations for these believers.

The influence of Christian Zionism in the evangelical world has also created a great deal of pressure on US politicians to support Israel's policies, particularly among those who depend on evangelical votes. Though Christian Zionist evangelicals are not the only group that has made it difficult for US politicians to criticize Israel, their influence on this debate should not be understated. And the consequently unique nature of support Israel enjoys from the US has ultimately served everyone poorly. Israel has sustained a military occupation to the point of permanence, knowing that the US and allies are reticent to critique its actions. Meanwhile, Israel's opponents point to oppressive systems and instances of violence to justify and rally international support for their own violent actions. It is a vicious cycle resulting in many unnecessary deaths and inhibiting progress toward peace.

The second way that Christians have been an obstacle to peace is the mirror opposite of the first. Many Mainline Protestants and other liberal

---

1. King, *Stride Toward Freedom*.
2. Webber, "On the Road."

Christians, often acting through denominational structures, have taken a reflexively critical attitude toward Israel's actions. For example, the Israel/Palestine Mission Network, an independent Presbyterian Church (USA) advocacy group, recently published a study guide called "Zionism Unsettled," which challenges the history and theological underpinnings of the Zionist movement. Some American Jewish leaders were outraged by the study guide, stating the publication ignored anti-Semitism and the Holocaust, and equated Zionism with racism; ultimately, they did not find the study to be an attack on particular Israeli policies, but on Jewish identity.[3] Attempting to delegitimize the premise for the existence of a Jewish state in the Holy Land, regardless of the merits of the argument, is counterproductive to creating peace in the region. Furthermore, when Mainline Protestants and others downplay or fail to acknowledge Israel's very real security concerns, it diminishes the validity of their critique and damages relationships between Christians and Jews in the United States.

Despite these problematic behaviors by Christians on both sides of the Israel/Palestine issue, there is also reason for hope for a more honest and fair approach among both evangelicals and Mainline Protestants. Among evangelicals, support for Israel's policies is no longer as unanimous and uncritical as it once was. As *Haaretz* noted earlier this year:

> While hard numbers are not available, evangelical leaders on both sides of the divide on Israel agree that members of the millennial generation do not share their parents' passion for the Jewish state; many are seeking some form of evenhandedness when approaching the Israeli-Palestinian conflict.[4]

Many young evangelicals are rejecting the message of Christian Zionism, just as they are rejecting the underlying theology that says that the afterlife and/or the end times are the only things that matter. These millennials are more focused on making the kingdom of God a reality on earth "as it is in heaven" by putting their faith into action for the cause of social justice. Consequently, they have a greater sensitivity to the plight of the ordinary Palestinians and Israelis who have suffered so much at the hands of their leaders and the most radical elements of their respective societies.

A big part of the evolving views of evangelical Christians on Israel and Palestine is the increased awareness of and empathy for Palestinian Christians. Christians have been living in Palestine since the third century, and about 50,000 of them became refugees when the State of Israel was founded

---

3. Goodstein, "Presbyterians Vote to Divest."
4. Guttman and Forward, "Israel is losing its grip."

in 1948.[5] The dwindling percentage of Christians currently living in Gaza and the West Bank are suffering the same indignities and oppression of the occupation as their Muslim brothers and sisters. As awareness of the circumstances of Palestinian Christians has percolated to US evangelicals, the views of evangelicals on the conflict have started to evolve toward a perspective that is less reflexively pro-Israel and more open to hearing a range of views.

Many Mainline Protestants also have a much more nuanced position on the Israeli-Palestinian conflict than is represented by the most vocally anti-Israel members of these churches. In many cases, criticism of Israel by Mainline Protestant churches is accompanied by a strong acknowledgement of Israel's right to exist and the very real security concerns Israel faces. These churches have not shied away from offering a powerful, prophetic challenge to some of Israel's policies in the occupied territories—especially those relating to Israeli settlements—but this critique does not make these churches anti-Israel.

For example, the Presbyterian Church (USA) recently passed a resolution to divest in three major corporations that supply Israel with equipment that supporters of the resolution say is utilized to further the occupation of Palestinian territory and oppression of Palestinians. Unlike the study guide I mentioned earlier, this resolution, while still controversial, is a much better example of words and actions that can be both prophetic and constructive. The purpose of the resolution is not to completely stop doing business with Israel, but rather to simply stop supporting settlement expansion in the occupied territories, which is among the most destructive factors to creating a lasting peace. In addition, this resolution explicitly "reaffirmed Israel's right to exist, endorsed a two-state solution, encouraged interfaith dialogue and travel to the Holy Land, and instructed the church to undertake 'positive investment' in endeavors that advance peace and improve the lives of Israelis and Palestinians."[6] This is an example of a more honest and fair approach toward the conflict that is needed by Mainline Protestants and Christians of all traditions.

In approaching the conflict, I believe that as Christians we are called to be both *honest and fair*, rather than being *balanced* or *neutral* in our witness. So what does a more honest and fair perspective on the Israeli-Palestinian conflict require of us as Christians? While I cannot claim to have all of those answers, I do think we can say that we first need to reject the distortions propagated by elements at both extremes of the conflict. And then we need

---

5. Morgan and Alford, "How Gaza's Christians."
6. Goodstein, "Presbyterians Vote to Divest."

to look at the situation with clear eyes and speak the truth in love, no matter how difficult we find this to be.

And one truth we need to speak is this: there is something terribly wrong with the settlements.

Settlements are Israeli communities established on the Palestinian side of the armistice line drawn after the 1967 war. This line, also known as the green line, forms the West Bank border. While Israeli settlements are built in the West Bank, they are not governed by the Palestinian Authority or Israeli military law. Instead, the protections and authority of Israeli civil law and governance are imported into the settlements with the aid and protection of the Israeli military. While only separated by meters, Israeli settlers are afforded the civil liberties and due process their Palestinian neighbors do not enjoy under Israeli military law and occupation. To be clear, there are two systems of Israeli law operating in the West Bank: one for Israelis, one for Palestinians. There is something terribly wrong with settlements. This truth has been reinforced for me by the things I have seen and the experiences I have had in the region. A few years ago, I was in Israel and the Palestinian territories for an international peace conference. As I traveled through the West Bank, everywhere I looked were enormous Israeli settlements, always on the highest ground, with the most modern, first-world living conditions anywhere, towering over the much poorer Palestinian villages down in the valley. There are over 500,000 Israeli settlers living in settlements across the West Bank, including East Jerusalem.

I saw how Israeli settlements loom over the West Bank and likewise loom over the chances for peace in the Middle East. They are the "facts on the ground" that shape virtually everything about Middle East politics today. Settlements are aggressive forays into Palestinian territory and each one makes lasting peace that much more difficult. Israeli soldiers are in the West Bank not to protect Palestinians from violence or crime, but only to protect the settlements and the settlers. They control the roads, control the movement, and control the daily life of the Palestinian population.

Many people in the Middle East and elsewhere have accepted the hope and logic of a two-state solution and the formula of land for peace. But there is no contiguous Palestinian territory in the West Bank or in Gaza. There are only pieces of Palestinian territory, transected by Israeli roads connecting Israeli settlements. As long as the settlements remain, the only possibility is disconnected territories housing the Palestinian workers who service the Israeli State.

The Israeli policy is called closure. Everything gets closed down in the West Bank and Palestinians are not allowed to move freely—to go to school, to work, or even to visit family. All Palestinians are required to have permits and pass through interminable checkpoints. I've been with groups stopped at every checkpoint, even though we were international delegations. We had some clout and were no threat to the Israelis, and they still held us up for hours. If you are a Palestinian, you wait. And you wait. I have heard so many stories of intimidation, indignity, and mistreatment of Palestinians from every religion and profession; even of women in labor stopped at checkpoints on the way to the hospital. Israeli journalist Amira Hass is one of a growing number of Jews both in Israel and America who believe the policies of settlements and closure are as morally damaging to the Israelis as they are oppressive to the Palestinians. Hass describes the closure policy as "the theft of spontaneity."[7]

There is indeed Palestinian violence against Israelis. Shootings and even mortar shells have been aimed into the settlements. People have been killed, and the fear is very high. There have been casualties even among Israeli children. I remember that two fourteen-year-old boys were found dead in a cave near their settlement, their bodies battered and mutilated with rocks, killed by Palestinians. There have been suicide bombings in Israeli cities, and rockets fired into Israel from the Gaza Strip. And in November 2014, two Palestinian attackers murdered four Israeli rabbis as they worshiped in their West Jerusalem synagogue, and killed one of the police officers who rushed to the scene.[8] The existence of horrific violence against Israeli civilians cannot be disputed. And such violence can *never* be justified. But the Israelis have used these tragedies to justify shelling Palestinians in massive, disproportionate retaliation. The casualties are enormous, including Palestinian children and infants caught in the middle of attacks. Violence against civilians is the definition of terrorism, and it must be named and condemned on all sides.

To be honest and fair, we need to speak clearly to the balance of power in this conflict. There is no "symmetry" in the violence between Israelis and Palestinians. It is simply an undeniable fact that the overwhelming power is on the Israeli side, and the majority of victims are on the Palestinian side. We should rightly condemn the occupation of the West Bank, and in particular the destructive nature of the settlements to the lives of the Palestinians and the health of the peace process. Yet we should also recognize that Israeli security fears are very real, and the violent actions of the Palestinians, particularly when they target innocent Israeli civilians, can be explained but can never be justified. In order to truly be peacemakers, we must be willing to speak the truth to both sides.

7. Wallis, *God's Politics*, 174.
8. Eglash and Booth, "Palestinian Attackers Kill 5."

So for American Christians, to truly promote peace in the region, we need to pursue an approach that is *pro-Israeli, pro-Palestinian, and pro-peace*. Many organizations and individuals, such as the Telos Group, J Street, and Christ at the Checkpoint use variations of this language, and the underlying message is clear: it is perfectly possible to be supportive of the hopes, aspirations, safety, and desire to live in peace of people on both the Israeli and Palestinian sides of the conflict—and indeed, as followers of Jesus, this is our mandate. And we can do so without ignoring the facts or the balance of power. Here are a few suggestions for how Christians in the US can contribute more productively to peace in the Israeli-Palestinian conflict:

1. *Respect everyone's God-given dignity.* Every human being is created in God's image (Gen 1:27). The ultimate source of human worth is rooted in this fundamental truth. Palestinians and Israelis both bear the mark of the Creator and the dignity of all must be affirmed. Everyone killed in this persisting conflict is a child of God, and that should matter to us; the human cost of this conflict makes pursuing peace a moral imperative.

2. *Recognize that leaders of both sides are moral actors.* Governments and rulers wield authority. In making choices that have consequences, they must understand and acknowledge the moral dimension to their decisions. We pretend that firing rockets, dropping bombs, implementing blockades, demolishing homes, and kidnapping or killing people are tactics for accomplishing strategic goals in order to hide from the admitting the obvious reality that war at its root involves moral questions. Too often nations rush into war having done plenty of military planning but little moral preparation. A lot of war and fighting could be avoided by spending more time on the latter.

3. *Remember that peace is a religious value.* Peace is not simply a political good. It is valued by people from a variety of faith traditions, including Jews, Christians, and Muslims. In the Gospel of Matthew, Jesus blesses peacemakers and calls them "children of God" (5:9). Genesis begins with humans living in harmony with God, each other, and all of creation. The presence of violence in our lives and world prominently demonstrates how deeply sin has marred this original beauty. Knowing that God seeks—and will ultimately deliver the restoration of—this harmony, we must work tirelessly for peace.

4. *Form relationships with Palestinians and Israelis.* Too many Christians understand this situation based solely on reports in the news media or the self-interested statements of political leaders. By intentionally

forming relationships with those most closely affected by the continued violence, Christians can better grasp the issues at hand and what is really happening to people caught in the middle of conflict. There is simply no substitute for relationships. Standing with Palestinian Christians at checkpoints and watching how men, women, and children are being treated changes your perspective. Talking to Israeli parents afraid for their teenagers at night clubs or shopping malls, where attacks against civilians have occurred, makes you understand those fears, as a parent. Sitting in the shelled homes of Palestinian families and looking at the huge hole from an Israeli bomb in their children's bedroom wall also hits you as a parent—feeling the fear of their children who were so scared they came that night into their parents' bedroom and were saved—but were still cowering, as were their parents fearing for their families' future.

5. *Speak truth.* It is easier to perpetuate violence when the advocates for peace are silent. Fostering peace requires speaking out against violence, condemning actions that cause death, and demanding leaders exhaust every alternative to violence. Congregations, political leaders, and individuals all need to be vocal advocates for peace. There are Muslims, Jews, and Christians who believe in peace, who believe the Qur'an forbids violence and terrorism, that the Hebrew Scriptures call for justice for the captive and the oppressed, and that Jesus asks us to take up the cross and not the sword. Any successful movement for peace will have to be Christian, Muslim, and Jewish. And there are hopeful signs of that, especially from a new generation on all sides—both in the Middle East and internationally. I've heard stories of young Christian Palestinian leaders in new personal dialogues with Jewish young people who were born in the settlements and see that something is wrong. These types of stories are hopeful indeed.

I am most lifted up by the tremendous determination of my Palestinian and Jewish friends who persevere in the midst of an almost impossible daily situation. Their energy, their faith, their passion, and their determination has always moved me and brought me hope. But they know that they can't win by themselves. It will take an international movement to press for a just and lasting solution for peace.

While Middle East political leaders and American politicians debate timetables for cease-fires and cooling off periods, the necessary momentum for peace will have to come from outside of politics, more from the bottom of society than the top, more from the new generation than the old, and more from faith communities who put their commitment to a just peace above their politics. We have many friends, both Palestinian and Israeli, who are putting their lives on the line for that kind of peace. We can't continue to let them suffer or struggle alone.

Our society too easily dismisses peace as impractical and its advocates as either idealistic or naïve. Re-establishing peace is hard work—about that there can be no doubt—but that reality does little to change the gospel's call for us all to be peacemakers. Following Jesus is never the easiest path to walk—after all, it requires a willingness to pick up our cross and follow—but it is the most rewarding way to experience abundant life. If we want to be children of God then we must be peacemakers in the Middle East and around the world. Our own lives and those of our brothers and sisters depend upon it.

Bibliography

Eglash, Ruth, and William Booth. "Palestinian Attackers Kill 5 At Jerusalem Synagogue, Including 3 Americans." *Washington Post*, November 18, 2014. http://www.washingtonpost.com/national/palestinian-attackers-storm-jewish-synagogue-killing-four-worshippers/2014/11/18/a1b7d502-6f01-11e4-8808-afaa1e3a33ef_story.html.

Goodstein, Laurie. "Presbyterians Vote to Divest Holdings to Pressure Israel." *New York Times*, June 20, 2014. http://www.nytimes.com/2014/06/21/us/presbyterians-debating-israeli-occupation-vote-to-divest-holdings.html?_r=0.

Guttman, Nathan and The Forward. "Israel Is Losing Its Grip On Evangelical Christians." *Haaretz*, March 11, 2014. http://www.haaretz.com/jewish-world/jewish-world-news/1.579182.

King, Martin Luther, Jr. *Stride Toward Freedom: The Montgomery Story*. Boston: Beacon, 2010. Google Play edition.

Morgan, Timothy C., and Deann Alford, "How Gaza's Christians View the Hamas-Israeli Conflict." *Christianity Today*, August 22, 2014. http://www.christianitytoday.com/ct/2014/august-web-only/hamas-israel-conflict-gaza-christians.html?start=2.

Wallis, Jim. *God's Politics: Why the Right Gets it Wrong and the Left Doesn't Get it*. San Francisco: HarperSanFrancisco, 2005.

Webber, Timothy B. "On the Road to Armageddon: How Evangelical Christians became Israel's Best Friend." *Beliefnet*, August 23, 2004. http://www.beliefnet.com/Faiths/Christianity/End-Times/On-The-Road-To-Armageddon.aspx?p=1.

27

Jews, Christians, and Muslims: Finding a Way to Peace

Dr. Joel Hunter

I Am Us For Them, There

Our problems are too big, too complex, and too immediate for any one faith group (or any one secular group) to solve. Not only do we need to build enduring coalitions, but we need to identify with them in a personal way, so that the solutions being built are not mechanical but relational. A global goal such as peace can only be secured through personal aspirations for people not in our own community, applying solutions that start in our own territory and extend beyond.

In 2015, I was listening to Greg Page, CEO of Cargill, the largest privately owned corporation in the US. It is a company that deals extensively with world hunger. He said, "We do not have a global problem; we have a multi-local problem." Brilliant. For me, there were several implications in this approach to impacting a problem too big for any one group or any alliance of major leaders to solve:

- "Peace" looks different in different parts of the world; each area has its own unique circumstances and stakeholders.

- Ongoing relationships are necessary for long-term solutions.

- Peace must be seen as important for the conduct of one's everyday life.

- World problems will not ultimately be solved by the gathering of global leaders, but by the implementation of local leaders.

I can't do much in my own community without the aid and friendship of the Roman Catholic Bishop John Noonan, Rabbi Steven Engel, and Imam Muhammad Musri, who have been my close friends for many years. And I don't want to do major efforts without them because I want to continue to build our friendship. I want them, as well as my own congregation, to live in a better community experiencing those benefits.

For the major Abrahamic faith communities to work together to help create world peace, we must each, in our own communities, see that our own future lies in the well-being of those of other groups in our communities. The directive from God in Jeremiah 29:7: "... Also, seek the peace and prosperity of the city to which I have carried you into exile. Pray to the LORD for it, because if it prospers, you too will prosper" (NIV).

Biblical Precedence

For many conservative believers, especially for evangelical Christians, whatever we do must have some scriptural basis or resonate with some biblical principle. The Bible records the lives of believers, for purposes of common good, working with people who didn't share their own personal faith. From Joseph to Nehemiah to Esther, from Saul to Peter, et al., our faith's ancestors cooperated with people who were not within heir faith communities.

1 Timothy 2:1-4 can be expanded beyond strictly secular rulers and authorities:

> I urge that entreaties and prayers, petitions and thanksgivings, be made on behalf of all men, for kings and all who are in authority, so that we may lead a tranquil and quiet life in all godliness and dignity. This is good and acceptable in the sight of God our Savior who desires all men to be saved and to come to the knowledge of the truth (NASB).

Notice that cooperation does not cancel out our mandate to share the gospel. The establishment of dialogue, mutual support, prayer, and benefitting everyone sets the credibility to share beliefs and let God do what he will.

Each of our faith traditions and unique Scriptures has examples and admonitions to collaborate with others outside our faith for the good common to all. This principled and practical collaboration carries on an example of our faith's ancestors and is in direct obedience to God.

Two Goods to Be True

A theological summary of common and special grace.

In Christian theology, there are two reasons why cooperation with people not like us is important:

First, if God is sovereign (all the Abrahamic faiths see God as sovereign over the affairs of this world), then surely we are not only free to operate with those not of our faith, we are expected to do so. And we are sure that God will guide those interactions toward his sovereign purposes. Learning about God from other religious adherents helps me grow deeper in my own faith and further grasp the extent of God's wisdom and omnipresence.

Second, each adherent to a particular faith wants to extend the boundaries and appreciation for his or her specific faith. We believe that God has specifically revealed himself in our particular faith tradition, in a special grace not like any other religion. In order to share that faith, to be a witness to the power and compassion of our particular understanding of God, we must be sent to others who do not believe as we do, but are beneficiaries of our God. In doing so, we hope to have the chance to speak about God as well as demonstrate his love. Our efforts, however, are not dependent on whether we can speak about Christ—our efforts are a result of his compassion in us.

Doubts and Accusations Around Us

> Each of us needs to face and deal with the voices of suspicion.
> "Christians are still Crusaders at heart."
> "Jews are only concerned about Israel."
> "Muslims don't just want respect, they want to create worldwide domination."

I have heard all of these statements verbatim in the last year, and you may have heard, or thought, similar ones. Many times such statements are followed by the all-telling disclaimer, "the exception being some of those whom I know personally." These statements are becoming commonplace.

The first time Pastor Terry Jones, in our own state of Florida, was going to burn the Qur'an to capture the national spotlight, my friend Imam Musri went to his church. Imam Musri stood outside in the heat for hours before talking to the "pastor" and failed in his attempt to dissuade him.[1] The second time, I went, along with the leader of the World Evangelical Alliance and a Malaysian pastor who explained the danger such an action would have for Christians in Muslim countries. We, too, failed to dissuade him. We faced what all people of a particular faith tradition must face: the moral obligation to dialogue with angry and fearful people in our own or other religions to try to help them see things in a different way.

To help bolster us for these kinds of conversations, we would do well to consider:

- Our affinity: Jews, Christians, and Muslims are all children of Abraham.

- Our opportunity: part of the infinite wisdom of God is to give us problems so big and complex that we must promote both grand (megagroup) approaches and granular (personal) activities in everyday life. Life-threatening challenges such as religious extremism and violence, war, global poverty, climate change, human trafficking, et al., warrant an "all in, including me" approach. The suffering are made in the image of God and should have the help of those who are safe.

- Our marching orders: "Love your neighbor as yourself" (Mark 12:31, NIV). Love is more than emotion; it strives to solve problems that endanger those we love. Worship of the God of our ancestors is more than responding to the divine with theological accuracy or personal devotion; it involves submitting to the maker's purposes beyond our own group. Peace is more than the absence of active conflict; it involves a type of ongoing coalition building that creates a culture of cooperative faith expression.

- Religion has been the greatest source of peace, healing, and help in history. Religion has also been used to justify some of the greatest conflicts in history. Turning to religion itself as a central component in peacebuilding is unsure at best and perilous at worst, but most of the world, religious beliefs reinforced within religious communities are the only moral authority strong enough to compel adherents to love instead of battle our neighbor. And our personal actions based on our faith are more powerfully constructive than we usually would think they are.

1. Johnson, "Muhammad Musri."

In the recent postmodern era of the West, the traditional sources of moral authority, such as religion, the family, the state, education, and even science have lost some influence with some of the segments of societies. Yet for the vast majority of Jews, Christians, and Muslims, a main guide to our best behavior is our understanding of our faith's moral imperatives. In thirty years of conversations with believers in various faith traditions, I can say with assurance that those most persistent in acting out of a specific moral conscience are those who believe their actions are fulfilling their mandate from a living God. This is especially true of those who believe their future existence in eternity will be impacted by their present actions on earth.

How much of the world's population is guided, at least in part, by what they believe their religion to say?

According to a study by the Pew Research Center, 84 percent of the world's population is religiously affiliated. Christian adherents are almost 32 percent of the world's population. Islam has adherents that number approximately 23 percent of the world's population, but their numbers are growing at a rate that by 2050 they will have reached a number that is approximately even with Christians. Combined, Christians and Muslims are projected to be 61 percent of the world's population by 2050. Jews will stay at around 14–15 million but will continue to exercise a great deal of influence in international affairs. So just from population numbers alone, religion stands to be a significant influence to the world's largest constituencies.

Major Barriers to Peaceful Relations in General

I've had a series of "shocking revelations" that should not have surprised me:

In the midst of a meeting at the White House, those of us on the Interfaith Dialogue and Cooperation subcommittee of the President's Advisory Council under the Obama Administration were talking over terminology to include in our written report. A phrase I always had taken as an automatic consensus value—"religious freedom"—was brought up . . . followed by an objection! How could anyone object to that phrase? "Because," said the objector, "you Christians always use that phrase to give you the liberty to proselytize people of other faiths." She had a point, at least with evangelicals like me. Experience had taught her to be careful about wonderful idealistic platitudes offered without paying attention to painful personal and cultural histories. Of course I am still an activist for international religious freedom, but how can it be implemented in a way that respects all religions and is not a "Trojan horse" for those who want to conquer another's religion?

While I was talking with a Jewish leader, he commented, "Those of you who are not Jewish can never understand what it is like to live every day with the weight of the Holocaust or the feeling that it will happen again. You can talk peace, but we always are thinking survival."

A Muslim leader from another country said to me, "I can learn from you, befriend you, and explain to you what we believe or why there is conflict in a given land. But I cannot think of you without knowing your blindness to the atrocities perpetuated by your own government and the ongoing persecution of Muslims you represent."

On an August 2015 trip to Egypt, while meeting with the Coptic Orthodox and Evangelical Synod leaders, I was thrilled by the degree of solidarity among Christian groups. Our group also heard wonderful stories of cooperation between Christian and Muslim groups during the Egyptian revolution of 2011.

In contrast, later, during that same trip when I was teaching "leaders of the future," I was pulled aside by a very respected intellectual. He said in a low voice, "You must tell the president to stop cooperating with Muslims. There are no moderate Muslims. There are only two kinds: ones that want to kill you now, and ones that are biding their time to dominate you later."

While I wish this man's voice was the voice of an outlier, the sentiment he expressed is one that is widely held by Christians about Muslims, by Muslims about Christians, and by Jews about Muslims and Muslims about Jews. Jewish leaders even carry an ongoing suspicion about Christians. What can reduce this distrust and turn the mainstream of faith groups toward acceptance of each other and ultimately peace?

Peace may be a "consummation devoutly to be wished," as Shakespeare once spoke through Hamlet. But in order to gain it, we must first die to the "thousand natural shocks that flesh is heir to."[2] We must lay down our earthly suspicions and we must have faith that there is something better that awaits us if we give up the normal struggles of this world. If we don't even trust the people within our own faith group (and we have anecdotal evidence why we can't), then how are we to trust those we don't know? Faith in a guiding God is the only way to make progress in building trust. And it is a faith that must be built upon by the efforts of innovative faith leaders.

The Dialogue and Proclamation of Faith Leaders

For years, a growing group of Jewish, Christian, and Muslim leaders have been building ways to peace and cooperation among our faith communities.

---

2. Shakespeare, *Hamlet* 1755–57.

One such leadership group from The Catholic University of America in Washington, DC, is made up of a Jewish law professor (Marshall Breger), a Catholic law professor (Robert Destro), and an Iranian-born ayatollah (Ahmad Iravani) who is now an American citizen. For years, these "builders of understanding" have convened groups of religious leaders, scholars, and public servants from the US and Iran. The groups have created dialogue about what our Scriptures have to say about particular issues, and consequently have built relationships resulting in friendships among the participants.

Other pioneers have been convened by national or international organizations.

Nationally in the US we have everything from the interfaith Office of Faith-based and Neighborhood Partnerships in every major agency of our government, to non-profit initiatives such as the Interfaith Youth Core. And, of course, the United Nations, realizing that cooperation between faith communities is essential for peace and well-being throughout the world, formed the Alliance of Civilizations, which included faith leaders. Dozens of other major efforts, such as the US-Islamic World Forum, A Common Word, The Parliament of World Religions, et al., have also added to the hope for peace.

Yet peace in the Middle East remains the most elusive of realizations. Peace will not come without an authoritative call from the top leadership of our three faith traditions, and a grassroots reorientation of congregations, and a compelling narrative that can inspire all people.

Faith leaders in the most conservative communities—the very communities whose cooperation we need if there is to be peace—are taking the biggest risks by leading bridge-building efforts. In many cases they risk their job security, evoking congregational backlash that stems from media-driven fears of other religious groups. But with the biggest risk comes the biggest potential gain.

No one has the level of influence on religious adherents' moral persuasion like a trusted local faith leader or a respected national faith leader. People of faith look to their religious leader to help them not only interpret their Scriptures but to help them interpret the headlines. The local congregational leader is the gatekeeper concerning what will or will not be addressed by his or her congregation.

So if we want to go from grand to the granular, from countries to congregations, from people groups to individual persons, we must go through religious leaders. We must address their fears and give them tools of understanding so that they can guide their congregations.

Multi-Level Bridges

From a faith leader's perspective, there are at least five levels to peace-building among religious cultures: relational, religious, cultural, policy advocacy, and political. In increasing levels of complexity and difficulty all, but the last one, tend to be more helpful than dangerous.

1. Building personal relational ties between persons of different faiths is the most constructive and effective road to long-lasting peace. Those I know who have a friend of another faith are more likely to interpret negative world events as aberrant to normal human conduct. At this level, each person can participate by simply getting to know someone of another faith. Pastors and other congregational leaders speak most persuasively when they speak from their own experience. We model the Scriptures best when we live the Scriptures. It is really difficult to align with God who "so loved the world" (John 3:16) or follow Jesus who "sent [us] into the world" (John 17:18, NIV) if we stick to members of our own group. My old pastor, Dr. Stanley J. Shoemaker, once said, "Nothing will come right in the world until you take care of the sin (separation) in your own heart."

2. On a second level, citing our own Scripture's reasons for building better relations between differing groups of people gives us a sense that such efforts fulfill our faith's specific scriptural mandates (or at least our moral ones). For the "people of the Book" such personal obedience to the God of our Scriptures is the strongest possible motivation for building peace. World Vision is a powerful example of a Christian organization that is indiscriminate in compassion by being personally faithful to spirit and truth of the gospel. What can apply to relief and development can also be applied to peace and reconciliation. When Jesus said, "Blessed are the peacemakers, for they shall be called the children of God" (Matt 5:9, NIV). He was advocating a general character and specific actions. So applying our Scripture is a passion for those who see Scripture as our ultimate authority for belief and behavior in everyday life.

3. On still a third level, Islam and Judaism are not only religions; they are comprehensive systems of culture. Christians, whose orientation has been less tied to a particular geography or language or culture, are more independent of specific traditions or cultural history. Yet in all three, it is not the leaders who will make the difference, but entire grassroots' understanding of other religious cultures and intents. So part of the way to peace for all three of these faith communities is to

take into account how we best communicate to our "faith cultures." Even terrorist organizations (e.g., Hezbollah, Hamas) have a political and social wing (both benefits and public services) and mass communications and for profit businesses, as well as a military wing. They offer something that the state cannot provide. Peace is a matter of unarmed forces of compassion because of our beliefs. It calls for practical benefits for entire groups, not merely the application of an individual's beliefs. As M. D. Yousuf Ali has put it, "Revelation Guidance should be considered as the main source of the three Abrahamic faiths for living . . . . The cultural transformation between the three faiths' peace, unity and coexistence would greatly and significantly contribute towards global peace and unity . . . it is not impossible to restart the universal cultural dialogue in order to understand and to be closer to one another."[3]

4. On the fourth level, we are all citizens of nations (or cities) whose policies can be brought more into line with the environment needed for peace. Policies and treaties don't "make peace." Even the most noble of them are subject to violation and change and self-advantageous amendments. Yet our very advocacy for more peaceful and respectful approaches are what makes for the real peace.

    Long before the Iran treaty, I became part a non-political group of US/Iranian Christian, Muslim, and Jewish clergy/scholars/policy experts that had been meeting for many years. Even though their delegation had members integrated into their government authorities, and our delegation had former congressmen, we kept our group collaborations to what our Scripture said about the scheduled topics. Our focus was about building relationships and understanding each other's scriptural perspectives.

5. Even in the Christian faith, meant not to be linked to any political system, there is an advocacy for peace that can and should come through relationships to people we know in public office. On a visit to Iran in 2014, one of the highest ranking officials in the country said to me, "We are not your enemies." It was not just a message for me; he meant it to be passed on from me to leaders in our country. You too, reader, may have some political connections through your normal relationships. Those are not an accident; they are a venue through which you can advocate understanding and peace.

For those of the Christian family, we must be driven by who we are in Christ . . . agents of reconciliation. Just as Jesus was our bridge between

3. Ali, "The Three Abrahamic Faiths," 193.

heaven and earth, so we must be those who risk our comfort to love people that may be hostile to us. In many cases, we will be surprised by how many people from other faith families are also trying to build bridges of understanding and cooperation.

A powerful reason for being an agent of reconciliation, a peacemaker like Jesus, is that it helps us become like him. "Blessed are the peacemakers, for they will be called children of God" (Matt 5:9, NIV). In doing so, we will exemplify the love of God, we will personify Christ's mission, and we will promote the respect of God among all people.

Bibliography

Ali, Dr. Yousuf. "The Three Abrahamic Faiths and Their Roles in Making Peace, Unity and Co-Existence." *World Journal of Islamic History and Civilization* 1.3 (2011) 193.

Johnson, Patrick. "Muhammad Musri, An Unusual Imam Brokers Quran Burning Debate." *Christian Science Monitor*, September 10, 2010. http://www.csmonitor.com/USA/2010/0910/Muhammad-Musri-an-unusual-imam-brokers-Quran-burning-debate.

Shakespeare, William. *Hamlet*.

28

How to Create a New Conversation about Israel-Palestine in Your Church

Bill Hybels

BECAUSE AMERICAN ATTITUDES TOWARD Israel and Palestine have an unavoidable impact on what happens in the Holy Land, we believe it is critical for American Christian leaders to promote a conversation that is authentically pro-Israeli, pro-Palestinian, and pro-peace.

Such a conversation must:

- Acknowledge and condemn all past and present anti-Semitism,
- Acknowledge and condemn the history of persecution perpetrated by Christians against Jews,
- Acknowledge and grieve the horrors of the Holocaust,
- Recognize the historical ties of Jews to the Holy Land,
- Agree that Jews in Israel, and anywhere in the world, should be free to live without fear of rocket attacks or other violence perpetrated against them, and
- Support and legitimize the existence of the Israeli state.

Such a conversation must also:

- Acknowledge and grieve the displacement of hundreds of thousands of Palestinian Arabs that accompanied the founding of the State of Israel,
- Acknowledge and condemn the current injustices Palestinians face as a stateless people without protection of basic civil rights,
- Recognize the centuries-old presence of Arabs in historic Palestine,
- Agree that Palestinians should be able to live without fear of heavy-handed military actions and collective punishment, and
- Support and legitimize the Palestinian demand for full civil rights and citizenship in their own sovereign state, or within the Israeli State.

Go and See

The first step in promoting this kind of conversation is to recognize that many Americans—including church leaders—think they know far more about the Israeli-Palestinian conflict than they actually do. Not only do many Americans overestimate their level of knowledge, they also tend to hold uninformed opinions with a great deal of fervor. We realized that if we wanted to bring greater truth and nuance to the polarized American Christian conversation about Israel-Palestine, we would have to proceed slowly and carefully.

In 2009, when my wife Lynne began traveling to the Holy Land regularly to learn from Israelis and Palestinians, she starting hosting informal meetings in our home with people she thought might be interested in what she was learning. She recommended books and films for those who wanted to learn more. Whenever friends from Israel or Palestine traveled to Chicago, she hosted informal events where they could tell their stories.

As she shared with me what she was learning, I became increasingly convinced that these educational opportunities should be expanded beyond the scope of our informal gatherings for friends. I wanted to bring this conversation into our greater church community.

Knowing how complex and controversial this issue is among American Christians, I decided to begin the educational process at the highest levels of leadership and influence at Willow Creek. So in 2011, Lynne began taking groups of staff, elders, and key leaders on "alternative trips" to the Holy Land, in partnership with The Telos Group, an NGO dedicated to educating Americans (including faith communities) about current realities in the Holy Land.

Our goal for these trips has been to learn from people on all sides of the conflict: Jewish settlers, Palestinians living in refugee camps, Muslim sheikhs, Jewish rabbis, Palestinian pastors, human rights activists on both sides, journalists, politicians, and followers of Jesus—both Israeli and Palestinian. The trips are frustrating and heartbreaking, inspiring and hopeful.

Along the way, the voices of peace bubble up from the others and linger long after we've left: the Israeli grandmother who facilitates relationships between Israelis and Gazans, the Palestinian activist who denounces all violence and teaches nonviolence according to the way of Jesus. The Christian, Muslim, and Jewish leaders who work together for mutual healing and transformation—of themselves and of their faith communities. The organization that takes Palestinian and Israeli young people into the desert where they can get to know one another without the distraction of the hostile voices in their respective communities.

We want our people to get past the stereotypes, to learn that not all Israelis are alike, and not all Palestinians are alike. In each community there are those who reject peace and those who are showing up daily to pursue peace. We want our people to be so captivated by the peacemakers that they will want to stand in solidarity with them.

Study and Learn

Prior to the trips, we require our people to read two books. *Blood Brothers*, by Elias Chacour, is a classic personal narrative about the founding of the State of Israel that calls for reconciliation between all the people of the Holy Land. *The Israeli-Palestinian Conflict: Tough Questions, Direct Answers*, by Dale Hanson Bourke, is a short primer on the modern-day conflict that provides a framework for understanding ongoing tensions.[1]

We usually find that after the trip, people are eager to learn more; we suggest additional resources at www.telosgroup.org/resources. We always tell our people that if they want to be active contributors to a constructive conversation about peace in the Holy Land, they can't just "dabble" in the issue. They will have to devote themselves to ongoing learning.

Theology Matters

One thing many Americans don't realize is that Israeli Messianic Jews (Jewish followers of Jesus) and Palestinian Arab Christians often have differing

---

1. See Dale Hanson Bourke's chapter 1.

theological and political perspectives. When hostility increases in the general Israeli and Palestinian populations, that hostility tends to be reflected between Jewish and Arab followers of Jesus, as well.

Followers of Jesus in the Holy Land deal with a complex blend of theology, politics, and history. Fear, hurt, and repeated disappointments compound this complexity. As American Christians engaging with the people of the Holy Land, I believe we need to do so in a way that supports the efforts of Messianic Jews and Palestinian Christians to live in unity.

One way to do that is to stand with those Messianic Jews and Palestinian Christians who are actively seeking reconciliation. Salim Munayer, a Palestinian theologian, and Lisa Loden, a Messianic Jewish theologian, have edited and written important books to encourage understanding between those who hold these differing theologies: *The Land Cries Out: Theology on the Land in the Israeli-Palestinian Context*, and *Through My Enemy's Eyes: Envisioning Reconciliation in Israel-Palestine*.

When the Willow Creek Association was invited to hold the Willow Creek Global Leadership Summit in the Holy Land, we hosted one site in Jerusalem, attended primarily by Messianic Jews, and one site in Bethlehem, attended primarily by Palestinian Christians. Because of the physical barrier separating Israelis and Palestinians, there are few places where Israelis and Palestinians can meet together. The best way to honor both communities was to host two separate events.

In the aftermath of the summer 2014 war between Hamas and Israel, the angry rhetoric rampant in both Israeli and Palestinian societies seeped into the Christian communities as well. But a group of young women—Israeli Messianic Jews and Palestinian Christians—said, "These voices of hostility within our respective communities do not represent us." They started a website to tell their stories—simple, everyday stories of women pursuing peace and relationships with "the other" in the midst of conflict. We'll probably never hear about these women on the network news, but they're there. I believe American Christians owe it to grassroots peacemakers like these to search for them, stand in solidarity with them, and join our voices with theirs.

Educational Events

During three years of educating staff and key lay leaders through alternative Holy Land trips, we were also sowing small seeds of information in the congregation as a whole. In weekend services, I used a Palestinian pastor as an illustration of servanthood. In a sermon about the kinds of walls that separate people from God and from each other, I mentioned various physical walls that have created division: the Great Wall of China, the Berlin Wall, the wall between Israelis and Palestinians. In a sermon on forgiveness, we interviewed two people whom many would consider to be permanent enemies—an Israel Jewish woman whose son had been killed by a Palestinian sniper, and a Palestinian Muslim man whose daughter had been killed by an Israeli border patrol. Their story of reconciliation and their commitment to peace presented a gripping and unexpected view of Israelis and Palestinians.

All these seeds of information created a degree of cognitive dissonance for people who assumed that all Palestinians were suicide bombers or that all Israelis feared and hated Arabs. It left people with questions that began to shake their firmly held opinions about the conflict.

Additionally, during weekend services, I began to teach about the discipleship of peacemaking. Inspired by the books of John Paul Lederach (*The Little Book of Conflict Transformation* and *Reconcile*), I challenged our people to become everyday peacemakers: people who don't run away from conflict, but approach it with wisdom and compassion, thus allowing conflict to lead to greater understanding and deeper relationships. In weekend and midweek services, we focused on the Sermon on the Mount; we began to consider more seriously the blessing Jesus proclaimed on peacemakers, and his command to "love our enemies." In sermons, we highlighted Paul's challenge "to overcome evil with good." All this was part of a slow, methodical process of helping people see the place of peacemaking in the Bible.

At our first educational event related to the Israeli-Palestinian conflict that was open to the entire congregation, we presented two sessions. First, a sixty-minute overview of the history of the modern Israeli-Palestinian conflict, presented by a Middle Eastern expert who honored both Jewish and Arab narratives related to the Holy Land. Second, we invited back the Israeli woman and Palestinian man our congregation had heard from a year earlier during the sermon on forgiveness. In an in-depth sixty-minute interview, these amazing peacemakers said, "If we who have paid the highest price a parent can pay are pursuing reconciliation and peace, anyone can—and must—pursue reconciliation and peace!"

We discovered that a captivating historical presentation followed by personal narratives that produced empathy was a powerful combination. After the event, one man confessed he had come to the event "ready to fight, fully expecting to hear a left-wing, one-sided, anti-Israel presentation." He left saying, "That was the most helpful presentation of the history of the conflict I've ever heard. And how could I not be moved by two people who I would expect to be enemies—but they're working together for peace!" That day on his Facebook page he posted a paragraph in praise of the event.

We're at the beginning when it comes to educating our congregation. Engaging in Israel-Palestine, or anywhere in the Middle East, is complicated. You can't engage long-term without addressing theology, politics, Christian/Jewish relationships, Christian/Muslim relationships, principles of peacemaking, and more. We have much to learn in all these areas and look forward to learning from and with other communities of faith committed to peace.

Handling Criticism

Though we've tried very hard not to be controversial, we haven't been entirely successful. We've discovered there are some people who simply don't believe it's possible to be pro-Israeli and pro-Palestinian at the same time. Others believe that any criticism of the Israeli government is an act of anti-Semitism. Still others are convinced that any criticism of Palestinian leadership is a slam against all Arabs. And of course there are those whose theological beliefs make it impossible to even consider the legitimacy of two peoples inhabiting the Holy Land. We've accepted that we can't avoid the criticism of such people.

On the other hand, we've learned much from our critics. In some cases we've learned that we did have a fact wrong, or we had ignored a significant part of the historical narrative; we've had to revise our telling of the story accordingly. We've also learned how important precise language and nuance is in this conversation. We've learned that it's never helpful to overstate a truth or to exaggerate. We've learned that no matter how much we learn, we are—and always will be—beginners. We must always speak with humility from the context of our ongoing learning process.

There are, of course, some critics who have repeatedly misquoted us, sent us sarcastic emails and Twitter messages, or accused us of beliefs and positions we do not hold. While we have not personally engaged with every disagreeable critic, such people have motivated us to be more forthright— more honest and specific—in our speaking and writing. If people are going to disagree with us, we want them to disagree with what we really believe and say rather than what a disgruntled critic writes about us.

Tips for Your Community's Engagement

Are you a leader who is ready to take your people on a peacemaking journey? Here are a few suggestions:

- Move slowly.
- Educate yourself.
- Go on a Holy Land pilgrimage that focuses on not just on where Jesus walked 2,000 years ago, but where he's walking—and working—today.
- Educate your leaders. Challenge them to learn, to go, and to see.
- Get to know followers of Jesus in both Israel and Palestine. Then open your hearts, minds, and relationships to Israeli Jews and Palestinian Muslims.
- Look for people of peace.
- Stand in solidarity with them.
- Tell their stories.

And finally, pray for the peace of Jerusalem. Pray that followers of Jesus in the Holy Land will incarnate Jesus in a way that draws people to him. Pray for a radical in-breaking of the life of the kingdom. Pray for the shalom of God's presence.

29

Christians as Agents of Reconciliation

Dr. Tony Campolo

THE CONFLICT IN THE Middle East has ramifications for the entire world, especially in light of the fact that it could be the launching site of the next world war. In the midst of conflicts we see unfolding almost daily in the Middle East between the Arabs and the Israelis, we Christians are called to be peacemakers. The Apostle Paul tells us that we Christians are called to be agents of reconciliation (2 Cor 5:18). In light of this admonition, we should consider the following issues:

I. Racism

We must attack the racism we see evident among Christians. Just as we must attack the racism we see greatly evident among Arabs, as well as the racism greatly evident among Jews.

From the earliest days of the Church, anti-Semitism has been all too evident among Christians. Among the earliest Church Fathers, such as Origen and Chrysostom, we find that Jews were condemned and often blamed for the crucifixion of Christ. Chrysostom, the Bishop of Antioch, and one of the most admired saints in Catholic history, once wrote, "All Jews are murderers and racists. They are filthy people and their synagogues are the dwelling places of Satan and houses of prostitution."[1]

Down through the ages, Jews have had to put up with Christians who have been prejudiced against them and, at times, have sought to annihilate them. It's not just the Nazis of the twentieth century who were out to destroy the Jews. History tells us that during the Middle Ages, as the "Christian" crusaders marched towards the Holy Land, they traveled down the Rhine Valley, and in every city and town in which they stopped along the way they sought out Jews and slaughtered them.

Jewish people since the Diaspora have sought to find a home in various nations, but wherever they went, they ended up being objects of hatred. Time and time again, when they trusted their Christian neighbors, they found that the latent racism in Christian hearts expressed itself in horrible ways. The latest expression of that hatred was in Nazi Germany, where an evil man named Hitler yelled hatred towards the Jews and released the people of Germany to express their latent racism on their Jewish neighbors. Of all the countries of the world, Germany was a country in which Jews seemed fully integrated into almost every social organization and professional vocation. They were scientists, musicians, academicians, as well as holding high positions in government. Yet none of that mattered when the opportunity was presented for anti-Semitism to rear its ugly head.

In light of the rampant anti-Semitism of the late nineteenth and early twentieth centuries, it is no wonder, therefore, that Theodor Herzl, along with Chaim Weizmann, came to believe that the only hope for Jewish people to live in safety and enjoy well-being was to have a nation-state of their own. These two Jewish leaders came to be the primary founders of the Zionist movement that eventually played the major role in creating a State of Israel in 1948.

Today, Israel even holds some suspicions about the United States as a loyal ally. They see anti-Semitic expressions by hooligans in cities across America, and they have come to believe that the only people that they ultimately can trust is themselves. To this end, they have armed themselves to the teeth, and have created the sixth strongest military establishment in the world today. According to a 2012 study conducted by the Foundation for National Security Research (FNSR) which reported Israel's military capability ranked sixth in the world and technological capability ranked fourth in the world.[2] They have vowed to never be passive again in the face of anti-Semitism. Before we can deal with the racism that is evident in the Israeli-

---

1. Chrysostom, "Homilies."
2. See Yashar, "Israel Among Ten Most Powerful."

Palestinian conflict, we Christians need to deal with the anti-Semitism that is operative in our own religious communities.

Not only are there racist attitudes among Christians towards Jews, but there is great evidence that we Christians have had, and still do have, racist attitudes towards Arab people. This racism has been exacerbated since the events surrounding 9/11. Whenever there are terrorist acts committed by Arab Muslims, whatever goodwill may have been extended to the Muslim community somewhat ebbs away.

We Christians have made matters worse with some of the things that are broadcast on "Christian" radio and television. Too many messages go out over the airwaves, pointing out that there are places in the Qur'an which justify violence against "infidels" and can be utilized to support wars against people of other faiths. Of course, we tend to overlook the passages in the Old Testament wherein Joshua, under what he believed was the command of God, committed genocide against the Canaanites and the Amalekites (see Deut 7:2; 1 Sam 15:3).

As ISIS kidnaps hundreds of teenage girls and forces them to convert and to marry Muslim warriors, animosity against *all* Muslims, and especially Arabs, is intensely heightened. I hope I need not say that the overwhelming proportion of the Arab Muslim community is no more committed to violence than are we Christians. There needs to be repentance regarding our attitudes towards Muslim Arabs as well as toward Jewish people.

Eric Hoffer, in his book *The True Believer*, endeavors to explain the origins of extremist movements. The most memorable thing I remember from that book is the idea that a social movement can exist without a god, but never without a devil.[3] We have seen movements in which one group or another has been deemed the devil, and demagogues have declared that if that devil can be removed all will be well with the world. As I suggested earlier, Hitler made the Jews into the devil, and he was able to unify anti-Semitic people around the desire to rid the Jews from the face of the earth. Today Muslims are being treated as the devil, and especially Arab Muslims.

In the anti-Arab attitudes so often expressed among we Christians, there is often failure to understand that there are roughly 14 million Arabs who are Christians and many of them are under severe persecution.[4] We Christians have remained incredibly silent as Arab Christians in places like Egypt, Iraq, and the greater Middle East have been persecuted and oppressed. We have said little about the fact that churches have been burned

---

3. Hoffer, *True Believer*.
4. For more information, see Pew Research, "The Future of World Religions" and Open Doors USA, "Persecution World Watch List."

down and many of our Christian brothers and sisters who are Arabs have been killed. Such things seem to get little more than a footnote in the discussions about what is going on in the Middle East.

We also must be concerned about the racism that is evident in the relationships between Palestinians and Jews. There are some schools in the West Bank and in the Gaza Strip in which children are taught untruths about Jews, depicting them as an evil people. On the other hand, there are some schools maintained by some extremist Jews, not only in Israel, but in Israeli settlements that have been illegally established in the West Bank, in which Arab peoples are described as an inferior race and a scourge on the human race. Before there can be peace, the racist propaganda that is evident in both the Israeli community and in the Palestinian community must be dealt with; and all possible efforts must be made to extinguish such racism; and we Christians should be doing all we can to make this happen.

II. Social Injustices and Divisive Political Policies

Those who travel to the Holy Land, particularly Israel and the West Bank, become aware that there are fences and walls that have been erected, making those Palestinians who live in the West Bank feel imprisoned. No one can see those fences and walls without sensing the injustice that they represent.

The Israelis, on one hand, contend the construction of this physical enclosure of the West Bank has significantly reduced terrorist acts against Israelis; and it has created a sense of safety for the Jews in the Holy Land that is greater than twenty years ago when the walls and fences did not exist. But these barriers have created tremendous limitations on the mobility and freedom of the Palestinian people. Add to that the reality that the land that was intended to be a homeland for the Palestinian people is being occupied by the Israeli army and hundreds of thousands of Israeli settlers.

On the other hand, we all remember the words of the poet, Robert Frost, who said, "Something there is that doesn't love a wall."[5] Whenever we see a wall that separates people, whether a wall in Berlin or in Belfast, we cannot help but think of what Christ did for us. According to what is written in Ephesians, through his death Christ tore down the walls and partitions that separate us from one another (Eph 2:14).

One of the major complaints of the Palestinians has been that whatever positive things can be said about the walls and fences by the Israelis, these walls of separation were not built along what has been called "the Green Line"—the border which was established at the end of the 1967 war. The

---

5. Frost, "Mending Wall," 24.

wall has been constructed in such a way as to take in land that previously belonged to what was intended to be part of a future Palestinian state. There has been no legal justification for the wall and fences to be located where they are, even if one is to accept the Green Line as a kind of official border between the two nations, as President Obama had suggested in his 2011 speech on the Middle East.[6]

Then there is the matter of the illegal settlements. When, in 1947, the United Nations established the Partition Plan with Resolution 181, promising land to the Jews, it was determined in that same resolution that land be provided for a future Palestinian state. It also was affirmed by the United Nations that both the Israelis and the Palestinians should share the city of Jerusalem as the capital of both the new nations. While the Jews accepted the UN Partition Plan, the Arabs rejected it. This division culminated in the 1948 Arab-Israeli War, which resulted in the establishment of the modern nation-state of Israel.

Despite the UN Partition Plan and subsequent international determinations that land be set aside for the Palestinians, over and over again the Israelis have encroached into the land that had been assigned to the Palestinian people. Since 1967, Israelis have built huge settlements in the West Bank and East Jerusalem, so that now more than half a million Israelis are living in these illegal settlements. The US government has funded the State of Israel very heavily and often without significant restrictions on the use of funding. For many, the exorbitant amounts of US foreign assistance seems to directly contribute to the tanks and bulldozers that come into Palestinian territory to demolish so many of the homes of Palestinian people and to clear the land for the building of settlements. Every time land is cleared for a settlement there are feeble protests from the US State Department, but our government does nothing to stop the building of these settlements.

Israel is the largest cumulative recipient of US foreign assistance since the Second World War. In 2016, the President's request for funding to Israel encompassed 53 percent of the total Foreign Military Financing (FMF) requested.[7] Since the United States sends billions of dollars every year to the State of Israel in order to sustain that country, we have tremendous leverage with the Knesset and with the prime minister of Israel. Yet the United States does not use that leverage to bring justice to the Palestinians, nor do we do anything to end the illegal settlements and the oppression that the Palestinians have had to endure.

---

6. Obama, "Remarks," May 19, 2011.
7. Sharp, *U.S. Foreign Aid*, 5.

III. Being Responsible with our Preaching and Teaching of Scripture

Being prophetic means being a voice for those who have no voice, and we must admit that the Palestinians have had very little voice in matters concerning their fate as the US Congress and other global powers attempt to sort out the future of what will happen to their people. Even today, there are gigantic affronts to the Palestinians in East Jerusalem, the part of the Holy City designated by the UN for the Palestinians to establish their future capital. The Israeli government continues to encroach upon Palestinian homes and communities by establishing new settlements. Whenever leaders of prominent Protestant denominations try to be prophetic and raise their voices against such injustices, they have to endure massive attacks from many ardent Christians who preach and teach on thousands of Christian radio programs promoting the idea all of the Holy Land should belong exclusively to the Jews because of the promise in the Abrahamic Covenant.

A few years ago, while being interviewed on a radio program for a Christian station in New Zealand, I interacted with an extremist who was part of what is called the Christian Zionist movement. He made the point that, according to Genesis 15:18, all the land that we call the Holy Land is land promised to the seed of Abraham and, thus, should belong solely in the hands of the Jewish people. When I asked him about non-Jews living in the Holy Land, he contended that only non-Jews who had been converted to Christianity and were, therefore, part of "the New Israel" should be allowed to live there alongside the Jews, whom he thought should be the sole possessors of the land.

My discussion partner on that New Zealand radio program failed to face the fact that not only were Isaac and Jacob the seed of Abraham, but so was Ishmael, from whom the Arab peoples have descended. In short, the Arab peoples can claim to be the seed of Abraham every bit as much as the Jewish people are able to make the claim. It might be argued that Abraham then passed on the blessing to Jacob, who should be the sole heir of the land that had been promised to Abraham. It should be noted, however, that Jacob married a Syrian wife (Gen 28:1–5), so that all the descendants of Jacob would be racially mixed. We must deal with this question of the Abrahamic Covenant and point out to our Christian Zionist friends that the land that was promised by God was promised to *both* Jews and Arabs, and that these two peoples should learn to live together in peace. We Christians should be asking what we are doing to be agents of reconciliation in the midst of the conflicts between these two peoples of God.

Going back to that man that I talked to on the New Zealand radio station, I wanted to know what he thought should be done with the Arab people who were not Christians who were living in the Holy Land. He told me that they would have to leave. And when I asked him what should be done if they refused to leave and decided to stand fast, he answered, "Then they must be *forced* to leave, and if they will not yield to force, they must be killed."

I was stunned at his answer and accused the man of promoting genocide. To this he responded, "Didn't Joshua, at the command of God, commit genocide when the Jews went into the Holy Land after their exodus from Egypt? If God ordained genocide back there and then, why should we not accept it as the will of God in the here and now?" I was speechless. I didn't give the man a good answer because I was so stunned at what he had said.

There are those who have read the book by Samuel Huntington, entitled *The Clash of Civilizations*, and believe that in the twenty-first century there will be an awesome war between those nations in the Judeo-Christians traditions of the West and the Muslim peoples in the Middle East and Far East. I cannot imagine the horror if that is to be the case. But the more that Muslim people in general, and Arab Muslims in particular, are deemed as a devil that needs to be destroyed, the possibilities of such a conflagration are highly increased.

We Christians have our work cut out for us. We are to combat racism at every turn. We are called to prophecy against the injustices that even now are being practiced against Jews. We must, however, also work against the injustices being practiced against Palestinian people. We must stand against those voices that call upon us to favor one ethnic group to the disparagement of another. We are to remember that in Galatians 3:28, we are told that in Christ such prejudices and discrimination are contrary to the Spirit of Christ, who seeks to make us one people.

If one is to believe in the prophecies of Scripture, let us remember what is written in Isaiah 19:23–25. There we find these words:

> In that day there will be a highway from Egypt to Assyria. The Assyrians will go to Egypt and the Egyptians to Assyria. The Egyptians and Assyrians will worship together. In that day Israel will be the third, along with Egypt and Assyria, a blessing on the earth. The Lord Almighty will bless them, saying, "Blessed be Egypt My people, Assyria My handiwork, and Israel My inheritance" (NIV).

From such Scripture we have to concur that such a day will come wherein those peoples in the Middle East who are struggling against each other right now will enter into a harmonious fellowship with each other, and that peace will abound in the land. It is my hope and prayer that we Christians will be privileged in helping to bring about that peace by the grace of God and through the power of the Holy Spirit who wants to create the fruits of the Spirit in all of us.

Bibliography

"Christian Persecution World Watch List." Open Doors USA, 2015. https://www.opendoorsusa.org/christian-persecution/world-watch-list/

Chrysostom, John. *Eight Homilies Against the Jews*, vol. 98. Amazon Digital Services, 2010.

Frost, Robert. "Mending Wall." In *The Road Not Taken and Other Poems*. New York: Penguin, 2015.

Hoffer, Eric. *The True Believer: Thoughts on the Nature of Mass Movements*. New York: Harper Collins, 2011.

Obama, Barack. "Remarks by the President on the Middle East and North Africa." Speech. The White House. May 19, 2011. Office of the Press Secretary. https://www.whitehouse.gov/the-press-office/2011/05/19/remarks-president-middle-east-and-north-africa.

Sharp, Jeremy M. *U.S. Foreign Aid to Israel*. Congressional Research Service. June 10, 2015. https://fas.org/sgp/crs/mideast/RL33222.pdf.

"The Future of World Religions: Population Growth Projections, 2010-2050." Pew Research Center, April 2, 2015. http://www.pewforum.org/2015/04/02/religious-projections-2010-2050/.

Yashar, Ari. "Israel Among Ten Most Powerful Nations in the World." *Israel National News*. Accessed June 28, 2016. http://www.israelnationalnews.com/News/News.aspx/176683.

Epilogue

Rev. Dr. Mae Elise Cannon

AS AMERICAN CHRISTIANS TURN their eyes toward the Holy Land and the Middle East, we must not ignore the voices of people from the land. *A Land Full of God* began with Aziz Abu Sarah, a Palestinian Muslim from the East Jerusalem neighborhood of al-Sarwahreh alongside Rabbi Doctor Daniel Roth, a Jewish rabbi from the United States who made Aaliyah to Israel and is raising his family in West Jerusalem. Christians must create space for such diversity of perspectives and experiences if a political resolution and reconciliation within civil society between Palestinians and Israelis is ever to be achieved. We must also create space to dialogue and learn from Jewish and Muslim leaders who live in the Middle East, Israel, and the occupied Palestinian territories. As we enter into interfaith dialogue, may the voices leading the way be the leaders of our own Christian communities and churches living in the land. On April 19-20, 2016, a historic summit took place at The Carter Center in Atlanta, Georgia, where American Christian leaders sat side by side with leaders from churches in the Holy Land. The following statement was released from those gathered as a cry for American Christians and people around the world to advocate for an end to the occupation of the Palestinians and to support a lasting political solution in the Holy Land.

Pursuing Peace and Strengthening Presence: The Atlanta Summit of Churches in the USA and the Holy Land[1]
The Carter Center, Atlanta, GA

———————— April 19–20, 2016 ————————

Preamble

1. We have come together in this unique first-time large scale Summit for Christian churches and church-related organizations from the USA and the Holy Land following the example and teachings of our Lord Jesus Christ on peacemaking, the dignity owed to all created in God's image and kindling the hope that some day there will be a just and lasting peace in the Holy Land.

2. 2017 will mark fifty years since the occupation of the West Bank including East Jerusalem and the Gaza Strip. In the Bible, the fiftieth year is a year of jubilee when land is given back to its original owners, a year of freedom, forgiveness, and mercy.

3. Also significant is that we are meeting in Atlanta—the birthplace of civil rights movement leader the Rev. Dr. Martin Luther King, Jr.,

---

1. © Atlanta Church Summit Executive Committee. Used with permission.

whose prophetic ministry challenged officially sanctioned racial segregation in the US, while working towards greater justice and freedom for African Americans through nonviolence. We continue to be inspired by his dream in spite of all the challenges and adversities.

Our Purpose in Meeting

4. We have come together for two days of prayer and open dialogue in a spirit of theological and ethical urgency for a just peace, and to express our ecumenical unity in action towards the end of occupation and a lasting political solution in the Holy Land. We honor the land that witnessed to the life and resurrection of our Lord Jesus Christ affirming his call to justice, peacemaking and to the ministry of justice and reconciliation.

5. For decades the Holy Land, the land of redemption and universal reconciliation, has been a land of war, oppression, injustice, and death. All the world's Christians trace their faith's roots to the Holy Land: it is the spiritual homeland for all Christians in the world. Therefore, Christians everywhere are called to prayer and action for healing in the Holy Land. They are called to act for justice and peace in the Holy Land. Peace with justice requires ending the long conflict, occupation, injustice, and all acts of violence and terrorism and bringing back the land we call Holy to wholeness, peace, redemption, and reconciliation for all of its inhabitants.

6. We affirm, therefore, that as Christian churches, we have a responsibility to take an active role in bringing this chronic conflict to a just peace. As Christians, we acknowledge the spiritual kinship we share with other children of Abraham, and the common imperative to love our neighbor and thus to respect other communities of faith.

7. We also acknowledge and affirm our obligation to continue the prophetic role of the church, in speaking the truth in love and speaking truth to power. We are called to speak out again and again. We refuse to be silenced and we refuse to cease working for justice and peace.

Our Beliefs and Affirmations

8. We believe that working towards a just and lasting solution to the Palestinian-Israeli conflict would not only serve the cause of peace

and justice in the Holy Land but also promote peace in the Middle East region in general. A just peace would take away from those who take advantage by exploiting this conflict to serve their own motives, thereby compounding the perpetuation of injustices.

9. We affirm that the two-state solution, built on the basis of international resolutions, in which both Israelis and Palestinians can live in neighborly relations and at peace with each other, must be viable politically, geographically, economically, and socially. As such, we believe that:

Affirmations

A. The continuing occupation of Palestinian lands beyond the 1967 borders and measures and laws that continue to constrain and control the Palestinian population, in contravention of the Universal Declaration on Human Rights, must end. These actions prevent economic and social development and constrain the exercise of political rights. We need to focus on bringing a new sense of equality, inclusivity, and mutual respect among all the citizens of the Land regardless of religious affiliation or ethnicity.

B. The continuing expansion of illegal Israeli settlements on Palestinian lands increasingly dims the hopes and realistic prospects for a two-state solution and is a major threat to peace.

C. Jerusalem, sacred for Judaism, Christianity, and Islam, is viewed as a capital city for Palestine and Israel and an open, shared city with no walls where the rights of all are equal and respected. To this end freedom of worship for people of all three faiths must be protected and attacks such as so-called "price tag" incidents (retaliation graffiti) against churches and holy sites prevented.

D. Churches and church-related organizations need to work together proactively to protect the existing and future presence of Palestinian Christians in the Holy Land. The current absence of a just political solution affects their presence and causes many of these Palestinian "living stones" (Luke 19:40) to seek dignified life in freedom outside the troubled Holy Land. A just and peaceful solution is imperative and will contribute to protecting the presence and active participation and involvement of the Palestinian "living stones" in the Holy Land and into a peaceful future.

10. We therefore call on both Palestinians and Israelis to do more to affirm the human dignity of the other, and urge their leaders to fulfill their responsibilities to do more to assure opportunity, security, and peace for all the people of the Holy Land.

Issues Requiring Our Attention

11. The issues that merit special attention in which we can effectively promote peace with justice in the Holy Land, and to advance the two-state solution for Palestinians and Israelis and the three Abrahamic religions to live in peace include the following:

In Peacemaking:

A. Develop a more effective advocacy in the USA.

B. Advocate and reach out to politicians and public figures and to a cross-section of the population.

C. Educate the members of our congregations on the necessity and merits of a peace process that would result in fulfilling the right of Palestinians to self-determination and to their own independent state as well as the rights of all people and nations in the region, including Israel, to live in security and peace.

D. Urge the US administration, Congress, politicians, and public figures to adopt balanced and just positions that would pave the way for, and meaningfully accompany the necessary steps toward, a just and enduring solution to the conflict and a lasting peace.

E. Strengthen initiatives with various faith-based groups and communities in the United States that would inform and provide substantive input to the political process of making peace between Palestinians and Israelis.

F. Support initiatives to nurture deeper insight and understanding of existing and future opportunities for interreligious collaboration, especially in providing humanitarian assistance to all people in need, including those in Gaza, the West Bank, Jerusalem, and all areas of the Holy Land.

G. Recognize, affirm, and support the solidarity that is being demonstrated among some Christians, Jews, and Muslims—and some of the leaders of these communities in the Holy Land—especially in addressing humanitarian needs, fighting poverty, and fostering peace.

H. Find appropriate ways to exert economic leverage on commercial and governmental actors to end unfair and unjust practices and policies which violate international laws and conventions.

I. Propose steps that can be contemplated by the governing bodies of various churches in the USA on issues of peace building, and relations with churches and communities in Palestine and the Holy Land.

J. Designate a common day of prayer and reflections across the churches in the USA and the Holy Land to focus all of our prayers on a just and comprehensive peace in Palestine, Israel, and the Middle East.

K. Exercise our obligation to educate our constituencies regarding the damaging consequences of certain versions of dispensationalist theology and fundamentalist Christian teachings that create obstacles to peace, the two-state solution and peaceful coexistence in present-day Palestine and Israel.

In Strengthening the Christian Presence in the Holy Land:

A. Engage in mutual visits and exchanges with the churches and their leaders, to strengthen the resolve for ongoing commitment and hard work for peace and justice in the Holy Land.

B. Increase community-based pilgrimages and authentic tourism to the Holy Land with the intent to stay in Palestinian towns and villages in order to engage with indigenous communities, to experience firsthand their hopes and fears and to contribute to their community and economic development.

C. Work with denominational, ecumenical, and interfaith partners to strengthen relationships and efforts towards a common witness for peace in Palestine and Israel.

D. Support development in Palestine through creative social and economic investment, thus witnessing to our commitment to operate at the intersection of faith and finance.

E. Strengthen existing efforts and identify new models of church solidarity in action.

F. Support local churches and church-related organizations not only to survive, but also to thrive and continue their ministries through educational, health, cultural, and social services.

G. Encourage reference to the Kairos Palestine message as an established initiative.

H. We remain committed to work on these issues and to follow up on this summit and on the issues presented above including a possible conference in the Holy Land.

Heads of Churches and Ecumenical Bodies

Vicken Aykazian, Archbishop, The Armenian Church

John R. Bryant, Senior Bishop, The African Methodist Episcopal Church

Oscar Cantú, Bishop of Las Cruces and Chairman of the United States conference of Catholic Bishops' Committee on International Justice and Peace

Iva E. Carruthers, General Secretary, Samuel Dewitt Proctor Conference, Inc.

Michael D. Castle, President, Alliance of Baptists

Michael B. Curry, Presiding Bishop, The Episcopal Church USA

John C. Dorhauer, General Minister and President, United Church of Christ

Suhail Dawani, Archbishop, The Episcopal Diocese of Jerusalem

Elizabeth Eaton, Presiding Bishop, The Evangelical Lutheran Church in America

Ibrahim Faltas, Treasurer, Custody of the Holy Land

Susan Henry-Crowe, General Secretary of the General Board of Church and Society, United Methodist Church

Michel Jalakh, General Secretary, Middle East Council of Churches

Thomas Kemper, General Secretary of the General Board of Global Mission, United Methodist Church

Carlos Malave, Executive Director, Christian Churches Together

John L. McCullough, President and CEO, Church World Service

Gradye Parsons, Stated Clerk of the General Assembly, The Presbyterian Church (USA)

Tyrone S. Pitts, General Secretary Emeritus, Progressive National Baptist Convention INC

Ervin Stutzman, Executive Director, Mennonite Church USA

Theofilos III, Patriarch, The Greek Orthodox Patriarchate of Jerusalem

Olav Fykse Tveit, General Secretary, World Council of Churches

Fouad Twal, Patriarch, Latin Patriarchate of Jerusalem

Sharon Watkins, General Minister and President, Christian Church (Disciples of Christ)

Jim Winkler, General Secretary and President, National Council of Churches

Munib Younan, Bishop, The Evangelical Lutheran Church in Jordan and the Holy Land

Heads of Church-Related Organizations

Tarek Abuata, Executive Director, FOSNA

Brian Bodager, President and CEO, The Pension Boards/UCC

Warren Clark, Executive Director, Churches for Middle East Peace

Yusef Daher, Executive Secretary, Jerusalem Inter-Church Center

Donald G. Hart, President of United Church Funds, United Church of Christ

Sam Jones, Co-Founder and President, Heartland Initiative

Michael La Civita, Communications Director, CNEWA

Anne Lynne, President, American Friends of Episcopal Diocese in Jerusalem

Beth Nelson Chase, Executive Director, Bright Stars of Bethlehem

Mitri Raheb, President, Diyar Consortium

Jack Y. Sara, President, Bethlehem Bible College

Michael Spath, Pilgrims of Ibillin

Ghassan J. Tarazi, Co-Founder, Palestinian Christian Alliance for Peace

Jeffrey D. Thiemann, President and CEO, Portico Benefit Services (ELCA)

Ed Thompson, Co-Founder and President, Americans for a Vibrant Palestinian Economy

Signators

Varsen Aghabekian, The Commissioner General, The Independent Commission for Human Rights in Palestine; Vera Baboun, Mayor of Bethlehem; Hanna Amireh; Fahed Abu Akel; George Ayoub; Ziad Bandak; Julia Brown Karimu; Cecelia Bryant; Charles Robertson; Stephen M Colecchi; David D. Daniels; Robert D. Edmunds; Hunter Farrell; Catherine Gordon; Cindy Halmarson; Ray Hammond; Amira Hanania; Mark Harrison; Cassandra Henderson; Salim Hodali; Jim Hooker; Eleia Iskandar; Sharon Jones; Issa Kasseessieh; Gregory Khalil; Zahi Khouri; Rula Maayah; Victor Makari; Peter E. Makari; Rafael Malpica-Padilla; Riyad Mansour; Katie McCloskey; John Mendez; Waltrina Middleton; James Moos; Tom Morse; Anthony Moujaes; Jessica Pollock-Kim; Nadia Saah; Marty Shupack; Joseph D. Small; Richard E. Walters; Steve Weaver; Tauren J. Webb; David Wildman; Leslie Withers; Jeremiah A. Wright.

The church leaders present at the Atlanta Summit were courageous in their willingness to gather and make such a strong statement advocating for peace. The authors who contributed to *A Land Full of God* have also been courageous in their sharing of ideas and experiences. While I may not agree with some of the different thoughts expressed here, I do believe all of the voices represented have a right to be heard. The Christian community in the United States must do a better job of creating space for divergent opinions and perspectives, all the while actively working toward resolution to real and pragmatic issues affecting people on the ground in Israel and the oPt including, but not limited to disparity in economic opportunities, human rights concerns, legitimate quests for safety and security, and hope for a prosperous life and future for their families and loved ones. With those aspirations in mind, may we collectively work together to constructively solve real problems.

One of the most encouraging stories in my own personal advocacy happened while on a speaking tour in the Midwest. I was traveling with two peace activists—a Palestinian Christian and an Israeli Jew. We gathered with about a hundred people or so at a large conservative evangelical church in Ohio. We talked about what it means to respect all of the narratives of people living in the land. We also talked about some of the realities affecting the Palestinian communities in the West Bank and Gaza. We then provided an opportunity for Q&A and discussion. At the end of the meeting, in the back of the room a young man stood up, raised his hand, and said: "I am a Palestinian Christian. I was born in America. And I have never heard the word Palestine mentioned in a church in the United States." He continued and said, "I am so thrilled that we're having this conversation. Thank you." What a beautiful thing to hear!

A few minutes later, a young woman sitting in the front rows raised her hand. She had long blonde hair. She said, "I'm a Messianic Jew." I was pleased she had joined the gathering and wondered to myself what her perspective might be. I assumed her thoughts might not be as favorable as the Palestinian Christian who had shared. The young woman continued, "Not only am I a Messianic Jew, but I grew up in Israel." As she continued, I began to have some apprehension. Had we honored her experience? Did our presentation and discussion respect her identity both as an Israeli and as a Jewish follower of Jesus? The girl continued: "I served in the Israel Defense Force during the Second Intifada." My heart sunk. I knew from relationships and personal study the horrors of the Palestinian bombing campaigns upon the people of Israel. The young woman continued to tell about how she had lost friends and loved ones in the fighting and to suicide bombers. What could we say to acknowledge her personal loss and grief? But then the woman continued and said, "Thank you for being willing to have this conversation in church. Thank you."

Both the Palestinian Christian and the Messianic Jewish woman had entered into a space where they felt like their stories could be heard. A new space—particularly in the context of the evangelical church in the United States. A space where we can talk about the realities that are affecting the Palestinian community. The Palestinian people are suffering. And a space where we can talk about the reality and experience of the Israeli people. The Israeli people are suffering, too. Not in the same ways and not for the same reasons, but both people have for decades experienced significant loss, pain, and the devastating effects of violence.

Yet violence will not be the end of the story. As a follower of Christ, I believe light can enter into the darkest of places. I believe there is hope for a vibrant future for both the Jewish and Palestinian people living in the Holy Land. Might we Christians follow in the footsteps of Jesus and be willing to courageously and boldly have hard conversations for the sake of justice. Might we be willing to pray, advocate, and pursue peace on behalf of a land full of God.

Bibliography

Heschel, Abraham Joshua. *Israel: An Echo of Eternity.* Woodstock, VT: Jewish Lights Publishing, 1997.

Mahmoud Darwish, "In Jerusalem" from *The Butterfly's Burden.* by Mahmoud Darwish, Fady Joudah, tr. Port Townsend, WA: Copper Canyon, 2007.

United States Central Intelligence Agency. *Israel.* Washington, D.C.: Central Intelligence Agency, 2001. Map. Retrieved from the Library of Congress. Accessed June 26, 2016. https://www.loc.gov/item/2001626219.

Subject Index

1948, 3, 8, 27, 32, 35, 37, 95, 99, 108, 119, 124, 125, 144, 180, 221, 223, 230, 239, 264, 267
1967, Six Day War, 73, 99, 100, 125, 193
9/11, 178, 265

Abraham, xxiv, 6, 7, 8, 36–38, 51, 55–65, 67–74, 75, 136, 139, 146, 150, 184, 189, 216, 249, 268, 273
Abrahamic Covenant, 162, 268
Advocate, xxiii, 2, 5, 25, 27, 67, 102, 105, 106, 108n1, 114, 117–18, 120, 159, 161, 174, 197, 219, 226, 244, 254, 271, 275, 280
Afghanistan, 178
African American (black), xv, 9, 73, 100, 101, 102, 105, 147, 150, 176–77, 181, 273
Aida Refugee Camp, 103
Allah (see also God), 22, 55, 184,
Ambassador, 174, 181, 199
Americans, xxv, 2, 5, 8, 9–10, 12–13, 19, 21, 26–27, 29, 31, 39, 78–79, 95–96, 115–16, 120, 127, 130, 160, 163–64, 180, 195, 211, 219–21, 223, 242, 244, 256–60, 271, 273

Anglicans, 145n11
Annex(ation), 101, 125, 143, 211–13
Anti-Semitism, xix, 4, 6, 27, 32, 34, 35, 52, 77–78, 83, 91, 92, 100–101, 120, 124, 130, 138, 144–45, 162, 165, 168, 223, 230, 239, 256, 261, 263–65
Apartheid, 4, 9, 12, 31, 94, 106, 146, 149–50
Apocalyptic, apocalypticism, 54, 118, 127,
Apologetics, 28, 80
Arab Spring, 5, 201
Atlanta, 271, 273, 279
Auschwitz, 80

Babylon(ian), 72, 110, 136n3
Balaam, 70–71, 206
Balak, 71
Balkan(s) War, 220
Baptists, 175–77
Bible (see Scriptures), *sola Scriptura*, 17, 29, 35, 36, 39, 47, 53, 56, 57, 59, 72, 75, 82–83, 84, 121, 130, 140, 149, 160, 162, 213, 214, 247, 260, 272
Blessed, 8, 58, 60, 62, 63, 67, 68, 70–71, 109, 169, 215, 253, 255, 269

Bosnia, 194, 220
British Empire, 67, 108n2, 116, 124

Camp David, 143
Canaan, Canaanites, 61, 69, 92, 96, 109, 139, 140, 265
Charismatic, 27, 105, 106, 116n19, 117, 118, 120, 158, 163
Checkpoint(s), 18, 128, 131, 143, 144, 149, 158, 159, 161, 164, 179, 183, 225, 233, 241, 244
Child detention(s), 231–33
Child(ren), 1, 22, 37, 39, 49, 59, 70, 95, 142, 144, 153, 157, 174, 180, 197, 199, 218, 219, 221, 225, 231–34, 242, 243, 266
Chosen, 7, 68, 70, 73, 91, 112, 117, 148, 176, 180, 205, 213
Christ, 13, 36, 37, 40, 58, 76, 92, 94, 110, 130, 138, 146, 186, 189, 221, 233, 238, 248, 254–56, 263, 266, 272, 273
Christ at the Checkpoint, 158, 160, 161, 205
Christian Zionists, 29, 35, 54, 108, 115, 117, 119, 120, 124, 161, 238, 264, 268
Church of the Nativity, 29, 179
Circumcision, 65, 81, 92
Citizen, citizenship, 7, 20, 79, 197
Civilians, 201
Colonial, colonialism, 89, 93, 100, 109, 123
Commandments, 52, 68, 162
Compassion, 141, 148, 150, 151, 174, 191, 205, 207, 210, 222, 228, 229, 233, 248, 253, 254, 260
Conflict, xxiv, 2, 18, 21, 25, 31, 41, 48, 50, 61, 64, 73–74, 93, 99, 124, 126, 130, 144, 159, 160, 162, 166, 174–74, 181, 185, 189, 219, 220, 225, 229–31, 239, 242, 263, 273
Conservative, 47, 52, 116, 181, 247, 252
Consul General, 102
Covenant, 38, 56, 57, 60, 62, 65, 69, 73, 75, 80, 92, 112, 136, 138–39, 141, 162, 188, 190–191, 191n1, 268

Croatia, 220
Crusades, 50, 189
Curse, 48, 67, 71, 73, 80, 138, 169

Democracy, 28, 78, 91–92, 95, 101, 128, 165, 224
Demolition(s), 103
Disciple(ship), 164, 221, 228, 233, 260
Dispensation(al)(ist)(alism), 28, 82, 115–19, 150, 176, 238, 276
Displaced, 27, 84, 103, 153, 215, 227, 230
Dome of the Rock, 189
DRC—Congo, 220

Economic(s), 33, 51, 77, 80, 97, 101, 106, 126, 137, 153, 154, 169, 238, 274, 276, 279
Egypt, 6, 10, 27, 48, 52, 58, 61, 62, 63–64, 71, 94, 100, 125, 143, 148, 150, 152, 191, 215, 220, 251, 269
Election, 56, 70, 76, 120
Emperor, 76, 81
Enemy, Enemies (Adversaries), 7, 22, 28, 48, 50, 61, 63, 130, 151, 200, 219, 220, 224
Epistemology, 94
Evangelical, 27, 28, 53, 54, 70, 72, 77, 89, 114, 115, 118, 119–20, 127, 130, 131, 140, 158, 160–161, 175, 178, 179, 238–41, 247, 249
Evangelism, 27, 213
Exile, 34, 37, 53, 72, 110, 112, 136, 136n3, 139–40, 147, 247

Fatah, 20
Feast of Tabernacles, 118
Female Genital Mutilation, 51
Forgive(ness), 55, 65, 184–85, 190, 191, 220, 224, 259, 272
Freedom, 20, 27, 28, 42, 50, 59, 90, 102, 105, 137, 142, 144, 147, 149, 156, 181, 214, 224, 226, 237n1, 250, 266, 272–74, 274

Gaza(ns), 1, 5, 21, 37, 100, 102, 106, 125, 142, 143, 144n9, 151, 153–56, 163, 169, 180, 189, 209,

218–20, 223, 239, 241, 242, 258, 266, 272, 275, 280
Genocide, 5, 89, 96, 227, 265, 269
Gentile(s), 37–37–40, 53, 61, 62, 64, 65, 70, 81, 82, 83, 92, 94, 108, 185, 186, 190, 213
German(y), 34, 39, 77, 79–80, 109, 111, 113, 114, 116, 150, 177, 264
God, 3, 7, 9, 22, 23, 29, 35–40, 42–43, 47, 48–55, 56–58, 60–65, 67–74, 75–77, 80–84, 89–94, 96–97, 99, 112, 113, 117, 119, 120, 135–41, 147–50, 157, 160, 161–62, 169, 174, 176, 181, 184–86, 188–92, 205–11, 215, 221, 226, 228–30, 234, 247, 248–51, 253, 259, 265, 269–71
Golan Heights, 125, 194, 200
Good Samaritan, 205, 208
Gospel, Good News, Great Commission, 55, 64, 70, 81, 100, 149, 162, 180, 181, 206–8, 213, 233, 245, 247, 253
Grassroots, 102, 105, 228, 252, 253, 259

Hagar, 55, 57–59, 61, 215, 216
Hamas, 1–2, 20, 73, 102, 143–44, 154, 167–69, 218, 224, 254, 259
Healing, 22, 57, 60, 83, 117, 185, 200, 208, 226, 249, 258, 273
Heaven, 17, 37, 51, 61, 81, 82, 84, 91, 189, 213, 239, 255
Hebrew, xxiii, 10, 35, 47, 48, 53, 59–60, 63, 75, 82, 111, 118, 184, 194, 199, 217, 232,
Hebrew Scriptures (see Old Testament), 3, 6, 52, 83, 135n1, 146, 149, 180, 188, 191, 244
Hebron, 11, 99, 102, 104
Hezbollah, 143, 224
Holocaust (Shoah), 7, 28, 30, 39, 49, 53, 71, 72, 77, 103, 106, 116, 124, 126, 130, 138, 142n7, 166, 214, 221, 239, 250, 256
Holy Land, xxv, 3, 7, 12–13, 17, 22, 29, 31, 38, 57, 95, 100, 107, 127, 130, 145, 159, 162, 163, 169, 174–74, 175, 176, 178, 180, 189, 195, 197, 205, 219, 221, 224, 226, 230, 233–35, 239, 256, 258, 259, 262, 266, 268, 269, 271, 273–78
Holy Spirit, 81, 159, 228, 229, 233, 270
Holy, holiness, 47, 76, 80, 83, 92, 99, 117, 127, 148, 163, 184, 188, 189, 225, 274
Homeland, 3, 7, 35, 38, 39, 48, 54, 72, 78, 80, 82, 83, 84, 108, 111, 114, 116, 124, 136, 138, 140, 147, 165, 222, 266, 273
Hope, 23, 28, 36, 40, 42, 47, 49, 52, 64, 80, 81–82, 92, 107, 110, 116, 125, 147, 153, 159, 162, 166, 167–68, 170, 191, 191n1, 208, 213, 214, 215, 219, 227, 237, 239, 241, 244, 252, 264, 270, 272, 274, 279
Human Rights, 9, 27, 31, 42, 106, 151, 167, 170, 180, 223, 224, 226, 257, 274, 279
Humanitarian, 141, 146, 153–54, 177, 198, 275–77

Imam, 178, 247, 248
International Law, 104, 125, 143, 158, 224, 276
Iran, 51, 212, 251–53, 254
Iraq, 27, 62, 93, 211–13, 220, 265
Isaac, 8, 35–36, 55, 56, 57, 58, 60, 61, 68–69, 73, 188, 268
Ishmael, 8, 51, 55, 56, 57, 58, 59–60, 61, 64, 68, 188, 268
ISIL, ISIS, 6, 73, 265
Islam, 5, 6, 50, 51, 54, 57n3, 60, 73, 106, 112, 129, 162, 183, 184, 189, 250, 253, 274
Israel, xxix, 1–2, 7, 17, 20, 22, 27–28, 30n1, 31, 35–36, 37, 40, 47–50, 53, 54, 56, 58, 61–63, 65, 67–74, 76, 79, 80–84, 89, 91, 92, 93, 96, 100, 101, 105, 106–7, 108, 110, 116, 118–20, 123–31, 135–37, 139, 140, 142–45, 147, 150, 152, 154, 155, 158, 159, 160–161, 162, 163, 164, 166–67, 168, 178, 179, 180, 188, 189, 191–92, 194–99, 208, 212, 213, 218, 221, 222, 223–25, 226, 229, 233, 238–41, 246, 258, 262, 264, 266, 267, 269, 275, 276, 279

SUBJECT INDEX

Israeli Defense Forces (IDF), 1, 29, 128, 168, 199, 225, 232, 280
Israeli Embassy, 1, 2
Israeli-Palestinian Conflict, 2, 19, 21, 26, 50, 104, 127, 159, 164, 166, 229, 230, 237, 239, 240, 243, 257, 260, 264
Israelis, 1–12, 18–19, 20–23, 25–33, 35, 36, 39–40, 41, 42, 49, 50, 53–55, 67–68, 73–74, 84, 89, 93, 95–97, 101–2, 103–7, 108–16, 123, 124–31, 138, 141–44, 149–51, 152–56, 158–70, 174, 177–83, 189–90, 191, 194, 198, 207, 208, 210, 212–14, 214–16, 217, 219–21, 221–27, 230–34, 237–45, 256–63, 264, 266–69, 271, 273–78, 279–81
Israelites, 61, 65, 70, 75, 90, 92–93, 148, 191n1, 216

Jacob, 7, 35, 36, 37, 54, 59, 68–69, 70, 71, 73, 268
Jerusalem, 6, 12, 25, 30, 32, 35, 53, 65, 71, 72, 74, 76, 82, 83, 99, 100, 102, 115, 118, 119, 124, 142, 149, 158, 165, 188, 189, 221, 223, 239, 241, 259, 262, 267, 274
Jesus, 2, 3, 5, 7, 8, 11–12, 17, 20, 23, 32, 35–40, 41, 52, 53, 54, 61, 62, 63, 64, 70, 72, 74, 79, 81, 83, 84, 91, 92–93, 130, 135, 138, 139, 141, 142n7, 146, 159, 160, 168, 169, 175–80, 183, 184, 186, 189, 191n1, 205–9, 210, 213, 215, 216, 220–22, 222, 226, 230, 233, 238, 243, 244, 254–56, 260, 262, 272, 273, 280
Jews, 3, 6, 8, 11, 23, 26, 27, 28, 29, 32, 34, 35, 36, 37–39, 47, 48, 49, 50, 51, 53, 55, 60, 65, 73, 76–77, 78–84, 99, 101, 108n1, 109–20, 124–25, 128, 135, 138, 140, 144, 146, 150–151, 159, 162–67, 169, 176, 177, 180–181, 184, 185, 188, 210, 214, 215, 217, 220–25, 239, 242, 243, 244, 249, 250, 251, 256, 259, 262, 263–70, 275
Jordan River, 3, 6, 39, 99, 194

Judah, 53, 72, 110
Judaism, 29, 52, 75–76, 77, 81, 84, 118, 128–29, 162, 163, 166, 253, 274
Judge(ment), 50, 53, 63, 135, 136, 149, 224–26, 232
Just peace, 12, 127, 129, 131, 244, 273, 274
Justice, 3–5, 12, 13, 20, 25, 38–40, 42, 51, 53, 65, 68, 74, 84, 97, 100, 127, 129, 140, 142, 148, 149, 159, 161, 166, 174, 180, 191, 210, 213, 214, 228, 229, 230, 233, 234, 237, 239, 244, 267, 273–75, 275, 276, 280

Kairos, 277
Kerry Initiative, 128
Kibbutz, 179, 198
King, kingship, 61, 64, 71, 76, 82, 90, 91, 92–93, 106, 147, 149, 150
King David, 61, 147, 150, 216
Kingdom, 37, 38, 62, 79, 125, 161, 176, 181, 191n1, 206, 213, 215, 221, 222, 233–35, 239, 262
Korea, 118, 237
Ku Klux Klan (KKK), 175

Lakota Sioux, 96
Land, 13, 36, 38–39, 54, 55, 61, 64, 65, 68–71, 72, 80, 82–84, 92–94, 109, 123–24, 127–28, 129, 130, 131, 136, 139, 140, 158–59, 162, 163, 166, 174, 178, 188–90, 191n1, 221, 222, 223–25, 230, 266, 237, 268, 270, 271, 273, 274, 279
Landmines, 194–200
League of Nations, 116, 143
Liberal, 17, 28, 78, 181, 238
Liberation, 25, 89, 91, 96, 97, 100, 189, 195, 200, 201
Love, 20, 22, 30, 36, 40, 53, 54–55, 65, 70, 79, 94, 114, 120, 130, 131, 136, 137, 139, 141, 145, 162, 164, 168, 169–70, 174, 175, 180, 181, 190, 191, 196, 210, 215, 216, 226, 228, 229, 233, 240, 248, 249, 253, 255, 273
Lutherans, 53, 80, 111, 113–14

SUBJECT INDEX

Madrid Peace Conference, 143
Mainline Protestants, 28, 78, 238, 239, 240
Marginalized, 80, 84, 167, 179, 207
Marshall Plan, 101
Mercy, 53, 55, 175, 191, 213, 218, 272
Messiah, 7, 35–38, 52, 62, 63, 64, 65, 70, 71, 72, 81, 91, 110, 116, 146, 176
Middle East, 3, 5, 6, 10, 17, 26, 28, 31, 32, 37–40, 41, 47, 48, 50–51, 64, 73, 101, 104, 116, 124, 127, 141, 143, 145n11, 151, 160–161, 165, 183, 185, 188, 189–91, 194, 207, 217, 220, 238, 241, 244–46, 252, 260, 263, 265–67, 269, 271, 274, 276
Military, 4, 34, 62, 80, 106, 124–26, 127–29, 145, 150, 168, 174, 197, 201, 212, 223, 231–34, 238, 241, 243, 254, 257, 264
Military law, 231, 241
Millennial, 10, 174, 239
Miracle, Miraculously, 7, 23, 53, 69, 71, 73, 126, 136, 207
Mission, missionary, missiology, 23, 27, 51, 58, 62, 113, 114, 160, 175, 213, 215, 255
Moab, 71, 216
Mohammed, xxiv, 189
Moses, xxiv, 62–63, 147
Muslim (see Islam), xvii, xxv, xxvii, 3, 6, 22, 27, 32, 36, 48, 50, 51–52, 54, 55, 57n3, 83, 105, 114, 135, 141, 145, 158, 161, 164, 165, 169, 176, 178, 181, 183, 184, 188, 189, 210, 212, 220, 221, 222, 224, 230, 239, 243, 244, 249–52, 254, 258, 262, 265, 269, 275

Narratives, xxiii-xxvii, 5, 20, 25, 32–33, 56, 58, 59, 60, 62, 68, 73, 83, 96, 126, 131, 142, 174, 178, 219, 222–24, 252, 258, 260, 261, 279
Nation, 39, 54, 58, 60, 61, 62, 64, 65, 67–68, 69–70, 71, 89, 94, 99, 109, 112, 123, 136, 139–40, 165, 168, 176, 186, 188, 189, 191n1
Nation-state, 82, 84, 89, 90, 91, 126, 189, 264, 267

Native American (indigenous), First Nations, aboriginals, 53, 56, 89–90, 91–92, 93, 94–96, 163, 215, 276
NATO, 197
Nazareth, 22, 36, 158, 223
Nazi, 7, 35, 39, 52, 80, 124, 145, 264
New Testament, 17, 29, 36, 38, 52, 57, 69, 70, 71, 74, 80, 83, 84, 117, 143, 146
New York, 28, 29, 196
New York Times, 31
News, Media, Press, 17, 30–32, 48, 106, 142n7, 143, 157, 166, 178, 181, 195, 198–200, 212, 227, 243, 252, 259
Nonviolence, 25, 100, 103, 105, 107, 224, 226, 258, 273

Obedience, 51, 247, 253
Occupation, 4, 9, 101, 103, 106, 125, 128–29, 131, 158, 162, 174, 189, 223–26, 230, 232–34, 238, 239–43, 272, 273, 274
Old Testament, 36, 38, 57, 62, 68–69, 75, 110, 111, 127, 146, 176, 188, 215, 221, 265
Operation Desert Storm, 211–13
Oppression, 77, 78, 82, 89, 90, 96–97, 142, 144, 147, 149, 174–74, 183, 212, 214, 215, 237, 239, 240, 267, 273
Orthodox, 53, 79, 104, 111n9, 128, 221, 251
Oslo Accords, 125–26, 128, 130, 152
Ottoman Empire, 115, 116, 123

Palestine, Palestinian, 1–12, 18–19, 20–23, 25–33, 35, 36, 38, 39–40, 41, 42, 49, 50, 53–55, 67–68, 73–74, 84, 89, 93, 95–97, 101–2, 103–7, 108–16, 123, 124–31, 138, 141–44, 149–51, 152–56, 158–70, 174, 177–83, 189–90, 191, 194, 198, 207, 208, 210, 212–14, 214–16, 217, 219–21, 221–27, 230–34, 237–45, 256–63, 264, 266–69, 271, 273–78, 279–81
Palestinian Authority (PA), 7, 104, 126, 129, 143–44, 152, 153–54, 241

Palestinian Liberation Organization (PLO), 126, 212
Paris, France, 34
Patriarchs, 56, 57n3, 58, 65, 69, 70
Paul (the Apostle), 17, 36–38, 56, 64, 69–70, 75–76, 80–81, 83, 111, 137–39, 185, 186, 260, 263
Peace, xxiii, xxiv, 3, 5, 10, 12–13, 18–19, 22, 23, 31, 33, 39–40, 42–43, 50, 57, 92, 101, 103, 104, 125–31, 143–44, 151, 152, 155–56, 159, 160–161, 165–66, 174–74, 179, 181, 182–83, 184–87, 190, 191n1, 196, 197, 201, 208, 210, 214–16, 219–27, 233–35, 237–46, 247, 249, 251, 252, 253–55, 258, 260–63, 266, 268, 270, 272–78, 279
Pentecostal, 117–20, 159, 160
Pentagon, 197
People of God, 3, 62–64, 71, 76, 92, 141, 149, 176
Plymouth (Christian) Brethren, 115
Policy, 51, 113, 129, 131, 159, 161, 165, 181, 195, 200, 241–43, 253, 254
Politic(s)(al), politician, xxiv, 3, 6, 9, 17, 21, 23, 31, 34, 38, 39, 50–51, 62, 65, 77, 79, 80, 97, 99, 100, 108n1, 114, 116–17, 126–28, 135, 138, 140, 142, 145, 147, 149, 162–64, 166–70, 194, 196, 198, 199, 208, 210, 212, 222, 226, 230, 238, 241, 243–45, 253–55, 258–60, 271, 273, 274, 275
Poverty, 144n10, 147, 174, 214, 228, 249, 276
Pray, prayer, 13, 17, 22, 23, 29, 35, 36, 42, 47, 49, 52, 54, 55, 63, 65, 74, 140, 141, 157, 159, 174, 184, 208, 209, 218, 219–21, 226, 228, 233–35, 238, 247, 262, 270, 273, 276, 280
Prejudice, 12–13, 40, 175–77, 180, 181, 183, 217, 230, 264, 269
Premillennial, 115, 118, 175, 176
Presbyterians, 53, 238, 240
Promised Land, 38, 68, 110, 146, 215

Promises, 28, 36, 38, 55, 58, 60, 68, 69–71, 73, 81, 93, 111, 136, 138, 139, 176, 189, 191n1, 200
Prophet, prophecy, 35, 37, 38, 64, 65, 70–74, 81–84, 92, 110, 114, 115, 118–19, 148–50, 166, 176, 209, 210, 216, 218, 221, 269
Puritan, 109, 112–15

Quartet, 32, 154
Qur'an, Koran, xxiv, 51, 184, 189, 244, 248, 265

Rabbi, 28, 29, 48, 49, 52, 58, 76, 91, 100, 104, 109n3, 116, 159, 161, 205, 242, 246, 257, 271
Race, 77–78, 80, 93, 176, 179, 266
Ramallah, 30, 102, 104, 158
Rapture, 213
Reconcile, 3, 92, 185, 226
Reconciliation, 5–6, 23, 27, 31, 33, 39–40, 57, 65, 106, 160–161, 174–74, 190, 191, 219, 224–27, 253–56, 258, 259, 260, 263, 268, 271, 273
Red Sea, 194
Redeem (redemption), 55, 58, 83, 136, 139, 140, 174, 191n1, 229, 234, 273
Reformation, 109, 113, 119
Refugees, 7, 23, 39, 50, 95, 144, 180, 227, 230, 239
Regather, gather, 72, 149, 279
Remnant, 7, 62, 64, 65, 70–71
Renewalism, 118
Replacement Theory, Replacement Theology, 76, 138, 141, 166
Resolution 180, 124, 267
Restore (restoration), 7, 10, 62, 65, 71–72, 83, 91, 94, 108n1, 109, 110, 114–17, 119, 136, 166, 176, 191n1, 215, 217, 229, 234, 243
Resurrection, 83, 126, 273
Retribution, 174, 189
Revanchism (revanchists), 126
Right, righteous, 21, 28, 37, 38, 53, 56, 65, 67, 73, 76, 79, 80, 84, 149, 190, 195, 198, 208, 229, 234, 253

SUBJECT INDEX

Rockets, 1, 154, 168, 188, 189, 215, 218–20, 223, 224, 242, 243, 256
Roman Catholic Church, 34

Salaam, xxiii, 43, 158
Salafists, 50, 51, 55
Samaria, 3, 163, 224
Satan, 51, 54, 73, 212, 263
Saudi Arabia, 51
Savior, 36, 38, 62, 168, 190, 247
Scattered, 51, 72–73, 82
Scofield Reference Bible, 115
Scripture, Scriptures, 3, 6, 8, 13, 29, 52, 56, 57, 61, 62, 65, 70, 72, 74, 80, 82, 83, 110, 111, 115, 120, 121, 130, 135–36, 140, 146–50, 162, 180, 184–86, 188, 191, 205, 214–17, 221, 229, 244, 247, 252, 253–55, 269
Security, 3–4, 29, 30n1, 39, 42, 101–2, 127, 143–44, 147, 149, 151, 153, 155, 156, 161, 189, 191–92, 194, 196–201, 224, 230, 233, 237, 239–41, 242, 275, 279
Self-determination, 54, 91–94, 275
Settlements, settler, 20, 23, 89, 95–96, 101–4, 106, 110, 114, 125, 128, 129, 142n8, 155, 158, 165, 215, 238, 240, 241–43, 244, 257, 266, 267, 268, 274
Sex Trafficking, 214
Shabbat, 48, 221
Shah, 51
Shalom, xxiii, 158, 234, 262
Shiites, 51
Sinai Peninsula, 37, 63, 73, 125
Soldiers, 21, 22, 26, 128, 150, 158, 168, 194, 217, 233, 241
South Africa, 12, 23, 105, 106, 114, 147, 149–51
South America, 118
Sovereignty, 62, 71, 73, 89–90, 93, 96–97, 120, 125, 136, 142, 165, 230
Spiritual, 17, 26, 38, 49, 52, 61, 65, 67, 69–71, 74, 84, 100, 111, 112, 114, 119, 121, 138, 150, 183–85, 190, 215, 221, 226, 273

Stalin, 73
State, 27, 32, 35, 36, 40, 42, 48, 50, 67, 73, 79, 82, 84, 89, 95, 104, 108, 116, 118–19, 124–26, 129, 131, 136, 142–43, 145, 158, 159, 162–63, 165–69, 191, 221–25, 238–40, 241, 256, 258, 267
State Department, 52, 102, 267
Student Nonviolent Coordinating Committee (SNCC), 102
Suicide bomb, 143, 150, 183, 221, 223, 242, 260, 280
Sunni, 50, 51
Supersessionism, 76, 80, 81, 83, 138, 166
Synagogue, 35, 47–49, 52, 167, 242, 263

Technology, 201
Temple, 49, 63, 76, 79, 92, 142n7, 176–77, 189
Territory (see land), 3, 33, 51, 93, 125, 126, 128, 129, 143, 165, 230, 240–42, 246, 267
Terror, terrorism, 6, 39, 51, 102, 106, 126, 144, 150, 174, 175, 189, 224, 233, 242, 244, 273
The Christian Century, 77–80
The Wall Street Journal, 31
The Washington Post, 31
Theology, theological, 6, 9, 26, 56, 57n3, 64, 73, 75, 76, 78, 82, 109–10, 112, 117, 120, 126–27, 130–131, 135, 138, 160–161, 162, 166, 179, 205, 207, 213, 216, 221–23, 237, 239, 248–50, 259, 261, 273, 276
Torah, 48, 52, 73, 84, 148, 149
Tourism, tourist, 30, 99, 188, 195, 199, 217, 276
Turk, Turkey, Turkish, 112, 123
Two-State Solution, 32, 129–30, 131, 143, 150, 155, 179, 240, 241, 274–77

UN Security Council Resolution 241, 125
Unitarianism, 117

United Nations, 32, 35, 108, 116, 123, 124, 211, 227, 252, 267
United States, 1, 10, 33, 36, 39, 78–79, 95–97, 103–4, 119, 130, 152, 153, 155–56, 174, 179, 181, 196, 212, 239, 264, 267, 271, 275, 279–81
UNRWA, 153
USAID, 198

Vietnam, 177–79, 181, 194, 207
Violence, 1–3, 5, 10, 25, 32, 41, 49, 82, 100, 105, 106, 124, 147, 149, 155, 162–63, 165, 168, 174, 189–91, 207–11, 215, 221, 223, 224, 227, 231, 237–39, 241–45, 249, 256, 258, 265, 273, 280

Wall, Separation Barrier, Security Fence, Apartheid Wall, 3, 4, 102–3, 106, 128, 131, 143, 150, 179, 189, 210, 259, 266
War, 5, 48, 95, 125, 139, 140, 167, 170, 180, 211–13, 218–20, 223, 230, 243, 249, 259, 269, 273
Washington, D.C., 1, 10, 47, 103, 125, 158–60, 224

Weapon(s), 54, 90, 168, 170, 197, 199, 209–11, 212, 214, 225
West Bank, 1, 3–4, 10, 23, 29, 30–31, 37, 100–104, 135, 142–44, 154, 155, 158, 160, 163, 169, 179, 180, 189, 199, 220, 222–24, 224, 230–32, 238, 239, 241–43, 266–68, 272, 275, 280
Women (Girls), 23, 39, 48, 58, 89, 95, 142, 153, 174, 180, 181, 214–17, 218, 219, 222–26, 233, 237, 242, 244, 259, 265
Word, 69, 72, 136, 139
World War I, 116
World War II, xv, xvii, 116, 124, 130, 220, 267

Yad Vashem, 103, 221
Yahweh, 53, 57, 60, 61, 96, 147–48

Zion, Zionism, 29, 54, 67, 108–9, 112, 114–20, 121n31, 124, 127, 136, 140–141, 145n11, 160–161, 166, 238–40

Names and Organizations

Abbas, Mahmoud, 41, 153, 154
Anti-Defamation League, xxx
Arafat, Yasser, 30, 126
Awad, Mubarak, 103–5
Awad, Sami, xxix, 22, 31, 103

B'Tselem, 31
Bastian, Maria, 34
Beinart, Peter, 128
Ben Ami, Jeremy, 31
Bethlehem Bible College, 23
Blackstone, William, 115–16, 120
Bruce, F.F., 70
Burge, Gary, 141

Cooper, Ashley, 115
Chacour, Elias, 7, 27, 258
Christians United for Israel (CUFI), 119, 161
Chrysostom, John, 76, 77, 80, 263

Dalai Lama, 196
Diana, Princess of Wales, 194, 199
Dreyfus, Alfred, 34–35
DuPlessis, David, 118

Ehle, Carl, 117

Evangelicals for Middle Eastern Understanding (EMEU), 26
Fishman, Herschel, 79
Fox News, xv, 181

Gandhi, 105
Gilder, George, 137
Gorenberg, Gershom, 128

Hawken, Paul, 56
Hedstrand, G.F., 77
Hitler, Adolf, 73, 264, 265
Holy Land Trust, 22, 31, 103
Hussein, Saddam, 212

Impact: Holy Land, 163
International Christian Embassy, 9, 119, 141
Iziz, Tariq, 212

J Street, 31, 242
Jewish Council of Public Affairs, xxx
Jewish Federation of Chicago, xxx
Julian the Apostate, 76

King, Martin Luther Jr., 3, 9, 99, 175, 238, 272
Kuttab, Daoud, 30

Kuttab, Jonathan, 27

Leahy, Patrick, 198
Luther, Martin, 77

MEJDI, xxv-xxvi, 217
MSNBC, 181

Nelson Darby, John, 115
Nobel Peace Prize, 11, 194

Obama, Barak, 12, 47, 156, 250, 267

Pope Francis, 7, 41n1
Prince, Derek, 118

Rabin, Yitzhak, 126

Religious Action Center (RAC) of Reform Judaism, xxx

Sacks, Jonathan, 75, 76, 80
Sadat, Anwar, 143
Schindler's List, 178
Simon Wiesenthal Center, xxx
Spurgeon, Charles 140
St. Ambrose of Milan, 76, 77
St. Augustine, 76, 77, 80, 110, 111
St. Jerome, 76

Wesley, John, 117, 140
Wright, N.T., 82

Zola, Emile, 34

Scriptural Index

Genesis

1:27	243
12:1–8	109, 188
12:3	46, 67, 68, 70, 72, 189
13:14–17	188
15:18	268
16:7–13	57
16:10–11	58, 59
16:12	59–60
17	60
17:8	139, 188
17:15–17,19	60
17:20	68
18:18	68
21:12–13	60
22:17–18	68
26:3–5	68
37:25–30	62
41:45	62
46:20	62

Exodus

1–12	62
2:1–15	62
2:15–22	63
2:13–26	63
3:1–10	63, 147
6:1–9	68
12:38	62, 65
16:32	6
18:8–12	63
19:6	61
22:21	191
23:9	191

Leviticus

19:33–34	94
26	72

Numbers

10:29	63, 65
22:12	70
34:6	6

Deuteronomy

6–8	62, 65
7:2	265
24:17–22	148
26:5	65
28	72

Deuteronomy (cont.)

28:63	139
30:1–3	139
32:10	135
32:39	72

Joshua

1:1–6	69
1:2	6
14:6, 14	64

Judges

1:16	63, 65
5:24–27	63
6–8	61
16:3–21	59

1 Samuel

15:3	265

2 Samuel

20:4–13	61

Job

1:3	64
1–42	65
39:5–8	59

Psalms

34:14	173
83:1–4	140
105	69
122	237

Proverbs

3:5–6	184
13:12	167
30:1	64
31:1	64

Isaiah

1:17	3
11:11–12	136, 139, 147
19:23–25	65, 269
30:1–3	62
31:1	62
35	73
42:6	61, 62, 64, 65
49:6	61
51:1–2	68
57:15	58
60:6	62, 63, 64, 135
62	74, 83
65:17–25	84

Jeremiah

2:24	59
12:16	60
25:1–26	62
30:11	72
31:10	72
35:1–11	63
35:18–19	63

Ezekiel

36	72

Hosea

8:9	59
11:1	62, 65

Joel

3:1–3	135
3:4	6

Amos

3:2	73

Micah

1:1–7	62
4:3	209n9

Habakkuk

3:3, 7	61, 62, 63

Zephaniah

3:19–20	137

SCRIPTURAL INDEX

Zechariah

2:8	135
12, 14	74, 83
14:16	82

Matthew

2:3	63
2:11	63
2:13–15	62
5:5	71
5:9	65, 243, 253, 255
5:44	174
6:1–4	32
8:10–12	37
19:28	71
23:8–12	91
23:37–39	72, 74
25:31–46	135

Mark

4:39	6
12:31	249

Luke

1:11–20	59
2:24	64
3:7–9	37, 65
10:25–37	205n2
11:31	61
12:48	73
13:34–35	191n1
19:40	274
21:24	71

John

3:16	139, 253
14:1, 27	184
16:33	13
17:18	253

Acts

1:6–7	71, 191n1
1:9–11	74
3:19–21	71, 74
7:9	62
7:29	63

Romans

9:6–9	65, 69
11:11	83
11:17	138
11:20–21	138
11:25–32	65, 70, 139
13:1–7	143

1 Corinthians

3:21–23	71

2 Corinthians

5:18–20	174, 263
11:32	64

Galatians

1:15–17	64, 65
3:6–9	65
3:26–29	37, 186
4:25	62

Ephesians

2:11–22	92
2:14	266
2:16	185
2:17–18	186
2:21	186

Colossians

3:11	186

2 Timothy

2:15	56

Hebrews

11:11	57
11:9–10	65
42:1–10	64
60:1–7	64

Revelation

3:7	72
12:6, 14	64, 136
21	82, 83, 84
22:1–2	83

www.ingramcontent.com/pod-product-compliance
Lightning Source LLC
Chambersburg PA
CBHW021345300426
44114CB00012B/1080